THE
TRAVELING
BIRDER

T·H·E

TRAVELING

BIRDER

★ 20 ★
FIVE-STAR
BIRDING
VACATIONS

★

CLIVE GOODWIN

DOUBLEDAY

NEW YORK
LONDON
TORONTO
SYDNEY
AUCKLAND

PUBLISHED BY DOUBLEDAY

a division of Bantam Doubleday Dell Publishing Group, Inc.
666 Fifth Avenue, New York, New York 10103

DOUBLEDAY and the portrayal of an anchor with a dolphin
are registered trademarks of Doubleday,
a division of Bantam Doubleday Dell Publishing Group, Inc.

Library of Congress Cataloging-in-Publication Data

Goodwin, Clive
The traveling birder : 20 five-star birding
vacations / Clive Goodwin.
p.   cm.
1. Bird watching. 2. Travel. I. Title.
QL677.5.G67   1991
598'.07'234—dc20   90-41715
CIP

ISBN 0-385-41146-4

BOOK DESIGN BY SIGNET M DESIGN, INC.
ILLUSTRATIONS BY MIKHAIL IVENITSKY

CONTENTS

FOREWORD

WHEN YOU HAVE SEEN MOST, IF NOT ALL, OF *the birds near home, why not travel? But why go with a group if you can drive yourself or go with a friend? Of course, if you would do the penguins in the Antarctic or the seabirds on remote islands, you cannot get there by car; travel by ship is the only way. However, even in Africa I prefer to have my own vehicle; but as an introduction to that continent or any other faraway place, I advise friends to go first (for an overview) with a tour group, then next time around in their own vehicle.*

If you are a lister or a ticker there may be some advantage in being with a group. A dozen pairs of eyes can pick up birds you might miss. But if you are a serious bird photographer, there is inevitably a conflict. The listers like to cover ground and to keep moving, while the photographer may want to stay awhile with a cooperative subject — perhaps even hours with some little brown job. So, if you are one of these obsessives as I am, your own vehicle — preferably a Land-Rover with roll-down windows and a roof hatch — is the answer. And not more than one other like-minded person, besides the driver, to share the work space.

One of the phenomenal spinoffs of the sport of birding is bird tourism. It all started in an organized way more than fifty years ago when the National Audubon Society promoted tours to Lake Okeechobee in Florida to see the endangered "Everglade kite" (now known as the snail kite), and to the Kissimmee Prairie to observe caracaras and cranes under the guidance of warden Marvin Chandler. The idea was to bring bird-watchers' dollars into the local economy, which by tradition had been supported in large part by duck hunters, some of whom had been putting undue pressure on the vulnerable non-game species. It worked; bird-watchers filled up the local hotels, and today the snail kite and the others are quite secure.

The idea of organized bird tours was quickly picked up by other tour entrepreneurs and travel agencies until there is now no avian hot spot in North America nor in all the world where you cannot be taken under competent guidance. Tourism, properly guided, has been an asset to the environmental movement.

Recently I instructed a studio assistant to go through my files and the wildlife and natural history magazines, listing all of the bird-watching and nature tours that were advertised. She came up with a total of more than 350 individuals and agencies that offered such services. In addition, there were another 200-plus advertised tours or workshops specifically for wildlife photographers, not including literally hundreds of field trips scheduled by nature centers, bird clubs, and museums.

This well-researched and informative book by Clive Goodwin is a Baedeker of his own favorite places, some of which you may already know. We all have our special hot spots, some of which may eventually become Meccas when the word gets around, as is the case of the J. N. "Ding" Darling Refuge on Sanibel Island in Florida.

As traveled as I am in all fifty states and abroad, I find in these pages a number of intriguing places that I have not yet tried. I will certainly explore them, with binocs and cameras at the ready. So perhaps we shall meet somewhere.

—ROGER TORY PETERSON

INTRODUCTION

I N THIS BOOK I HAVE DESCRIBED A SERIES OF
birding vacations in locations that are among the best on
the continent, together with four contrasting locations
overseas. Some of the areas presented can constitute a major holiday of two weeks or more, and some can be covered
in a long weekend if desired. Similarly, you can take the
trips any time of the year.

For North American destinations the detailed information
on routes and hotels is presented in the boxes. Where possible, I have selected hotels with a view to their quality for
birding. Where no accommodation with birding potential
exists, accessibility is the chief criterion for choice, and in
North America I have selected mid-price-range hotels where
available. Since many birders like to camp, I have also included campground information on North American destinations.

Bird names follow the American Ornithologists' Union
Check-list of North American Birds (1983) and its supple-
ments. Species overseas, where the names used differ from
the Check-list or are not included in it, are listed in the Ap-
pendix with their scientific names, together with the names
of the other species of animals and plants mentioned in the
text.

SOMETHING ABOUT HAZARDS

Birders generally take the minor hazards of birding in stride
and think little of them, and some of the more macho hard-
core birders seem to ignore them completely. As a result,
those who write about birding travel often overlook hazards.
Not everyone can afford to be quite so casual, however, and
the newcomer may do hazardous things without realizing it,

so being forewarned is important. Matters specific to particular destinations are covered in the appropriate chapters. In most cases precautions are simple once the need for them is understood.

Biting flies are present in all the destinations described, and chiggers are widespread in more southern areas. Insect repellents are usually reasonably effective for these, with a hot shower at bedtime being a good second line of defense against chiggers. Very hot water is a good antidote for pesky bites (but don't scald yourself).

Ticks should be taken seriously, as they can carry Lyme disease in the Northeast and Rocky Mountain spotted fever and other diseases in the West and South. Tuck your slacks into stocking tops and search yourself thoroughly for freckles with legs each evening. Remove any that are attached by gently pulling with forceps or tweezers.

Watch your step in the more southern states. Rattlesnakes like to bask in the early spring sunshine on some of the paths you may choose to use. Other nasties include black widow and brown recluse spiders, primarily in the desert, as well as scorpions and centipedes. Avoid stepping or putting your hands in places you cannot see, try not to use animal trails, and be alert, particularly if you're camping.

The more arid regions of the South have their share of additional hazards. Winds can be troublesome in the desert, and dry washes can become torrents in minutes when it rains. Don't be tempted to camp in them! You should be very careful about dehydration and sunstroke. Cactus disperses itself by attaching bits to passing animals: try not to be one of them. Fleas in the Southwest can carry plague, so avoid close contact with wild mammals. All of this sounds rather dramatic but really amounts to little more than using some common sense.

A WORD ON EQUIPMENT

Birding books are usually written by experienced birders, and it's easy to forget the problems newer birders experience. If you're a newcomer to birding you'll likely find Peterson's Field Guides to the Birds, East and West, easier to use than the admittedly very fine National Geographic Guide— the beginners in our courses seem to do so. In our experience the other guides on the market at present are less useful.

By the same token binoculars with a wide field of view are valuable if you have difficulty finding birds in them. The power of a pair of binoculars and their field of view tend to vary inversely to each other, and you're probably better off with a 7× or 8× binocular with a good field of view, rather than a more powerful 10× with a smaller field of view, even though I use 10× binoculars myself.

Birding equipment basically consists of a good pair of binoculars and one of the above field guides. Other things such as telescopes, cameras and so on come later. I'll only note here that for photography a telephoto lens that comes anywhere closer to your binoculars in power must be a minimum of 300 mm. in length.

Clothing will range from parkas at Churchill to lightweight cottons in Trinidad. A pair of gloves can make the difference between a comfortable trip and a miserable one, even when the weather seems quite mild, and hats can be important for both heat and cold. Good walking shoes or light hiking boots are usually adequate in most situations, with sneakers for hot and rubber boots for very wet conditions.

Finally, birding is fun. You don't have to master *Empidonax* flycatchers if you don't want to. You don't have to go for a bird list, or get involved in a "serious" project, or even do anything more ambitious than sit at the window watching the bird feeder.

But birding travel is one of the most rewarding of travel experiences; a source of endless fascination and stimulation. At least my wife and I find it so, and one of our delights is being able to share that excitement with others. I hope this book will enable you to share in it too; and better yet, help you go and find your own rewards.

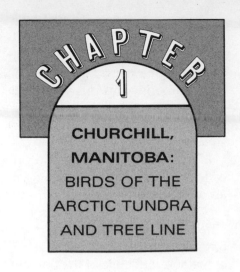

CHAPTER 1

CHURCHILL, MANITOBA:
BIRDS OF THE ARCTIC TUNDRA AND TREE LINE

FIRST VISITED CHURCHILL IN 1968. THE PLACE was booming: Texas oil drillers were holding all-night parties in the motel, the military base was busy, scientists at the rocket range were firing missiles to study the atmosphere, and there were high hopes for the town's future as a major grain shipping port. The citizenry viewed our little group of bird-watchers with puzzled but tolerant amusement; a tourist destination this frontier town was not.

Today the oilmen and military are gone, Rough-legged Hawks nest on the deserted rocket silos, and there is even some doubt about the future of the grain elevator; but the birders are here in force. During our visit at least five groups have been trundling around in little buses, and there is a scattering of individuals loaded down with binoculars, telescopes, and cameras. Churchill is now very aware of its importance to naturalists, and tourism is a growth industry.

Most of this started with one small gull. Not that the birding community was unaware of the town before, but when Ross' Gulls first attempted to nest here in 1980 a flood of birders descended and things have never been the same since.

Even if Ross' Gulls vanish overnight, however, Churchill will continue to attract birding groups. It is by far the most accessible place for the birder to see the breeding birds of the Arctic, and they can be seen here in relative comfort. Sitting as it does close to the tree line, Churchill is home to birds of both the tundra and the taiga, that zone of low trees at the northern edge of the boreal forest.

You'll find good birding at Churchill from late May through the end of June, when fall migration is already under way. Later in the year—peaking in October—the town is famed for a somewhat larger attraction, as polar bears gather waiting for the ice on Hudson Bay to freeze. Tourist operators take bear enthusiasts out in "tundra buggies" to view the huge animals. The bears, however, are not beyond ambling into town: a sign in the community center brags that "our pests are ten feet tall and weigh a ton," and life in Churchill during bear season calls for vigilance.

Churchill literally is the end of the line. The railroad tracks that terminate at the grain elevator just below the mouth of the Churchill River start some 700 miles to the south on the prairies around Winnipeg. The town itself nestles, a huddle of low clapboard buildings, between the broad river and Hudson Bay. The countryside around is dominated by low ridges of smooth gray rock, surrounded by a tidy carpet of red-green crowberry and willow, a Thumbelina tundra forest of tiny, ancient trees. Open to the bitter sweep of winds across the Bay, the houses themselves have a look of freshly painted impermanence or of imminent abandonment: things age quickly in this hostile land. The motel is a low, weathered building with a huge mound of snow outside.

A seashore town this may be; a seaside resort it's not. It

Access to Churchill is by train or air from Winnipeg. Most people use the latter, a flight of a little over 2 hours, and there is long-term parking at Winnipeg airport. It is extremely expensive to bring an automobile to Churchill; you should prearrange to rent a vehicle if you need one. Because the town is so remote, and facilities limited and often uncertain, travel information tends to date rapidly and should be rechecked before your departure.

This is one of the reasons there is a real advantage to visiting with a group. **Churchill Wilderness Encounter**—P.O. Box 820, Cumberland, British Columbia, Canada, V0R 1S0, (604) 336-8414—is excellent. It is run by Bonnie Chartier, author of the very useful *A Birder's Guide to Churchill* (L&P Press, 1988).

There are several motels and hotels. We favor the following, on the main street at the far end of town and only a short walk from the grain elevators:

Churchill Motel & Churchill Restaurant—P.O. Box 218, Churchill, Manitoba, Canada, R0B 0E0. (204) 675-8853. Open all year. Rooms: 26 units, private bath with shower. Amenities: Licensed dining room, coffee shop (open 6 A.M.–10 P.M.), complimentary limo service from the airport, vehicles available to rent, laundry facilities available for guests staying a week or more. Terms: (here and below all C$) Single $55, double $65.

There is a good restaurant opposite, **The Trader's Table,** the Community Center has a cafeteria (open 8 A.M.), and there is a restaurant at the motel itself.

★

can snow here at any time, and at the beginning of July there are still ice floes in the river and, likely as not, mini-icebergs twice the height of a man decorating the Bay shoreline. But at the beginning of July too it never really gets dark, and a visitor walking down the dusty main street will have his own little retinue of blackflies, each eager for its own share in the largesses of tourism.

A short distance inland the dark green forests of spruce replace the open tundra, stretching in an irregular line west and north over 1,400 miles. To the south these boreal forests dominate the landscape within 100 miles of Winnipeg itself, a vast, still region of silent Spruce Grouse and finches that sometimes flood south to enliven the balmy winters of the northern United States. At their northern limits the trees are low, stunted, knee-high—ideal Christmas trees for a small apartment except for their irregular shapes and angular gray snags. Many are very old, and when they finally fall their tissues split into long, symmetrical spirals, elegant even in death. Later, tiny yellow anemones and fragile calypsos will bloom among them, in that brief tumultuous celebration of life as the long winter ends.

It is early June when we arrive. The polar bears are a hundred or so miles out on the ice and even the hardiest flies are still dormant. As the plane lands we are greeted by a lifeless vista of snowdrifts, gray rocks, and brown tundra—an unpromising landscape to say the least. But pairs of Canada Geese fly up from beside the runway, and as we drive into town the tundra pools are full of shorebirds, some already claiming territories with display fights, others resting and feeding prior to continuing their journey north.

Ross' Gulls have been seen near Akudlik, and we immediately plunge into birding; checking into the motel can wait. Shivering in the bitter wind, we plow through a snowdrift and head out onto a dike. But there are no gulls anywhere to be seen, although we're rewarded by a pair of Pacific Loons swimming out through a lead in the ice, their plumage an exquisite blend of grays, black, and white.

Even familiar birds can look so totally different at Churchill that you have the illusion of seeing them for the first time. The plain blacks and whites of Pacific Loons diving in the surf off San Diego hardly generate rapture. But here their heads are an exquisite silvery white shading to soft gray, and the heavy necks curve gracefully to the slender, dark bills. So it is with other species. The nondescript brown Lapland Longspurs of the Toronto winter waterfront are now decked out in dapper blacks, whites, and chestnuts;

and the plain gray Hudsonian Godwits of the fall are resplendent in cinnamon-brown, with bold black barring.

Later we head out to the Churchill River. A leaden sky
spits a few wet snow flurries, and the raw wind off Hudson
Bay makes us glad that we have come fully equipped for
winter birding. In the choppy gray waters ahead a few Bonaparte's Gulls are sitting, newly arrived from their southern
wintering grounds. Suddenly we realize that a couple of the
distant birds seem larger, their wing tips flecked with white
mirrors. In the 'scope these heads are gray, the bills tipped
yellow; Sabine's Gulls on their way north to the high Arctic.
And at that moment the birds fly, revealing a distinctive,
elegant wing pattern, familiar from repeated thumbing of
the guides but rarely seen on a real, living bird.

The next day dawns warm, by the standards of a Churchill
spring. Once more we head out to Akudlik, and this time
our efforts are rewarded. As we plow through the snowbank
once again a pair of small gulls flies over our heads. Suddenly we recognize the light, buoyant flight, the narrow,
ternlike wings, the delicate bills. In the early morning sunlight their breasts are suffused with a glow of softest pink,
and a fine black line encircles their necks. Some "life
birds"—birds seen for the first time—are counted and soon
forgotten, a check on a list made at some ill-remembered
time long past. But some you recall twenty years later in the
same vivid detail of that first sighting, gloriously relived in
memory. We know that Ross' Gulls will stay with us.

These birds now appear consistently each summer at
Churchill, and for a while this pioneering colony was closely
guarded at great expense. Their fortunes have been uneven
and their numbers are still too few to generate compla-
cency. Sadly, their presence has elicited the full range of bad
behaviors that at times can blacken the image of birders.
Eggs have been stolen and photographers have driven nesting birds to desertion, and there's a sorry chronicle of folk
who insisted on close sightings at all costs. It's all a strange
approach to pursuing an avocation.

The road network at Churchill is quite small, and mostly
graveled. The Goose Creek road extends some distance

along the river, and the Twin Lakes road heads along the coast past the airport to the rocket range, and then inland some twenty miles in all. A number of shorter roads, many of uncertain quality and in early June still closed by snowdrifts, branch off these two. In spite of this circumscribed network, however, there is much variation in the accessible habitats, and the birder really does need a vehicle to cover Churchill well, particularly since the better sites are widely dispersed.

Some birds are everywhere, as characteristic of the Churchill scene as Red-winged Blackbirds and Song Sparrows are over much of the continent to the south. Arctic Terns are constantly in sight, patrolling the edges of the innumerable lakes and hovering airily over tiny pools in the ice. The air is filled with wild, bubbling rhapsodies as Whimbrels and Hudsonian Godwits circle in display flights over the tundra. Common Ravens patrol constantly, on the lookout for anything edible.

As soon as it warms up a little we can hear the limpid little songs of American Tree Sparrows from the willow tangles, and somewhere from among the snowbanks behind the motel a White-crowned Sparrow sings huskily, "poor Peter . . ." Stop at a stunted clump of black spruce and there will be redpolls darting around erratically overhead, with wheezy, goldfinch-like songs. In a few days Lapland Longspurs will have dispersed over the tundra as well, soon to be joined by Least and Semipalmated sandpipers.

With raptors you can never tell from year to year what you're going to see, or how many. We constantly sight Merlins—small, dark and lethal—dashing across the tundra. A Peregrine Falcon is hanging around the grain elevators, putting up clouds of Ruddy Turnstones from time to time, and earlier in the year there were Gyrfalcons. There's a pair of kestrels here as well, commonplace enough in the South, but noteworthy birds in this topsy-turvy world.

For the rest, their numbers depend on the availability of food, which here means the numbers of lemmings. Some years you'll see no lemmings at all, and hardly any raptors.

This year we are lucky. Everywhere lemmings scuttle across the roads and dash out of clumps of vegetation. The Southerner's image of a lemming is a tiny mouselike creature, but they're surprisingly large, looking for all the world (as our friend Mark Ancoll puts it) like a hot dog with legs!

The result of all this abundance is that the raptors are plentiful too. There are several pairs of roughlegs around, and across the tundra we see the ghostly shapes of Short-eared Owls, wings raised akimbo, wobbling around erratically low over the ground. From time to time jaegers appear and vanish, skimming along almost lazily, their flight seemingly effortless, their sheer power only apparent by the speed of their movement. One day we encounter an incredible twenty-five Pomarines drifting steadily northward.

To find other birds it is necessary to visit more specific locations. The road to Twin Lakes heads into taller boreal forest, where species such as Spruce Grouse, Bohemian Waxwings, and Pine Grosbeaks can be found. Go down the right trail and there are birds all over; try someplace else and the woods are still, silent. On the way there the road passes through a mixture of open tundra and low spruce trees, and along here are numbers of Willow Ptarmigan. The females blend so well with the tundra that they vanish before our eyes, but their attending males, an unpredictable mixture of deep russets and white, are easier to spot. Many are still very white, and often one will sit on the top of small snag, like a giant snowball even whiter than the snow itself.

Smith's Longspurs are one of the much-sought-after birds of the Churchill area. No words can adequately describe the exquisite shade of peachy buff on the breeding male, with its elegant black-and-white head. They prove to be hard to locate, but eventually, after much fruitless trudging over wet tundra, we encounter three of these beautiful birds close to the road.

Birds or no birds, the tundra carpet itself is a source of constant fascination. Under the taller conifers the ground cover consists mainly of crunchy pale yellow reindeer moss; from a distance the dark trees seem to be sitting in a sea of lemon meringue! Out on the more open tundra the carpet is more uneven, and the lichens are interspersed with minute shrubs and perennials. The result is a rich, intricate tapestry of color that varies from one part of the tundra to the next; here red-brown, there gray-green. In spite of its bouncy resilience the tundra carpet is a fragile one, easily damaged by too much trampling. Recovery can take many years.

The most usual pattern of color is one of yellow and gold spangles on a darker background. If you think this sounds like the back of a Lesser Golden-Plover you're correct—and if you want to get an idea of what the Churchill tundra looks like, take a good look at the next spring-plumaged golden-plover you see. They're sitting on eggs as we drive around, and well-nigh invisible until they leave the nest. Then they stand nearby, seeming ridiculously tame. The eggs themselves are even harder to see, and we don't try—they chill

There is a rarity sightings board outside the Arctic Motel, next to the Churchill Motel. Churchill is not, of course, a place for big lists, although some astonishing rarities have shown up there. It is the quality of the birds seen, plus the opportunity to see many species in high breeding plumage, perhaps for the first time, that makes the place so exciting.

June is the time to visit, with most visits taking between three days and a week. Early in the month migrants are pouring through, but the Ross' Gulls may not be back until the end of the first week. Later the migration tapers off but there are more nesting birds to be seen. There are also mosquitoes and blackflies—millions of them. Even then cold days can occur, and earlier visitors should be prepared for extreme cold; it can drop to 0°F at this time, and the wind is formidable. On the other hand the day after our departure (June 15) it was over 90°F! The tundra is very wet: take rubber boots, preferably knee-high.

★

quickly in the cold air, and the parent birds have enough hazards to contend with without curious birders.

At this time of year only a few species of flowers are out. Here and there in drier areas patches of purple saxifrage glow against the rocky ground. Woolly willow catkins are already well advanced, and closer searching reveals the minute flowers of crowberry and alpine bearberry. A couple of weeks from now these early blooms will be replaced by a multitude of other low-growing species: yellow and white rock cresses, several species of saxifrage, the purple spikes of hedysarum, together with the beautiful little Lapland rhododendron and delicate pink alpine azaleas.

The Goose Creek Road is another favorite birding area. It parallels the Churchill River, here a wide, rock-strewn waterway with swampy thickets along its banks. The road passes through a mixture of habitats. There is dense low spruce forest where we can hear the plaintive cadences of Harris' Sparrows, rather like whitethroats that never quite get going. The birds sit up high in the spruces—large, striking sparrows with pale bills boldly outlined against the black of their faces. Farther along there are areas of open fresh water adjacent to the creek itself. Here flocks of Bonaparte's Gulls are feeding, and with them a Little Gull, a bird that has nested here in the past.

One consistently productive place is around the grain elevators and the ponds adjacent to them, an easy walk from town. Here several species of ducks are usually feeding and Red-necked Phalaropes spin and dab. This is a place to look for shorebird migrants, and around the grain elevators themselves are small flocks of sparrows and Snow Buntings. The loitering gulls are always worth inspection. As usual, several Thayer's Gulls grace our visit, together with a late Iceland, giving a wonderful opportunity to compare the plumages of Herring, Thayer's, and Iceland gulls all together at close quarters.

A little farther on, Cape Merry overlooks the mouth of the Churchill River. It's a park of sorts, and a great place for waterbirds and stray migrants. It is probably everyone's favorite birding spot and it's unusual to have the place to yourself for long. On our last morning we spend a couple of hours there, watching the ice floes as they drift down on the current to join the ice jams out in Hudson Bay. It's a tranquil scene, one of muted colors: smooth dark gray rocks, the dark water, and everywhere the ice—white, blue, and green, piled along the shore, drifting in grotesque sculptures, and massed out in the bay as far as the eye can see. The only evidence of man is the thin line of Fort Prince of Wales far away over the river. The only sounds.are the distant low grinding and crashing of the floes.

Little groups of Common Eiders sit on some of the floes, dark brown females, and males resplendent in black, white, and chartreuse, hitching a ride while digesting the morning's meal. Light comes early here and the days are long; now it's the eider equivalent of coffee break. Out in the river mouth a large group of Pacific and Red-throated loons are diving vigorously together, attended by a melee of milling terns. Meanwhile, moving upriver as steadily as the floes move down, the white backs of beluga whales regularly break the surface. It's a scene that somehow crystallizes the essence of Churchill.

At present you can reach Churchill by both rail and air. Either way it is necessary to start from Winnipeg, the capital of Manitoba, some 700 miles to the south. The birding opportunities offered by a stop in Winnipeg are not to be passed over lightly. Some of the largest one-day lists recorded anywhere inland on the continent have been from here. Only some fifty miles to the east are the eastern forests, with their imposing array of breeding wood warblers, and while the long-grass prairie around Winnipeg itself is long gone, even those of us on tighter schedules can still find some outstanding opportunities for prairie birding close to the city.

One of the best of these is Oak Hammock Marsh Wildlife Management Area. It lies about twenty-five miles due north of Winnipeg and consists of almost 9,000 acres of marsh, grasslands, and lure crops. You can pass a day comfortably at Oak Hammock, with its miles of dikes and a variety of habitats. It is productive at any season, whether as a magnet to migrant waterbirds, a fine wetland for nesting, or even in winter for open country species.

On our visit the long-grass prairie is dotted with prairie-clovers and lilies, and in the wet fields along the road Le Conte's and Sharp-tailed sparrows are singing. Waterfowl jump up from the ditches ahead of us and here and there Marbled Godwits are feeding off in the fields. Across in front of the car steady streams of Franklin's Gulls, and Yellow-headed Blackbirds fly between the fields and the marsh itself. In the distance we can hear the muted clamor of the gull colonies and other waterbirds from behind the dikes.

Finally we arrive at the north end, to an observation mound revealing all the teeming life and frantic activity of a large prairie marsh in the spring. In one corner a group of Ruddy Ducks are courting, the vivid males snapping their

---

The following is close to the airport and to the good birding locations northwest of the city: **Airliner Inn—** 1740 Ellice Ave. (at Century), Winnipeg, Manitoba, Canada, R3H 0B3. (204) 775-7131; toll-free 1-800-665-8813. Open all year. Rooms: 155 units with two double beds or 1 double bed and a pull-out sofa. Amenities: Dining room, lounge, indoor swimming pool, whirlpool, sauna, exercise room, free airport limo. Terms: Single $44–50, double $52–55. AMEX, VISA, MC, DINERS.

The best camping is east of town, in a large seminatural park with good birding: **Birds Hill Provincial Park—** Birds Hill, Manitoba, Canada, R3C 0V8 (go 15 miles north on Route 59 from Winnipeg). (204) 222-9151. Open May 14–September 15. Campsites: 459 sites, 45 full hookups, 104 electricity, 310 no hookups. Shaded or sunny sites. Amenities: Coin laundry, store, flush toilets, showers, sewage disposal, beach, swimming, ski trails, nature trails, riding, playground. Terms: $6–14, ten-day limit.

★

heads and shaking those incredible powder-blue bills. In another there is a dispute between Eared Grebes, ear tufts glowing golden against their dark faces. Pairs of Wilson's Phalaropes fly around, Black Terns hawk insects overhead, rails call from the cattails, and further out the water surface is covered in a multitude of ducks, with herons and shorebirds feeding along the edges. Over all this the constant parade of gulls and blackbirds continues, backward and forward.

At lunchtime we head back to the visitor center and the picnic area, overlooking the dikes in another section of this huge marsh. There's a colony of Richardson's ground squirrels here, the familiar gophers of most prairie folk, and lunch is punctuated with shrill squeaks and lively chases. Afterward it's out on the dikes again, adding Western and Red-necked grebes and a closeup of that elusive creature, a Least Bittern, as it flies over the reedbeds. Marsh Wrens, Common Yellowthroats, and Swamp Sparrows bounce around in the vegetation and pop up to sing from the tops of the cattails.

To reach Oak Hammock, drive north on Route 90 (Century St. in Winnipeg), and at the 101 bypass continue north on Route 7 to Route 67. Turn right and continue to Route 220 (a gravel road) where the RESERVE sign is on the left. Turn north here on a good gravel road to the interpretive center. Stop there for a map and checklist, and inquire about the condition of the roads ahead. The dirt roads around Winnipeg are notorious for becoming slick when wet, and it is worthwhile to check on road quality before continuing.

For the airport areas, from the corner of Century St. and Notre Dame Ave. go west on Notre Dame to the cemetery. The road finally turns north up the airport fence as Brookside Blvd. Continue to the first dirt road north of the airport fence, and head west if it is passable. Do not attempt to drive it when it is wet.

★

For prairie landbirds the periphery of Winnipeg airport itself is a rewarding area. Brookside Cemetery, tucked into the northeast corner of the airport fence, yields nesting birds of the prairie shelter belts, species such as Northern Oriole and Warbling Vireo. Then just west of there, along the north boundary of the airport, there are Chestnut-collared Longspurs in the fields and a variety of other field birds such as Upland Sandpiper and Grasshopper Sparrow. Like airports everywhere, this one attracts hawks to its periphery, although in the breeding season only the familiar Red-taileds and Northern Harriers can usually be seen.

For the birder with more time, there are other prime locations within an easy day's drive. Riding Mountain National Park lies about a hundred miles to the northwest of Winnipeg, and really deserves a chapter of its own. Here eastern deciduous forest, boreal forest, and grasslands—together with the birds that belong in these habitats—are all to be found. Then to the east the roads in the Pinawa area, fifty miles from the city, yield an array of boreal forest species. And at the southern end of Lake Manitoba, about halfway to Riding Mountain, lie the large Delta marshes, with similar habitats to those at Oak Hammock and an equally fine array of prairie waterfowl.

OTHER THINGS TO DO AND SEE WHILE IN MANITOBA

Winnipeg, as the capital of Manitoba and one of the largest cities in western Canada, has all the usual big-city attractions including some fine parks, golf courses, interesting old buildings, and historic sites. The Manitoba Museum of Man and Nature (Main St. and Rupert Ave., 10 A.M.– 8 P.M., $2.50. 956-2830) has galleries on both the boreal forest and the grasslands. Ironically some of the few remaining areas of tall-grass prairie are within Winnipeg city limits, and the botanically inclined should visit the Living Prairie Museum, situated southwest of the airport, where an area of native prairie is protected. (2795 Ness Ave. at Prairie View Rd. The little building itself may or may not be open; it's the prairie itself that is of interest.) This is similar habitat to the area at Oak Hammock, but it is older and is managed more intensively to maintain succession. Hence it has a wider diversity of plants, although in early June most of these are still in the early stages of their annual cycle.

In spite of Churchill's location and small size, it too has features of interest other than birds. The photographer and botanist will find the area fascinating a little later in the season, although you should be prepared for some of the most voracious hordes of mosquitoes and blackflies that you are likely to encounter anywhere. Mammals are also of interest, and we saw both silver and cross foxes as well as a variety of smaller creatures. Larger species such as caribou and wolf are not likely to be encountered close to town, and the seasonal influx of polar bears and movements of belugas are mentioned above.

It is difficult to remember that the European contact with this frontier town pre-dates settlement of much of the rest

of the continent. While there is no trace of the boats that visited the area in the early 1600s, Fort Prince of Wales, a national historic park, was built by the British in the first half of the eighteenth century. It is on the other side of the river from Churchill itself, and when the ice is out of the river it is possible to arrange to be taken across to view it. There are some other features in the area, such as ancient graffiti apparently dating from the same period.

The museum at Churchill has interesting information on the native peoples of the area and is worth a visit, and the gift stores in town feature Eskimo and Indian handicrafts, some of particularly fine quality.

The newcomer to Manitoba and Canada should obtain Travel Manitoba's *Vacation Planner* and *Accommodations and Travel Services* booklets. Phone toll-free 1-800-665-0040 Ext. 36 for these and general information.

★   ★   ★   ★   ★

CHAPTER 2

SOUTHEASTERN ARIZONA: BIRD ISLANDS IN A DESERT SEA

OUTHEASTERN ARIZONA IS A LAND OF MOUN-
tains and desert. The mountains are counterpoint to the
broad, flat valleys with their towns and cities, roads and
development. Some are low, no more than rocky carbuncles
on the countryside, even more arid than the flats around
them. Others soar up, capturing the clouds. Each of these
towering masses is a world apart, each with its own flora
and fauna, magnets to birders from across the continent.
Their crowns are blanketed with forest and, in winter, snow;
and over the centuries runoff has etched deep canyons into
their slopes where limpid streams run, shaded by silver sycamores and dark cedars, only to vanish into dry washes on
the slopes beneath. These canyons are refuges from the
heat and aridity of the desert, full of hidden, secret places
and unexpected pleasures.

But first there is the desert. Our images of deserts, born of childhood pictures of the Sahara, are of sandy, empty wastelands. The approach to Tucson from the air does little to dispel those ideas. Red mountains tower over a red-brown plain, promising only dust, heat, and lifeless aridity. Yet the reality proves to be very different. As we leave the airport we drive past green paloverdes spangled with yellow blossoms, open flats of dark green creosote bushes, and saguaro cacti standing like giant candelabra along the roadsides. This is the Sonoran desert, a land rich in life despite its dryness.

There is an abundance of accommodation and facilities in Tucson. The following is well situated:

Best Western Ghost Ranch Lodge—801 W. Miracle Mile (Miracle Mile Exit 1—10 east), Tucson, Arizona 85705. (602) 791-7565; toll-free 1-800-528-1234. Open all year. Rooms: 79 units, all ground floor, double rooms, some kitchenettes and cottages. Amenities: Dining room, lounge, swimming pool, putting green, shuffleboard, laundry. Terms: Single $41—85, double $43—87. AMEX, CB, DINERS, MC, VISA.

Campers may choose between the following, the latter close to the Desert Museum. Both have good birding around the campgrounds, and there are also picnic areas and washrooms nearby: **Catalina State Park**—9 miles north of Tucson on Route 89. P.O. Box 36986, Arizona 85740. (602) 628-5798. Open all year. Campsites: 50 sites, no hookups. Amenities: Flush toilets, no showers, nature trails, disposal station. Restrictions: RV limit 30 feet. Terms: $3—6.

Tucson Mountain Park, Gilbert Ray Campground— Pima County Parks and Recreation Department; 12 miles west on Route 86 to Kinney Rd. then 8 miles north. Route 13 Box 977, Tucson, Arizona 85713. (602) 883-4200. Open all year. Campsites: 118 sites, electricity 100. Amenities: Rest rooms, no showers, nature trail, disposal station. Restrictions: No campfires. Terms: Electricity $6, no hookup $4.50. 7-day limit.

★

It doesn't take us long to find that the desert abounds in birds as well. We head out early the next morning through the low mountains west of Tucson, toward the Arizona-Sonora Desert Museum. The slopes and washes ring everywhere with song. Black-throated Sparrows fly to the tops of spindly ocotillos, Canyon Towhees rummage below low shrubs, and Verdins and Black-tailed Gnatcatchers dash from bush to bush. Overhead a Red-tailed Hawk circles in lazy spirals, capturing the first rising thermals of the warming day.

In the bright early morning light the monochrome desert proves instead to be a rhapsody of soft greens, grays, and golds, each bush a different shade from the next, and the whole punctuated by glistening patches of cholla, their vicious spines glowing silver in the sunlight. Cactus Wrens chatter and scold, Curved-billed Thrashers sing, and Gila Woodpeckers swoop between the tall saguaros, their tips crowned here and there with clusters of white blossoms where White-winged Doves sip nectar.

The Desert Museum is not a bad place to start an exploration of this fascinating countryside. The exhibits provide a great introduction to the plants and animals of the Sonoran Desert, and the feeders attract Gambel's Quail, Inca Doves, and wintering sparrows. On the grounds you can find such species as Costa's Hummingbird and Canyon Wren, which can be difficult to locate elsewhere.

Tucson is full of good birding spots. In the city itself places such as Evergreen Cemetery attract migrants and wintering birds, and close by there is the Best Western Ghost Ranch motel, with an attractive cactus garden and citrus orchard. If you stay there you'll see birds from your room, with Curved-billed Thrashers in the garden and Gambel's Quail roosting among the orange trees!

North of the city the sewage lagoons are waterbird meccas, and out to the northeast Santa Catalina State Park has a mixture of riverside habitats and rocky, saguaro-covered slopes. Here Vermilion Flycatchers, Bell's Vireos, Lucy's Warblers, and Rufous-crowned and Rufous-winged sparrows can all be found, together with flocks of wintering sparrows visiting feeders in the campground. To the east tower the Santa Catalinas, where Sabino Canyon and the road running up to the top of Mount Lemmon take the birder through a rich mix of habitats and a corresponding variety of birds. The conifers toward the summit are one place Olive Warblers can be found even in the wintertime.

Winter's a good time to visit southern Arizona, although some of the mountain roads will be closed to travel at that time, and most of the hummingbirds are absent. Later summer is also productive, and wandering Mexican species may appear in the mountain canyons. This is the time for some of the more exotic hummingbirds, but it is also a time when the heat may be too much for a birder unaccustomed to such extremes.

Mid to late April can be just about perfect: hummingbirds are pouring through, and you can hope to see other northbound migrants as well. It is hot even then—over 90°F as we drive in from the airport—but there's none of the oppressiveness that such a temperature means elsewhere.

A Tucson road map will be handy if you propose to visit the spots mentioned. Directions to Catalina State Park appear above, and the Desert Museum is 2.5 miles past the Gilbert Ray campground on the Gates Pass road, which is Speedway Blvd. in Tucson. Evergreen Cemetery is on the northwest corner of Miracle Mile and Oracle Rd. (entries on both streets).

The sewage lagoons are north of town, west of Interstate 10 between Prince Rd. and El Camino del Cerro (Ruthrauff Rd.) From Prince turn north immediately west of the frontage road serving the Interstate and drive to the plant to get a pass. Open 7 A.M. to 3:30 P.M., when the gates are locked.

Both Sabino Canyon and the road up Mount Lemmon are reached from Tanque Verde Rd., the former to Sabino Canyon Rd. and then north, the second to Catalina Highway and then northeast.

The graceful peaks of the Santa Ritas can be seen in the distance south of Tucson. Heading south, we're soon on the road that leads up into Madera Canyon on the west flanks of the mountains. The range is dominated by the imposing 9,400-foot peak of Mount Wrightson looming above the canyon. The road climbs gently, past a desert that in spring can be a garden of yellow and white daisies and sturdy, handsome mauve thistles. As we curve up toward the flank of the mountains themselves the vista of low shrubs and cacti is replaced by long grasses, bleached sere and yellow and dotted with mesquites and ocotillo. Finally the mountain slopes close in on either side and we enter an open forest of live oak, the route of the creek below us marked by the silvery trunks of sycamores.

At Santa Rita Lodge we step out into a new world. The heat of the desert has gone, the air is heavy with the perfume of cedar. Shady log cabins perch on the crest of the little valley, and dotted around under the oaks are feeders, promising hummingbirds and finches, woodpeckers and titmice.

At once we're overwhelmed in new experiences. Hummingbirds swarm like bees, Yellow-eyed Juncos forage on the ground, families of Acorn Woodpeckers argue and jostle at the suet, and from time to time a dark-backed Strickland's Woodpecker flies in for a brief visit. A noisy procession of Gray-breasted Jays flits across the road one by one, and a sweet song from a nearby sycamore reveals a Painted Redstart flitting restlessly along the boughs and trunk. Chickadee-like calls announce a group of Bridled Titmice.

We're torn between staying in our room with our noses glued to the windowpane, watching the constant activity below, and exploring outside. We've four species of hummer already, and a flash of dazzling yellow through the trees in the valley reveals a Scott's Oriole. Later, as we sit outside in the evening, flocks of Turkey Vultures glide in silently to spiral in a giant pinwheel, a vortex of vultures, before settling to roost in the trees along the creek.

At dusk small groups of expectant birders gather in the

parking area for the nightly owl vigil. On the one side of the road Elf Owls nest in a power pole. On the other side a larger hole is home to a Whiskered Screech-Owl. It's almost dark when the two owls finally emerge for their evening hunting, but long afterward the irregular hooting of the Whiskered Screech-Owl can be heard, punctuated occasionally by the calls of Elf Owls.

On one day during our stay the weather changes abruptly, and a bitter north gale with black clouds and heavy rain sweeps in. The peaks vanish into a swirling cloud of white, and at the trailhead a short way up the road the ground becomes covered in snow. It's a day to sit at the feeders, and

---

Madera Canyon is south on Interstates 10 and 19 to the Continental turnoff at Green Valley, then follow the canyon road southeast. There are two delightful picnic areas, but only pit toilets.

Santa Rita Lodge—Madera Canyon, HC 70 Box 5444, Sahuarita, Arizona 85629-9323. (602) 625-8746. Open all year. Rooms: Motel units with two single or one double/queen size bed. Cottages: one queen size plus one double bed. All units with fully equipped kitchenette, tub and shower, color TV, maid service every four days, linens, and barbecues. Amenities: Restaurants and grocery stores in Green Valley, 20 minutes away. Restrictions: No pets. Terms: Motel rooms $44, cabins $53 (one or two persons). Credit cards accepted. From March 15 to October 1 advance reservations only for minimum of 2 nights, on holiday weekends 3 nights. Deposit of $20 (minimum) per night within 5 days of reservation.

Bog Springs Campground—National Forest Service—Madera Canyon, Green Valley, Arizona 85614. (602) 281-2296. Open all year. Campsites: 13 sites. Amenities: Pit toilets, no showers, nature trails. Terms: $5/family. 14-day limit.

the flocks there are joined by high-country visitors such as Steller's Jay and Townsend's Solitaire.

One of the ultimate prizes of these southern mountains is that most colorful of North American birds, the Elegant Trogon. It seems exotic, almost unreal, the stuff of legends, one of those special species that create the mystique of Arizona. Everyone wants to see it. Sometimes it seems as though everyone is here looking for it, and "Have you seen it?" refers to only one thing.

Sometimes a lucky birder finds one down near the lodge itself, but normally you must drive up to the trailhead and then hike up the trail itself. Constantly we meet others on the same quest: there's much comparing of notes . . . one was seen this morning about half a mile up the trail on the left, or last night someone saw it hanging around the parking lot all evening. Exactly how far is that half mile, we wonder?

But the best way of locating the trogon is not by sight at all but by sound, a distinctive low hooting. And indeed, as we start up the path calls come from the valley to our right, and as we dash back down again the bird appears, perversely, to be moving toward our original location. Finally we emerge again on the trail to a flash of red crossing the path. And there, briefly, in full view a few yards away, the trogon sits. Its breast glows red beyond imagining, and its green plumage flashes iridescent in the sun, the long tail flared elegantly outward and its ivory bill shining. This is a splendid tropical creature, out of place in this early spring vista of delicate greens and muted browns. Suddenly it is gone, and we in turn look like the self-satisfied birders who drive newcomers to despair with assurances that "it was just here five minutes ago."

This is a land of dry stream beds. Even quite vigorous streams degenerate into sandy washes shortly after leaving the mountains. A permanent stream is a thing to be treasured and, above all in this dry country, to be used. So a permanent stream with its original woodlands, with giant old Fremont cottonwoods, tangled understory and all the creatures that go with it, that is a rarity indeed. Only extreme remoteness or determined effort will protect such a place.

Just such a stream flows through the Patagonia-Sonoita Sanctuary of the Arizona Nature Conservancy. It runs, green and inviting, south through the town of Patagonia, and it is through the determined effort—and money—of the Conservancy that it exists today. Patagonia-Sonoita is one of those rare places that give you the feeling that, no matter how often you visit, something new will appear. Most of us don't have the opportunity to put that feeling to the test, but at different times we have indeed seen such unexpected things as Common Black-Hawk and Barn Owl.

Patagonia-Sonoita Sanctuary is just south of Patagonia. Go south on Interstate 19 to Nogales, then northeast on Route 82. Turn west in town on N. 3rd Ave., go 2 blocks to Pennsylvania Ave. and the reserve entrance is on the left about 0.5 mile south. There are neither washrooms nor picnic facilities on the reserve.

The best accommodation is:

The Stage Shop Inn—3rd St. and McKeown Ave. (1 block east of SR 82, exit 3rd St.), Box 777, Patagonia, Arizona 85624. (602) 394-2211. Open all year. Rooms: 43 units, double and single rooms, 11 have kitchenettes. Amenities: Dining room, bar, swimming pool, special Ghost Ranch Tours by appointment ($15/person). Terms: Single $36, double $42—44, with kitchenettes $59—64. AMEX, MC, VISA.

The nearest campground is some 7 miles south of town, with picnic areas and washrooms: **Patagonia Lake State Park**—(12 miles northeast of Nogales on Route 82, then north on a gravel road for 4 miles). P.O. Box 274, Nogales, Arizona 85624. (602) 287-6965. Open all year. Campsites: 82 sites, 9 full hookups. Amenities: Rest rooms, showers, supply store, sewage disposal, water sports, fishing, boat rental. Terms: $3—8.

From Patagonia head north on Route 82 to Sonoita and continue east to Route 90. Turn south on 90 to Sierra Vista. The gatehouse to the fort is west at the junction of Routes 90 and 92, and the Ramsey Canyon road is about 7 miles south on 92.

Mile Hi is open 8 A.M.—5 P.M. At other times there's a chain across the road. Parking is very limited, and the number of persons on the trails is carefully controlled. Pick up a permit at the office, and then try to tear yourself away from the excellent gift shop! There are privies but no picnic area. The preserve has cottages and these are the ideal places to stay, but you'll need reservations a year or so ahead of time:

Mile Hi Cabins—RR 1, Box 84, Hereford, Arizona 85615-9738. (602) 378-2785. Open all year. Cottages: 6, fully equipped housekeeping, flush toilets, showers. Terms: $60/2 persons.

Failing that, there is accommodation of all kinds at Sierra Vista. The following is south of town:

Ramada Inn—Sierra Vista—2047 S. State Hwy. 92 (1.5 miles south of junction of Route 90), Sierra Vista, Arizona 85635. (602) 459-5900. Open all year. Rooms: 152 units. Amenities: Dining room (Open 6 A.M.), cocktail lounge, heated swimming pool, spa, limousine service. Terms: Single $64–69, double $68–73. AMEX, CB, DINERS, MC, VISA.

Camping is rather limited. The following is just off the Ramsey Canyon Road:

Apache Pointe Ranch Campground—(602) 378-6800. (7 miles south on Route 92 from junction of Route 90, then 0.5 mile west on Ramsey Canyon Rd. and 1 mile south on Richards Rd.) Open all year. Campsites: 34 sites, water and electrical. Amenities: Flush toilets, hot showers, sewage disposal, recreation hall, horseshoes, volleyball, hiking trails. Terms: $8/vehicle.

★

As we enter the refuge Dusky-capped and Brown-crested flycatchers are calling, and out in one of the open areas a Vermilion Flycatcher zooms around in its display flight, looking for all the world like a brilliant little round red clockwork toy. Suddenly out of a bush an annoyed-looking little flycatcher pops, its crown feathers raised in indignation. It's a Northern Beardless-Tyrannulet, and I'd feel annoyed too if I were stuck with a name like that! Meanwhile newly arrived Summer Tanagers are arguing about territory, and a Blue Grosbeak feeds below the embankments of the old railroad. In the tall cottonwoods a pair of Black-shouldered Kites are courting, and further on a Gray Hawk sits quietly, the bright yellow of its legs and cere vivid against the soft gray barring of its breast.

Gray Hawks are one of the specialties of the sanctuary, but no visit to Patagonia-Sonoita will yield all the birds that occur here. Different seasons have their own specialties. A little later Thick-billed Kingbirds and Rose-throated Becards will nest along this valley, while winter brings waxwings, finches and sparrows. There's good birding also around the campgrounds in Patagonia Lake State Park to the south— definitely the place to stay for a camper (Olivaceous Cormorants occur).

A little way north of Nogales there is an old, unhappy saguaro. It's the last saguaro that we will see as our journey continues eastward, and it marks the end of the Sonoran desert. Now, heading into the dry rangeland around Sonoita, we unknowingly cross the invisible boundary line between east and west. When we next encounter desert there will be vistas of creosote bush and ocotillo, with tall spikes of Spanish bayonet and agave. Here, in extreme southeastern Arizona, is the westernmost edge of the Chihuahuan desert, a vast expanse that extends east to Texas. From here on the ravens are more likely to be Chihuahuan, and the meadowlarks Eastern.

Southeast, close to the Mexican border, the Huachucas hide their high tops in cloud. At their foot is the bustling city of Sierra Vista, servicing Fort Huachuca military base. There's good birding on the base itself: Garden and Sawmill canyons are one of the better places for Buff-breasted Fly-catchers, and Spotted Owls can be found.

The highlight in a visit to the Huachucas is Mile Hi, the Nature Conservancy's famous preserve in Ramsey Canyon. It really is about a mile high, but easy enough to get to. Early one morning we head up the Ramsey Canyon road until it ends abruptly just past a shallow ford across the stream. We're there!

In the narrow, shady canyon small cottages nestle in an arc under the trees, with the Center building just beyond. Hummingbird feeders are festooned everywhere, each with its complement of hummingbirds constantly dashing in and out, and there are rows of chairs placed thoughtfully to allow ringside views, together with an interpretive plaque to help you sort out the more usual visitors. At one feeder a Magnificent Hummingbird scintillates green and blue, at another tiny Black-chinneds quarrel with a Rufous, the vivid red of its gorget contrasting with its fox-red body. Mile Hi is *the* hummingbird spot in Arizona: 15 species occur here, and we're tempted to settle down for the day.

But there's even more to see farther up, so we head out along the wide trail beside the creek. A Greater Pewee calls from the trees at the far side, "Ho-say-Maria," and Black-throated Gray Warblers sing. Soon the trail turns and, narrowing abruptly, becomes a steep boulder-strewn track climbing up through the pines to the saddle far above. At eye level a golden-cheeked Hermit Warbler is foraging and a lively Virginia's Warbler flits by. Bridled Titmice scold while a Hutton's Vireo peers out of a live oak. You can spend a good day at Mile Hi!

We now must head east toward the Chiricahuas, the easternmost and most remote of Arizona's "Mexican" mountains. My first unforgettable view of this range was in a March blizzard, looming dark and forbidding out from a sudden, brief break in the white wall of snow. In pleasanter weather there are magenta patches of sand verbena along the road and occasional groups of distant pronghorn out over the open range. In the sunlight the mountains are more beautiful than forbidding, flushed in reds, pinks, and mauves, but they're still imposing.

The Chiricahuas are formidable even in terms of their neighboring mountain ranges. Chiricahua Peak, at 9,795 feet, towers five thousand feet above the desert floor. For over thirty miles they stretch north and south, penetrated by few roads and crossed by only one, the winding gravel road across Onion Saddle, usually closed in winter.

The entrance to Cave Creek Canyon is appropriately dramatic. On either side towering pinnacles of pink rock bound the long, wooded valley. As the road winds down toward the

---

To reach here drive east from Sierra Vista on Route 92 and then at Bisbee continue on Route 80 through Douglas to Rodeo, and the Portal road is on the left a couple of miles north of town. You can return to Tucson by continuing north on 80 to Interstate 10, and then west.

Facilities at Cave Creek are few. The **Portal Store**— P.O. Box 364, Portal, Arizona 85632, (602) 558-2223— has 6 bed-and-breakfast rooms, and the only restaurant. The **Southwestern Research Station**—Portal, Arizona 85632, (602) 558-2396—often has available dormitory-style accommodation with a cafeteria. The following has housekeeping units in an idyllic setting: **Cave Creek Ranch**—Box F, Portal, Arizona 85632. (602) 558-2334. Open all year. Rooms: Apartment and cottage units, all fully equipped housekeeping. Amenities: Swimming pool during the summer months. Terms: Summer $50–72/two persons. Winter $50–76. Pets $4 each. For one person deduct $6/day.

There are limited picnic areas, and camping is also quite limited (there is more up the mountain, but not accessible in April): **Idlewild–Cave Creek Campground** (National Forest Service)—2.5 miles west of Portal. (602) 364-3468. Open April 1–October 31. Campsites: 10 sites. Amenities: Pit toilets, nature trails, no showers. Terms: $5 per family. 14-day limit.

★

creek these pink walls close in on either side, sometimes hidden by tall cedars and dense live oaks and sometimes emerging, precipitous ramparts blocking the route ahead, until the road again turns to follow the course of the stream. Few birding sites are so spectacular.

Each canyon in these ranges has its distinctive character. At Madera the slopes are forested and the creek itself runs deep among huge boulders. At Ramsey the creek seems small, its riparian vegetation hemmed in by the dry slopes above. Here at Cave Creek the stream is broad and shallow, and it winds along a narrow wooded floodplain between those overpowering pink cliffs. It penetrates deep into the mountains themselves, and when the road finally forks the birder is offered a choice of visiting the South Fork—a name evocative of hosts of rarity sightings—or continuing on to the point where the gentle grade finally ends. Then the road turns to gravel, to snake its way upward in the long climb to the Onion Saddle and the forests of spruce and fir that crown the high tops.

As we arrive at the entrance to the canyon we stop in the tiny village of Portal to watch the hummingbirds buzzing around the feeders at the store and locate the pale Great Horned Owl that nests in one of the sycamores. Portal General Store is a local center of a kind, selling everything from gas to maps, and T-shirts with the slogan "where the hell is Portal." The little restaurant at the back serves mouth-tingling Mexican food, and glorious mounds of pancakes that totally overwhelm both the eater and the plates they are served on.

Another center for birders is the Southwestern Research Station, at the end of the pavement just before the road starts up the hill. It's a busy research operation, but much of its work is ornithological and birders can stay here as well. Often the folk here know the latest on what is around.

Cave Creek is named for the deep caves in the rock faces—the onetime summer home of Cochise and his Apaches—but among birders it is known for its array of Mexican rarities, including the elusive Elegant Trogon. Formerly these forests were also home to the Thick-billed Parrot, and Arizona Fish and Game is trying to reestablish this species, using wild birds confiscated from illegal imports. It's an effort that seems to be bearing results.

One morning we drive up to look for a flock of parrots that have been seen feeding near one of the trails. It's a little like looking for needles in a haystack, but parrots never seem to keep quiet for long, and finally loud screeches lead us to a flock of ten of these magnificent birds. They're steadily working over the cones in the top of a pine tree, their brilliant green and red plumage blending amazingly well with the darker green of the pine. They deftly manipulate the cones with their massive dark bills until suddenly the flock takes off with a chorus of screeches, long tails streaming and wings flashing yellow in the sunlight. We're so entranced that their "countability" never enters our heads at all!

Picnics here can be eventful. At one table a flock of Gray-breasted Jays soon arrives looking for handouts, and an Acorn Woodpecker flies over to find what is going on. All the

Two very useful references are James A. Lane's *A Birder's Guide to Southeastern Arizona* (L&P Press, 1988) and W. A. Davis and S. M. Russell's *Birds in Southeastern Arizona* (Tucson Audubon Society, 1984). The Tucson hotline is (602) 798-1005.

If you have never visited southern Arizona before there are 15–20 species that occur only or mainly here, although some are very rare. If you're new to the Southwest as well there are about as many other species that will be new. You can expect a list of around 180 species or more in the two weeks or so that a comfortable round trip might take.

Although the route runs in and out of mountains there are only two actual mountain drives, both optional: the trip up Mount Lemmon and the drive up to Onion Saddle in the Chiricahuas.

★

fuss brings a trio of javelinas, which wander around for a while in a bad-tempered sort of way, manes bristling, before departing in disgust when no food is forthcoming. A Blue-throated Hummingbird appears, but is equally disappointed at finding a red hat contains no supplies of nectar!

Some of the special birds of the Chiricahuas are found only at the top of the mountains. If you want to see a Mexican Chickadee or a Red-faced Warbler you must climb that winding road to the Onion Saddle. Or at least, so the books say. We head up, but soon the wind becomes a gale, the mist swirls low above, the only sounds are the wind, the only movements the wind in the spruces. If there were birds they must be around the other side of the mountain! We retreat in defeat.

Down in the valley all is pleasant and sunny, so we turn to birding the woods along the creek. This is the same principle as looking for your lost dollar under a lampstand because you can see better there! Certainly there are birds here: jays call, a Strickland's Woodpecker melts away, and soft warbler songs drift down from the fresh green of the cottonwoods. First there's a Townsend's Warbler, black and gold; then more Black-throated Grays in fastidious formal wear; then a sudden glimpse of red in the leaves, and an exquisite Red-faced Warbler cocks its head perkily under a branch as though to say "Gotcha!"

OTHER THINGS TO SEE AND DO IN APACHE COUNTRY

Southeastern Arizona is just as fascinating to a botanist as it is to a birder, with two very different sets of desert vegetation, a range of life zones—Hudsonian, Transitional, Upper and Lower Sonoran—up the slopes of the larger mountains, together with some species endemic to the area. Your chances of finding the desert in bloom vary greatly with the wetness of the winter and the amount of rainfall just preceding your visit, as desert plants are finely attuned to rainfall conditions.

Other animal life is equally rich, from coatimundi in the canyons to a formidable list of reptiles and amphibians. The Arizona–Sonora Desert Museum—(602) 883-1380. Open 8:30 A.M. to sundown. $6—provides a first-class opportunity to become familiar with many of these species. Don't miss it!

The dramatic scenery of Cave Creek becomes even more spectacular on the other (western) side of the Chiricahuas where the Chiricahua National Monument, billed as the "Wonderland of Rocks," protects some of the finest formations. There's much of interest to the rock hound generally. Tucson has gem and rock stores, and mining has been a major industry from the days of early settlement. Bisbee is a major mining center with a museum.

The region is full of history. To the extent that there really was a Wild West, this was it. North of Sierra Vista is Tombstone, of "gunfight at the O.K. Corral" fame, and the countryside is scattered with historic markers commemorating the wars with the Apache.

One of the best-known reminders of the days of Spanish settlement is the San Xavier del Bac mission just southwest of Tucson; the Indian Reserve here is also a good place for Bendire's Thrasher. Farther south the Tumacacori National Monument preserves the remains of a mission, and has a museum.

Tucson itself is a major city, with all the usual facilities. There is an abundance of golf courses here, and winter skiing on Mount Lemmon. Horseback riding is popular, and there are many guest ranches; the most noteworthy for a birder is the Circle Z Ranch—Patagonia, Arizona 85624. (602) 287-2091—which occupies the creek below the Patagonia-Sonoita Sanctuary.

There is recreational boating and fishing at both Patagonia and Peña Blanca state parks (the latter west of Nogales) and both have good birding as well.

Handicrafts and gem and silver work are most readily available in Tucson, although many stores in adjacent Mexican towns specialize in such things. The main ports of entry are at Nogales and Douglas, where Agua Prieta lies on the Mexican side of the border.

★   ★   ★   ★   ★

CHAPTER 3

TRINIDAD AND TOBAGO: A TANTALIZING TOUCH OF THE TROPICS

HERE IS A TRIP TO THE NEW WORLD TROPICS without most of the hassles and shots. To a place where they talk English and you can drink the water. A place where the birdlife is tropical, but you don't have to sort out fifty species of almost identical flycatchers. Just ten miles off the coast of Venezuela is the island nation of Trinidad and Tobago, and its birds really are South American. There's none of the impoverished birdlife of the rest of the Caribbean here, and while you're not going to find the thirteen hundred or so species recorded in the Venezuelan avifauna, even a trip to Venezuela itself would be likely to yield only a small fraction of that total.

Trinidad, the larger of the two islands, is separated from the mainland to the south and west by narrow straits, and

33

from neighboring Tobago—billed "the Robinson Crusoe Isle" in the tourist folders—by twenty-six miles of sea to the northeast. Its three hundred or so species are a remarkable number for a relatively small island, and offer the birder an introduction to birding in the tropics without many of the health, language, and cultural difficulties that often arise on such trips.

In Trinidad the language is English (even if the patois often sounds like something else), accommodations are adequate, the water is potable, and the island has few of the formidable health problems that the traveler can encounter farther south. As inconsequential as the hard-core birder sometimes regards these matters, they can make the difference between a relaxing and enjoyable trip and one memorable mainly for primitive outhouses and discomfort!

But there is an even more compelling reason for using Trinidad and Tobago as a jumping-off point for South American birding. Tropical birds and habitats are so unfamiliar to someone who has only birded in more temperate regions that they can be overwhelming. Trinidad's manageable avifauna provides challenge enough, and is an excellent introduction to birding in the tropics. Here, in a relatively small area (about 40 miles wide and 55 long) are mountains and lowlands, forests and savanna, fresh and saltwater swamps, and—never very far away—tropical ocean beaches lined with coconut palms.

But all these words do nothing to convey the real magic of the place. The balcony of the Asa Wright Nature Centre in Trinidad's Northern Range looks south down a broad, heavily forested mountain valley, with the town of Arima and the cultivated lowlands beyond just visible in the far distance. My first visit to this place was at the end of November, in pouring rain. The drive up the mountain had been dominated by sodden vegetation and dark tunnels of foilage over the road, with none of the enchanting interplay of light and shadow that I came to know later. The valley was gloomy and the trees on the slopes above had vanished into heavy clouds. I was coming down with a bad bout of flu, and in no mood to be enchanted by anything.

I stepped onto the balcony, overlooking a tropical orchard full of bird feeders. And at the feeders there were birds— not just three or four species of birds as one might expect at a North American feeding station, but a multitude of birds of different sizes and vivid hues: hummingbirds dashing in and out to the nectar, honeycreepers and Bananaquits fighting over slices of fruit, and tanagers everywhere, out of the eaves of the building, into the bushes, up onto the feeders. Farther down the orchard, still more species fed in some of the fruiting trees and there was a constant procession of Crested Oropendolas, big blackish birds with outsized whitish bills, startling blue eyes, and a rear end decked out in rich cinnamon and yellow. Colloquially called "yellowtails," they flapped laboriously across the clearing as though their bills were almost too much to carry. Periodically a metallic "tonk" sounded from the forest below, the improbable call of a Bearded Bellbird. Every one of these birds was new to me. All the sights and sounds were new. It's a bird-watcher's El Dorado.

Bookings for the **Asa Wright Nature Centre & Lodge** are handled exclusively in North America by Caligo Ventures, Inc., 387 Main St., P.O. Box 21, Armonk, New York 10504-0021. Toll-free U.S. 1-800-426-7781; Canada 1-800-548-5340. Rooms: Simple, comfortable rooms in the original plantation house and several adjoining cottages, with twin beds and bathroom including shower. Amenities: Dining room—all meals are included; viewing veranda for afternoon tea, and complimentary rum punch served before dinner. Terms: (All U.S.$) Single $98/person, double $73/person. Transfers round trip Piarco International Airport—Asa Wright Nature Centre $27.

There are many other accommodations on Trinidad, including the Mount St. Benedict Guest House which caters to birders, but we prefer Asa Wright for its location and atmosphere.

★

On our February visit the birds around the Centre are fewer, but the sky is a vivid blue, and the seasonal rain forest below us is painted an exquisite salmon by flowering immortelles. All around a lush green glows, while overhead vultures and hawks circle lazily, playing hide-and-seek behind the tall trees. The oropendolas are nesting now, busy around their long, pendulous nests of yellowish fibers, but the procession across the clearing is still part of the morning routine.

The sound of rain is replaced by the oriole-like song of a Rufous-browed Peppershrike in the trees outside the door— "d'y wash every week?" Bananaquits still dash around with sizzly little songs, sounding vaguely like treble Tennessee Warblers; and hummingbirds whirr and flicker in and out of the flowering shrubs—here the vivid green of an emerald; there, briefly, a tiny jewel of a Tufted Coquette.

If you're to get the most out of a trip with so many new birds, some advance preparation is vital. Fortunately there are several good books. The main guide is: *A Guide to the Birds of Trinidad and Tobago* by Richard ffrench (Harrowood Books, 1976), and its 1988 supplement—available at the Centre. (Unfortunately this book has just gone out of print, and so at present the Venezuela guide listed below is the only alternative). ffrench's small *Birds of Trinidad and Tobago* (Macmillan Caribbean) has some good photos but is inadequate for an even mildly keen birder.

A Guide to the Birds of Venezuela by Rodolphe Meyer de Schauensee and William H. Phelps, Jr. (Princeton University Press, 1978) is useful for some species, such as hawks in flight, even if ffrench is reprinted.

A Birder's Guide to Trinidad and Tobago by William J. Murphy (Peregrine Enterprises Inc., 1986) is a good "where to" book, and the same author (P.O. Box 1003, College Park, Maryland 20740) has a useful cassette recording of 41 species available for $10.

★

At twelve hundred feet, Asa Wright sits at the boundary of a zone known technically as lower montane rain forest. Below it lies a band of seasonal deciduous forest that traces the valley of the Arima River upward, and near the pass above, at about two thousand feet, is a limited area of montane rain forest.

While the term "deciduous forest" usually evokes maples and oaks, and "rain forest" conjures pictures of sodden, impenetrable jungles, neither is remotely close to reality. All these forests are enormously rich when compared to those of more temperate zones, with a multitude of tree species. The dry season deciduous forest never has the starkness of the deciduous forests in the northern winter: many trees are still green, and many of the deciduous trees themselves choose this period to bloom. There's a wonderfully incongruous quality to a leafless tree completely covered in brilliant yellow blossoms!

The rain forest, on the other hand, is a dark, silent place, with huge buttressed trunks towering up to a dense canopy far above. A multitude of lianas dangle down, and wind backward and forward around both themselves and everything else, like the massive hawsers for some huge, untidy ship. There's little understory, and once you're through the riot of vegetation around the edges walking is easy.

Together with much of the neighboring property, the Asa Wright Nature Centre itself was formerly a coffee and cocoa plantation. The beautiful tree that so dominates the view with its huge salmon pea flowers, the immortelle, is an alien introduced by the plantation owners to provide shade for the coffee trees. Income from the plantation is still a part of the Centre's revenue, and on our morning walks we pass cacao trees dangling their dark red pods, pass neat nutmegs with their round yellow fruits, and in places the wonderful perfume of the white coffee flowers fills the air.

Again, the word "plantation" conjures up images of monotonous rows of carefully pruned trees, with all competing growth relentlessly removed; but these plantations have a relaxed, almost overgrown quality to them, and it doesn't take us long to discover that the tall immortelles yield some of the best birding. Every nectar feeder around, it seems, heads for the flowering trees—no wonder the bird feeders around the Centre itself are not as well patronized!

One of the secrets of tropical birding is to watch for flowering and fruiting plants. Certainly not all tropical birds are fruit or nectar specialists, but many are, and they concentrate at the current food sources. In the tropics something is in flower or fruit throughout the entire year: find the appropriate plants and you find the birds. After a day or so we discover that the real places for Tufted Coquettes are the tall mauve spikes of verbena, a surefire draw. A little patience and you see the exquisite little male bird zip in, its vivid green plumage accented by a fiery crest and a jaunty cravat of rich rufous feathers.

Soon after our arrival we also discover a fig tree on the path to the Oilbird cave loaded with small fruits, and an hour or so sitting nearby yields a steady procession of birds: squat little White-bearded Manakins, a Chestnut Woodpecker, the vivid yellow and deep blues of a Violaceous Euphonia, a Bay-headed Tanager with bright golden-green plumage, and a pair of Violaceous Trogons, their golden brilliance muted in the shade of the tree. Nearby a Ferruginous Pygmy-Owl starts calling from a clump of bamboo, and its persistent hoots momentarily distract the tanager hordes, which dash over to scold from the branches above.

One of the specialties of the Asa Wright Sanctuary is the Oilbirds, which nest in a deep cave cut by the river far below the Centre itself. These strange fruit-eating relatives of the nightjars nest colonially on the walls of dark caves, emerging at night to fly to their feeding trees. The colony in the gorge is one of few accessible ones anywhere, although the bird numbers here are much fewer than formerly, and the Centre now restricts visits to try to avoid disturbance. A visit to the Oilbird cave is no longer a certain attraction of a trip to Asa Wright, but visits can usually be arranged once there.

Such a visit is unforgettable. A narrow path winds down to the cave through dense forest. In this heavy cover there

Tours can be arranged by the Centre to Dunston Cave and the Centre Grounds, Blanchisseuse, Caroni Marsh, Aripo Savannah/Arena Forest, Nariva Swamp, and the Heights of Aripo. The tours cost $11.25–32.25/person, depending on destination and length. There is a minimum charge of $90 a day per vehicle.

It's possible to rent a car and drive yourself, avoiding the costs of the field trips. We think you will see many more birds by going with an experienced leader here; and you should also be aware that Trinidad roads are busy, often narrow, that you'll be driving mountain roads, and that people drive on the left-hand side of the road, which can be unnerving until you grow accustomed to it. Car rentals (Hertz, Budget, and Singh's) are available at the airport.

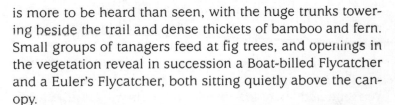

is more to be heard than seen, with the huge trunks towering beside the trail and dense thickets of bamboo and fern. Small groups of tanagers feed at fig trees, and openings in the vegetation reveal in succession a Boat-billed Flycatcher and a Euler's Flycatcher, both sitting quietly above the canopy.

Trails like this always offer chances of encountering some of the shyer forest species, birds that normally melt away unseen. At one corner a series of clear whistles invites imitation, and in response a dumpy little blackish bird struts indignantly out onto the path. The Black-faced Antthrush looks as though its maker couldn't decide between a rail and a thrush, yet it is related to neither, and soon proves to have a distinctive personality all its own. It doesn't really appreciate being imitated, and after flicking its stubby tail a couple of times it quickly vanishes back into cover again.

Finally we make the last steep descent to the cave, and one by one venture into the narrow entrance. Ranged along the ledges ahead the birds sit, their enormous eyes glowing red in the beams of the spotlight, their eerie shrieks echoing off the walls of the cave. They're surprisingly large, and their formidable bills would do justice to a hawk. As night falls this whole colony will fly out to feed at some suitable fruiting tree, perhaps many miles away. They concentrate on oil-rich fruits, and are themselves so rich in oil that young birds were apparently formerly used as candles!

The Oilbirds have used this cave for many years, and such constancy is not unusual in the tropics. The males both of manakins and the group of hummingbirds known as hermits use communal display grounds. A good friend of ours, Jack Satterly, visited the sanctuary regularly when Asa Wright was still alive in the late sixties and her place was known as the Spring Hill Estate. At that time he mapped the locations of some of these leks, and we were fascinated to find those same traditional sites still in use today.

There are several manakin display grounds below the Centre, and the White-bearded Manakin males visit these areas, spending much of each day tidying the ground of litter and performing snappy little display flights for one another. Not only do the birds snap from one branch to another as though propelled by a slingshot, but an active bout of display sounds like the discharge of a host of tiny firecrackers. One lek (display ground) is beside the main trail, and if you sit quietly here for a while the birds will start performing. The male manakins are showy little fellows, decked out in tiny black-and-white tuxedos, but the girls—with other responsibilities to attend to—are a muted dark green. The smaller Golden-headed Manakin's displays are rather different, but equally entertaining.

Asa Wright is a good base for visiting other parts of the island. Every trip has its own distinctive character, and the Centre's drivers—Jogie and Roodal Ramlal—are skilled at both spotting the birds and identifying them. One of the best outings is along the road past the Centre, which winds up over the pass to the north and down through heavy forests to Caribbean beaches near the village of Blanchisseuse. From the heights we look down on flocks of bright green parrots feeding in the trees below, and see the whitish shapes of bellbirds staked out on their territories high above the forest canopy. Flocks of Channel-billed Toucans flop over the treetops, massive black bills contrasting with the white and orange of their face and breasts. Sitting quietly on the branches under the canopy we find trogons and a Blue-crowned Motmot: yellow and blue, red and metallic green, chestnuts, blues and green, an incredible array of color combinations, each perfect in its own way. They are all striking birds, even among a host of showy species.

Finally we're down at the beach, lunching under the shade of coconut palms and swimming in the warm Caribbean surf. Occasional squadrons of Brown Pelicans lumber by, and overhead Magnificent Frigatebirds hang suspended in the breeze like huge black kites flown by some celestial kite flyer. A Spotted Sandpiper teeters past, seeming strangely out of place in this tropical scene, even when we know it must spend more time in Trinidad than it does along the streams of North America.

Down on the lowlands south of the Centre there are many exciting trips in store. The Aripo Savannah has a distinctive mixture of grasslands and shrubs interspersed with plantations of Caribbean pine. Here we watch slender Fork-tailed Palm Swifts twisting and turning around the moriche palms and little chattering flocks of Green-rumped Parrotlets feeding on weed seeds. White-winged Swallows hawk over the old runways of an abandoned airbase, while overhead a Gray-headed Kite flies over with distinctive flickering wingbeats.

The village of Cumuto has its birding attraction right in the center of town, in an old pine outside the police station! Here lives a busy colony of showy Yellow-rumped Caciques, smaller relatives of the oropendolas, with even brighter blue eyes and brilliant yellow around the base of the tail. Nearby a Piratic Flycatcher sits, an unwelcome resident that appropriates cacique nests for its own use.

The lowland forest of Arena is home to many of the same birds we encounter at Asa Wright, but also has other species that do not occur in the mountains. Our first find is a grace-ful Plumbeous Kite sitting kestrel-like on the wires, and we spend some time searching for the owner of a buzzy, up-and-over warbler song that at home would announce a Northern Parula but here must be a Tropical Parula.

Leaf through the bird guide and your eye will be caught by "ant" birds: not only are there antbirds, but antvireos, antshrikes, antthrushes and ant-tanagers. The names, we are informed, originate from the habit of many of these spe-cies of associating with columns of army ants. My own mind immediately jumps back to childhood adventure stores where the intrepid explorers desperately fight off huge hordes of these tiny creatures, advancing in vast columns and consuming everything that moves—slowly, inexorably, horribly. I guess that's the reality if you're a caterpillar, and standing in one of the columns is not a good idea; but other-wise they're interesting rather than terrifying.

As everywhere, there are some real "nasties" here. Malaria is not present, but yellow fever is endemic in the animal population and shots are sometimes rec-ommended. Check with your doctor. There are four poi-sonous snakes (the fer-de-lance, bushmaster, and two coral snakes) but they're mainly nocturnal; neverthe-less, you should be aware of them. Ticks and chiggers are here too. Use fly repellent, and be careful about overexertion in the heat.

You don't expect brilliance from an ant. One day we found a column straggling across one of the paths at the Centre, and decided to follow it to see where it went. Finally it headed straight to our cottage, and after looping around the outside went up under our door into the room. We pondered this for a while, and decided that we'd prefer them to go somewhere else. How do you stop an army ant column? We gently headed those nearest the door over to link up with the other end of the column, which they joined with evident gusto. Soon the ants inside the room came scurrying out to find where everyone else had gone to, and when we finally left for lunch the entire column was still busily going in a circle around the building.

For the smaller animals in their path, however, army ants must really be terrifying, and the birds that associate with the columns are able to exploit the bounty provided by creatures trying to escape the ants. On our trip to Arena we come across such a gathering, and spend a hectic few minutes trying to nail down all the birds present. Birding in tropical woodlands really can be a feast or a famine!

Another day we visit the experimental farm for such open country species as Red-breasted Blackbird and ground doves, and wetland birds such as Wattled Jacanas and Southern Lapwings. Savanna Hawk is a highlight here, a rufous-and-black raptor vastly more striking than the plates in the guide. On a longer trip we drive west to the Atlantic beaches to visit the freshwater Nariva Swamp. Huge flocks of Dickcissels winter here, and Masked Yellowthroats skulk in the tall reedbeds. In the evening flocks of Red-bellied Macaws fly in to roost, and along the beach we put up a Yellow-headed Caracara, graceful and falconlike.

One of our most unforgettable trips is to the enormous Caroni Swamp. We leave in the later afternoon for the boat moorings to meet Winston Nanan, who knows the mangrove swamps and their birds intimately. Heading down one of the broad channels through the mangroves in a large flat-bottomed boat, we pass an hour or so searching for such species as Black-crested Antshrikes and Bicolored Conebills, birds that nest exclusively in the mangrove swamps. Finally we move out into a large area of open water where other boats are gathered to watch the roosting flights of egrets and ibises.

Behind us a burnished sun goes in and out behind scattered clouds, painting them with fire and radiating shafts of brilliance against a golden sky. To the north, insubstantial in the distance, lies the Northern Range, forming undulations of soft lavender, mauve, and gray-blue against a sky of the most delicate turquoise. Above, small scattered clouds float, pink, salmon, and orange, and ahead of us lie the mangrove islands, dark green mounds against the low dark wall of the swamp.

The water lies still, reflecting the multitude of hues from the sky, together with a silvery radiance seemingly its own. The boats lie still, silent. We wait. For some reason it seems necessary to talk in whispers.

The first Scarlet Ibis appears. Long neck and curved bill outstretched, the entire bird that incredible hue of scarlet save the neatly contrasting black wingtips, it flies quickly past to vanish among the islands. Then a small flock appears; and then more and more fly in, their brilliant plumage even more vivid in the setting sun, dropping into the darkening clumps of mangroves ahead. Soon the nearest island is covered with them, for all the world like a giant poinsettia covered with enormous blossoms.

Gradually the light fails, the flight tails off. Finally something disturbs the birds and they all fly up briefly, a sudden huge whirl of dark rich reds and crimsons again a salmon sky, before settling back to their roosts once more. It is dark, and somewhere in the distance a Tropical Screech-Owl calls.

But for us the evening's adventures are not yet over. We head even farther into the mangroves, now barely distinguishable from the dark sky above. Far away, we hear a melancholy cry. Suddenly it is closer, a haunting, descending cadence, an eerie, hollow sound. This is no disembodied spirit, but rather a Common Potoo, revealed in our spotlight sitting up on the top of a dead stub, looking exactly like an extension of the branch itself. Its large eyes glow as it calls again, to be answered by other birds farther down the channel. Soon it darts off for its evening hunting, materializing as the large nightjar that it really is. We too return, through the lights and the noise and the traffic, to head back up to our late dinner, but with the desolate cry of the bird in the stillness of the swamp echoing in our ears.

Sound is, of course, the most evocative element of birding. A picture of a bird may do a good job of recalling the bird, but its calls or song have the ability to transport you back in time to the very place it was last heard, with all the sights, sounds, smells, and feelings of that moment vividly recaptured.

The forests of Trinidad provide a rich and bewildering supply of material for such recollections. Some noises, like the call of the potoo, are unmistakable and unforgettable. Many others remain as little more than disembodied sounds throughout our visit. The soft calls of the Little Tinamou, sounding rather like a distant cockerel, we have yet to attach to a living bird. The author of the clear, downward piping that is heard so regularly in the evenings only rarely

shows itself as a Buff-throated Woodcreeper. Still other sounds trigger inappropriate recollections. The author of House Sparrow-like chirps usually proves to be a Palm Tanager, robinlike chuckles are Cocoa Thrushes, and Silver-beaked Tanagers sound alternately like cardinals and Song Sparrows. But altogether these sounds simply merge with a multitude of others to become unmistakably Trinidad.

Reservations at **Kariwak Village** can also be handled by Caligo Ventures (see above for details). <u>Rooms</u>: 18 rooms in 9 cabanas which surround a pool, with a queen-size bed or a queen plus single. All rooms have shower. <u>Amenities</u>: Authentic Caribbean cuisine in an open-air dining room. All meals are included. Bar specializes in Caribbean alcoholic and nonalcoholic drinks. Beach nearby. Fishing, snorkeling, diving, wind surfing and sailing can be arranged. <u>Terms</u>: Single $98/person, double $78/person. (Prices may be lower May–November). Transfers round trip Crown Point Airport–Kariwak Village $4. All major credit cards accepted.

Trinidad's twin island of Tobago is very different from its larger neighbor. You might expect that a smaller island (26 miles by about 7.5 at its widest), sitting farther out at sea, would have a much smaller avifauna. And you would be correct, but twenty species occur on Tobago alone, and the birding there is very different. Most of the countryside on Tobago is more open, and many of the birds are tame. Some Trinidad skulkers, species such as the Barred Antshrike and Stripe-breasted Spinetail, turn out to be much easier to see there.

The crossing from Port of Spain to Crown Point airport is a short half-hour flight, and our landing is enlivened by Blue-gray Tanagers arguing under the eaves of the building as we pick up our luggage. Our base here is in the delightful

Special tours can be arranged to Hillsborough Dam, Grafton Estate, Buccoo Reef, and Little Tobago Island. The tours cost $11.25–31.75/person depending on destination and length. The dam and estate both emphasize landbirds, including the more elusive species. The minimum fee for vehicle use applies here too.

cabanas of Kariwak Village, with birds bobbing in and out of the dwarf poincianas and other shrubs.

One of the Tobago specialties—and conspicuous almost everywhere—will seem familiar to North American eyes, as the Red-crowned Woodpecker looks rather like a small Red-

---

The airline offering the widest range of flights to Trinidad is BWIA (British West Indian Airlines). A regular air service links the two islands.

U.S. and Canadian visitors require only a current passport or proof of citizenship. Currency is in Trinidad and Tobago dollars, but U.S. dollars can be exchanged readily at the airport and are accepted by many hotels.

January through March is the driest period and the most popular for visits, but there is good birding year-round, and South American migrants are present only in the rainy season of May through September.

---

bellied, and behaves in much the same way. Some of the others are harder to find as they are confined to heavier cover. These range in size from the large Rufous-vented Chachalaca to the diminutive Blue-backed Manakin, an elegant little creature with a scarlet head patch and sky-blue back contrasting to its black plumage. Adolphus James, the driver who escorts most of the Tobago birders, has a wonderful ability to call these, and other species, into view.

The real high spot of a trip to Tobago is not land birding at all, but rather a boat trip to Little Tobago. This lies off the town of Speyside, at the northeast tip of the main island, and it is here that we join a fisherman's boat to take us across. It doesn't look very far, but distances are deceptive and the passage is quite choppy. Landing depends very much on weather conditions, and is not possible if the sea is too rough.

Today we have no difficulty, and we start up the track that leads to the summit of the island, and views of the seabird colonies and the open ocean beyond. As we continue the steep climb Adolphus unsuccessfully investigates burrows for nesting Audubon's Shearwaters. Finally we emerge to a vista of rocky headlands and surf far below us, with all the turmoil and excitement associated with a seabird colony.

Brown Boobies are ranged along the ledges lower down and fishing out over the water, joined from time to time by smaller Red-footed Boobies, together with Brown Noddies and a few Sooty Terns. Far more spectacular, however, is the steady procession of Red-billed Tropicbirds flying in and out to their nests on the cliffs just below us, and dozens of frigatebirds soaring overhead. Tropicbirds are one of those species that can elicit a rather "ho-hum" response from a North American birder with images of terns in his mind. So the striking size and dramatic appearance of these beautiful birds, soaring a few feet away and screaming like banshees, is memorable indeed, and a fitting conclusion to a trip to these magical islands.

Depending on how much you wish to cover and at what pace, Trinidad and Tobago are good for a week to two weeks of steady birding. You can visit the major spots on Trinidad itself in a week, while Tobago requires three days or so. The current birdlist for the two islands stands at 366 species; of these you may see some 160 to 200 species on a ten-day trip, and—more significantly—if you have never been outside North America before the majority of these will be new.

OF STEEL BANDS, PARADES, AND CARNIVAL

The islands have even more fascination for the general naturalist than the birder, but trying to sort out all the plants and animals is both challenging and frustrating! In most cases no field guides exist at all. Nevertheless, there is a long history of biological investigation on Trinidad—some of it based at Simla, the research station situated in the valley below Asa Wright itself—and so the plant and animal life is far better known here than in most other areas of the neotropics. Even the moderately interested visitor cannot help but be fascinated by the rich flora, with the abundance of epiphytes growing on the trees—there's even an epiphytic cactus—and the many vivid butterflies.

Trinidad's main city is Port of Spain, which has a number of historic sites and good tourist facilities, but the island places less emphasis on conventional tourism as its economy is more broadly based, with emphasis on both oil production and agriculture.

Tobago too has a long and colorful history, and there are a number of historic sites dating back to the late eighteenth century. Here tourism is the major industry, with facilities ranging from resort hotels with their own golf courses to small family-run businesses in some of the towns.

The islands' rich ethnic mix has resulted in a lively and distinctive culture. The calypso originated here, and the festivals, with their steel bands, showy displays and limbo dancing are central to Trinidad life. The main festival is Carnival in the week before Lent, and the entire island becomes caught up in the lively competition with colorful processions through the streets.

Tobago has many excellent beaches, and most of the hotels also have their own swimming pools. Scuba diving is especially popular and reputed to be some of the best in the Caribbean. One noteworthy locality off the west shoreline is the Buccoo Reef, where an elevated area of reef forms, in effect, a crystal-clear swimming pool out in the middle of the ocean. You might even see some seabirds as well!

★   ★   ★   ★   ★

CHAPTER 4

POINT PELEE, ONTARIO: LANDFALL FOR THE WARBLER HOSTS

AT DAWN THE LOW SUN OVER THE LAKE TO the east turns the water into a carpet of silver, the waterfowl a multitude of black dots spotted over its surface. On the sandspit to the south a small flock of gulls gathers: Ring-billed, Herring, and Great Black-backed—scruffy-looking teenagers with nothing better to do. Beyond them Bonaparte's Gulls swirl low over the turbulent waters off the tip, swinging back and forth, up and down in a restless ballet, while out to the west are vast flocks of Red-breasted Mergansers, in constant movement with the males jerking their heads forward and then abruptly backward in excited display.

Periodically a whole flock suddenly rises from the water for no apparent reason, and at times the sky is full of mer-

gansers crossing the point in both directions simultane-
ously. Overhead a constant succession of blackbirds is flying
south down the point, some in flocks, others singly, to arrive
at the tip and mill about uncertainly, as though they had
only just noticed the expanse of water ahead. The nearest
landfall, Pelee Island, is no more than a hazy mirage on the
horizon some ten miles to the southwest.

We look over the gull flock for possible Iceland or Lesser
Black-backed gulls; scrutinize the Bonaparte's for stray
Franklin's or Little gulls, or perhaps something even rarer;
scope the thousands of merganser for larger or smaller dots,
loons or grebes, scaup or scoter, or something rarer. Sometimes warblers arrive in the bushes behind us, to dart out
nervously over the sand before diving back into cover, and
overhead the milling flocks must be watched for occasional
orioles or grosbeaks, maybe something rarer. Another day
of spring birding at Point Pelee has begun.

Pelee—more properly, Point Pelee National Park—is a
long sandspit jutting over six miles out into Lake Erie. It is
the narrow triangular tip of a long point that starts from the
town of Leamington to the west, where most of the accommodation is situated, and from the village of Wheatley on
the east.

Like promontories into major water bodies generally, the
entire area concentrates birds, but Point Pelee itself, with its
patchwork of woodlands, marshes, and open places concentrates them most. In fact, as the southernmost tip of Canada
(and on the same latitude as northern California), it is the
major concentration point on the Great Lakes, and one of
the very best on the continent. But also like such places
everywhere, Pelee can be good one day and dead the next.
You can carefully time your visit for a few days in the peak
migration period—usually the second week in May—only to
find a birdless point with cold, rainy weather.

The Point itself also is constantly changing, coming and
going. In some springs the sandspit will stretch far out beyond the last line of trees, curving to a narrow hook at its
end. In other years late winter storms will have bitten into

the bulwark of shrubs itself, and no beach will be visible. Because the Point is really composed of a series of dune ridges separated by low, wet areas, a year following severe storms in the early spring will leave huge areas flooded and

Pelee is south of the town of Leamington, itself easily accessible via Routes 401 and 77. Continue south through the town on 77 to its end at County Rd. 20. Turn left, then bear right on County Rd. 33, which leads to the park gate. The nearest airport is at Windsor, about 25 miles west.

There is an excellent range of accommodation in Leamington, but for peak periods in spring—usually the second and third weeks of May—reservations must be made months in advance. The following is the nearest place to the park, but although it is fairly well situated it has no outside windows and tends to be rather noisy: **Pelee Motor Inn**—P.O. Box 616, Leamington, Ontario, Canada N8H 3X4 (3 miles south of Leamington on County Rd. 33). (519) 326-8646; toll-free 1-800-265-5329. Open all year. Rooms: 60 units, double; some suites with king-size bed, sitting and dining area, private whirlpool bath. Amenities: Dining room, lounge, coffee shop, night club, indoor swimming pool, sauna, whirlpool, fitness facilities, badminton, putting green, table tennis, pool table. Terms: (all figures C$) Double $64.50, suites $125–150. AMEX, MC, VISA.

The following is the nearest to the park in town, and there are restaurants in the plaza opposite:
Journey's End Motel—279 Erie St. S., Leamington, Ontario, Canada N8H 3C4 (2 blocks south of Route 3 on Route 77). (519) 326-9071; toll-free 1-800-668-4200. Open all year. Rooms: 62 units. Amenities: Clean, comfortable rooms. Terms: Single $39.88–41.88, double $46.88–48.88. AMEX, MC, VISA.

Pelee allows only prearranged group camping. The following is the most pleasant camping location in the area, and it can often yield good birding, but it is a fair distance from the park and is sometimes very noisy.

The opening and closing dates vary from year to year, but are usually around the dates given: check with the park ahead of time:

Wheatley Provincial Park—Box 640, Wheatley, Ontario, Canada N0P 2P0 (1 mile east of town on Route 3, then south on Klondike Rd.). (519) 825-4059. Open May 10—October 15. Campsites: 210 sites, 52 electricity, 158 no hookups. Amenities: Rest rooms, hot showers, playground, beach, boat rentals, hiking trails, sewage disposal. Terms: Electric $10, no hookup $7.

The following is close to the Point, but you need reservations in the peak periods:

Sturgeon Woods Tent and Trailer Park—R.R. 1, Leamington, Ontario, Canada, N8H 3V4 (5 miles southeast of Leamington on Point Pelee Rd.). (519) 326-1156. Open April 15—October 15. Campsites: 385 sites, 100 full hookups, 250 water and electricity, 35 no hookups, separate tenting area. Amenities: Rest rooms, hot showers, recreation room, playground, boating, dock, fishing, limited grocery store, sewage disposal. Terms: Full hookup $12, electric and water $11, no hookup $10.

inaccessible. At other times even the ditches are dry, filled with tangled vegetation, but no matter what the conditions on the Point itself, the birds still concentrate and the birders still arrive to watch them.

To the regular visitor these migration hot spots are full of memories. There was the day when a flock of avocets flew down one side of the Point to circle briefly at the end before vanishing. There was the Summer Tanager that sat sleeping on a bare bough at the side of the path for an hour or two at dawn, like a marathon swimmer who struggles ashore to collapse exhausted. Throughout that time it had its little knot of admiring observers, until it awoke, and finding itself surrounded by a host of predators—the swimmer awakening in a pride of lions—vanished instantly into the vegetation. Individual bushes and trees take on character: there was the clump where we saw the white head of a small hawk, either a Black-shouldered or Mississippi kite, but failed to find the rest of the body; there was the tree where a Virginia's Warbler sat before disappearing, never to be found again.

There's also a history of the ones that were missed: the huge reverse migration off the Point on the only morning we decided to sleep in, and the Scissor-tailed Flycatcher that flew past just after we left. Every birder in every migration hot spot has such memories, and in a place like Pelee the newcomer can become frustrated by the bounty of birds that are reported but that completely elude him. The area is so intensively birded that many rarities are found, but often seen by very few.

After scanning the Point, we work slowly north through the tangled vegetation at the tip. In one of the taller trees sit a couple of male Northern Orioles, three male Rose-breasted Grosbeaks, a small flock of goldfinches and, in the outer branches, a male Indigo Bunting. They look for all the world like Christmas tree ornaments arrayed on a leafless tree. Warblers dart in and out of the heavy tangles and flirt with observers from the depths of the low cedars, and little flocks of Chipping Sparrows forage along the sand and in short grass along the path.

Already the grapevine is working: someone just saw a Golden-winged Warbler (or Prothonotary, or Worm-eating, or Kentucky, or Hooded) in the trees by the train loop; there's a Clay-colored Sparrow in with the chippies in the West Beach parking area; someone saw a Glossy Ibis (or Snowy Egret, or Tricolored Heron) in the marsh on the way in. The temptation is to go chasing after each one of these: sometimes they are still there! But you'll often spend your day chasing from one group of frustrated searchers to another, and miss the day's real birding in the process.

A major element in that real birding is the brilliant array of high-plumaged warblers foraging in small flocks through the shrubs and in the treetops. It's an element that's taken for granted because it's almost always there, an integral part of a "good" day; without it something, a great deal, is missing. The glowing orange of a Blackburnian's throat, the vivid yellow of a Yellow Warbler, the black and orange of a butterfly-like redstart, the exquisite contrasts of yellow, grays, and blacks of a Magnolia and the elegant, subdued beauty of a Black-throated Blue: without these and the rest of the radiant throng, Pelee would be immeasurably less enchanting.

Park entry is $5 (annual $30, and valid for other national parks). The Interpretive Centre has a paper showing the road networks in the area, as well as checklists (75¢, with a small map on the back) and other books and information. The trains to the tip normally start at 9 A.M., but during at least part of the birding season they usually start early; however, this decision is made seasonally so you should check with the Centre on your arrival (it is not open at dawn) regarding the current schedule.

There is only a small snack bar in the park itself, and very few places to eat until you get into Leamington. This can be particularly troublesome at breakfast, as it's inconvenient to leave the park, and sometimes difficult to find a restaurant open at 4:30 A.M. However, there are several picnic areas and rest rooms in the park north of the Interpretive Centre.

My own *A Bird-Finding Guide to Ontario* (University of Toronto Press, 1982) also has a map of the area and more detailed directions, as well as information on other areas in the province. The hotline for this area is (519) 252-2473, and for the province (519) 586-3959.

★

The tip is linked to the Interpretive Centre by a small propane-powered train that covers the last mile and a half or so to the tip. Automobiles are excluded from this area, and in the busier periods the train service originates even higher up the Point, from the Laurier parking area. Access to these parts of the park is otherwise on foot, and walking is the best way to see Pelee.

Over the years traditions have developed in covering the Point, often their origins lost in antiquity, and newer birders may wonder why, for example, birding has usually commenced at the tip. True, the tip becomes very disturbed and the birds tend to leave, but it can be quite rewarding there later in the day. One year on impulse we went down at noon, and found the only Bell's Vireo of the spring—also the only bird at the Point, just as we were the only birders!

Sometimes in both spring and fall the Point is anything but warm, especially at dawn. Conditions are very changeable at these times, so be prepared for both cold and rain, as well as possible hot weather.

We start at dawn for those very rare times when a major grounding or overflight occurs, and under these circumstances every branch can seem to be covered with birds, and such improbable things as rails and moorhens can be found sitting in the trees. These groundings disperse rapidly, and indeed enormous reverse migrations have been seen off the tip in the early morning, with birds flying out into a south wind. You can spend a lifetime without chancing upon one of these remarkable movements, and we have never had the good fortune to experience one. It's the possibility that keeps people coming back to Pelee year after year.

More and more people keep coming. Pelee in migration is no place to visit if you don't like birding in a crowd, and indeed many veteran Ontario birders now rarely visit in spring, preferring to exchange the rarities for less outstanding, but still exciting birding at other promontories along the lakes: places such as Rondeau Provincial Park near Blenheim, and Long Point near Port Rowan. But for sheer number and variety of birds Pelee is unequaled, and at its best unbelievable. Careful estimates of the birds on the Point at such times have run into millions.

After covering the Point we are faced with choices, as the birds disperse as the land widens and the trees become taller. Where to go next? Sometimes it seems to be a good idea simply to continue walking up the road to the Nature Centre. Sometimes wind and general weather conditions assist in the decision, and birding is often better on the more sheltered side of the Point, in spite of the periodic disturbance of the trains.

We opt to cover the main nature trail from the Interpretive Centre. Our path loops through an enchanting open woodland of hackberries, hickories, and oaks, with a lush ground cover of wildflowers—violets, bellworts, trilliums, Jack-in-the-pulpit and many others. The warblers here are moving in small groups through the treetops, often associated with chickadees, White-breasted Nuthatches, and the occasional Downy Woodpecker.

Finally the path emerges through tangles of wild grape and creeper into an old orchard. Here dense thickets of stagshorn sumac and red cedars dominate, and we encounter different birds. Rufous-sided Towhees are singing from the tops of the grape tangles, and a Brown Thrasher roots around below. Farther away we hear the distinctive tootings of a Yellow-breasted Chat and the sweet accelerating song of a Field Sparrow. Here the skies are easier to see, and as the day warms hawks are beginning to move. Two high specks turn out to be Red-shouldered and Red-tailed hawks soaring together, and a few Turkey Vultures tilt and turn in the breeze. Lower, just over the treetops, flock after flock of Blue Jays flies past. Other migrants are scarce through this more open area, although it can attract such birds as Sedge Wren and LeConte's Sparrow.

The orchard ends at the Post Woods, now an open area where narrow dune ridges separate water-filled depressions, the path winding across boardwalks linking the sandy ridges. Once this was a giant old hardwood forest, shady even in the early spring, but a severe storm blew down most of the trees. Now it is a place of light and air, of dense shrubby tangles and young supple saplings, of huge deadfalls and bleached stubs and snags, and sloughs fragrant with the blossoms of spice bush. A few giant remnants of the original forest still stand, reminders of Post Woods past and future.

In spring the place becomes a vast Tree Swallow colony, and the birds swirl constantly around the multitude of dead trees, greeting mates with soft musical calls and quarreling over nest holes. House Wrens sing and scold at every bend of the path, and the wet sloughs are home to Swamp Sparrows and Common Yellowthroats. Our walk through here yields such skulkers as Lincoln's Sparrow, and in one or two places a Carolina Wren sings vigorously. A few Rusty Blackbirds, lingerers from the flocks of April, gurgle from one of the denser thickets.

Southwestern Ontario is the richest agricultural country in Canada, a level, fertile plain dissected by drainage canals. Much of it is reclaimed marsh, and this is particularly true

of the fields north of the park boundary that were once part of the Pelee marsh itself. They are fields now by virtue of the high dikes holding back the waters of the lake. Sometimes, in particularly stormy years when lake levels are high, these dikes are breached by the waves, which inundate huge areas. At the best of times many of these fields are wet in the spring, and so they provide another habitat, complementing the swampy woods and cattail marshes of the park.

After lunch we head out onto the "onion fields" to drive around the network of gravel roads leading toward Wheatley. At once we see Horned Larks and Savannah and House sparrows, birds not present in the park itself, but our real objectives are the water and shorebirds that can appear in the wet drainage ditches, unplowed corn and soybean fields, and muddy wet spots. Eventually we come across a group of Black-bellied Plover and a few Ruddy Turnstones feeding among the dead stocks of a cornfield, and farther along lie wet areas where we find Short-billed Dowitchers and Dunlins busily probing the mud, both resplendent in the rich cinnamons and rufous of spring. At one point a few American Pipits call overhead, at another a Merlin dashes past.

Finally we arrive at Hillman's Marsh, a wetland that is frequently better for birds than the rather inaccessible marshes in the park itself. Here the marsh borders a creek, and roads run parallel to it along either side. From the dike we see flocks of Bonaparte's Gulls resting on a mudflat, and Forster's Terns constantly patrol the open water. Suddenly birds are flying wildly in all directions: the gulls swirl up and flocks of shorebirds appear from somewhere in a panic. The dark shape of a Peregrine Falcon rockets across the marsh and disappears low over the fields toward the Point. Soon all is quiet once more, but not before we have picked out the mothlike flight and dark underwings of a Little Gull flying among the mass of Bonaparte's.

Around on the north side of the creek, wet sedge meadows are good places to see rails and other waterbirds not visible from the shoreline. King Rails nest in long marsh grasses near the road, but seeing them can be another matter. Some birders with more determination than responsibility and common sense plow out into the wetland to flush the birds, but populations of this species are few in Canada and vulnerable to disturbance.

Hillman's Creek creates other small wetlands as it winds through the fields in this area, all of them worth a stop to scan and listen, but the isolated groves of trees along the lakeshore are usually more productive of landbirds. We find flocks of warblers moving through, and they're a lot easier to look at here than in the heavy vegetation of the Point. Quickly we have a dozen species, all brilliant in high spring plumage. Lake Erie is worth more than a passing glance as well, for diving ducks and grebes not visible from the Point, and we stop periodically to look over the open water.

Our last stop is at Wheatley harbor, one of Lake Erie's major fishing ports, and a constant scene of activity as boats move in and out. Gulls loiter here, and it is often a place to pick out a rarity or two. Even if there's nothing to be seen, the small woodlot by the bridge just to the north usually has a few Black-crowned Night-Herons roosting near the water.

While major groundings at Pelee can be hard to predict, the general progress of migration is influenced by the broader weather patterns, and usually it is at least possible to identify the best day to go shopping in Leamington. Continuous poor weather inhibits migration, of course, and in spring the arrival of cold air masses from the north brings everything to a halt. Not that a beautiful warm day with southerly winds is necessarily ideal, because sometimes the birds simply overfly the Point in fine weather, although birding still tends to be better than in a period of prolonged cold. Springs with a mixture of warm and cold air movements are often the best, the warm air stimulating migration and the frontal systems themselves often grounding the birds. By the same token the really big groundings are often the product of sudden changes in the weather: fog, or even a localized storm overnight may precipitate a bonanza.

On our return to the park we head into Tilden's Woods. These lie immediately north of the Post Woods, and are now the finest woodlands on the Point. Huge red maples and sycamores grow along the sloughs, and areas of dense shrubs and cedar create heavy cover. Nesting Wood Ducks fly off with creaky quacks of alarm, and Red-headed Woodpeckers play peekaboo from the shelter of the tall trunks.

Tilden's is one of those places where you always have the feeling that anything can turn up around the next bend, and indeed many of Pelee's rarest birds have occurred here. Soft warbler songs can be heard everywhere as we walk in along the main trail. Most of the birds are high among the flowers of the tall maples, but lower down in the chokecherries a Blue-winged is feeding, and an Ovenbird sings briefly from somewhere on the ground.

Finally we arrive at a group of shady pools, well known as one of the most productive areas in the entire woodlot. Here Northern Waterthrushes teeter along the water's edge, and after some searching we finally spot the bubble-gum-pink legs of a Louisiana, a rarity here in Ontario. Waiting around eventually pays off again as a shaft of sunlight illuminates a spot of brilliance. Perhaps the deep, dark, still, silent, secret swamps of the South were created as a fitting setting for this one supreme golden jewel, a Prothonotary Warbler.

Priorities differ widely among the park's birders. Canadians come searching for the southern birds, overshoots more reliable here than anywhere else. In a week at Pelee a keen Ontario birder can hope to add twenty or more species rare anywhere else in Canada. But a visitor from the Southwest will drool over the gaudy array of wood warblers, and some folk have very specific objectives indeed—like those who come in the third week of May for a chance to add Connecticut Warbler to their life lists. And some will settle for everything: we were talking to a young English birder on his first day at the Point when a Cedar Waxwing went sizzling over.

"Am I likely to see one again?" he asked. I thought about the hundreds of waxwings that were likely to line his route, and assured him that I'd be surprised if he didn't, but when I left he was still gazing wistfully in the direction of the long-vanished bird.

Late evening can have some special attractions at Pelee. Black-crowned Night-Herons and shorebirds sometimes gather at the tip, and as darkness falls and the chorus of cricket frogs starts in the marsh, woodcock stage their evening flights from the woodlands along the road. Before dawn the birds are performing again, and it is frequently possible to hear Whip-poor-wills calling from the woodlands north of the group campground at that time as well.

Travel in Ontario is easy, and the province publishes a free Traveller's Encyclopaedia which is very useful to anyone visiting the nation and province for the first time, as well as accommodation and camping books. Phone toll-free, 8 A.M.–6 P.M., 1-800-268-3735.

★

Although Pelee is the focus of birding in southwestern Ontario in the spring, it's not the only good place there. Lake St. Clair is about twenty miles north of the park; here, east of the village of Stoney Point, are other productive marshes with nesting Yellow-headed Blackbirds; the St. Clair Wildlife Refuge farther to the east can also yield excellent birding, with thousands of Tundra Swans in March. Back on the Lake Erie shore, the roads to the west through Kingsville reveal the lake now and then, and, particularly around Cedar Creek, there is good waterbird habitat and nesting Bald Eagles. The park naturalists can usually give more explicit directions to these places.

Thirty miles to the east, Rondeau Provincial Park near the town of Blenheim has superb old hardwood forests and extensive marshes. Its record as a nesting area for southern species such as Chuck-will's-widow, Acadian Flycatcher, White-eyed Vireo, and Prothonotary Warbler is much better than Pelee's, although the extensive habitat here does not concentrate migrants as well. Pelee Island shares much of the Point's quality, but is difficult to get to and has only limited accommodation. Well to the west, near Amherstburg at the mouth of the Detroit River, is Holiday Beach Park. Though only moderately interesting in the spring, it is the site of major hawk flights every fall, with numbers exceeding those from many of the better-known hawk-watching areas in the Appalachians.

Point Pelee itself, while known principally as a spring birding area, is excellent in fall, although the dense vegetation at that time makes landbirds much harder to see. Another reason that the landbirds tend to be secretive then is that the Point is a major pathway in the southbound flight of accipiters, particularly for Cooper's Hawks. In fall the weather conditions that stimulate migration are, of course, reversed, and the birds flood in with the bodies of cold air and the passage of high pressure systems from the North. At such times it's possible to stand at the Point and watch a steady procession of accipiters and falcons flying out over the lake. At this time the Point also funnels thousands of monarch butterflies, which sometimes cover the asters and goldenrods in living blankets.

Whenever conditions are suitable in early autumn, shorebirds gather on the onion fields, and in some years noteworthy concentrations of Buff-breasted Sandpiper have been recorded. Later fall is rewarding as well, when Tundra Swans fly along the Point and the mergansers again gather in huge flocks off the tip.

Even winter brings its delights. While it is not a particularly good area for the real northerners—such species as winter finches, which usually only get as far south as this in heavy flight years—wintering species that normally are far to the south often appear here. Ontarians like to refer to the Southwest as the banana belt, and it indeed gets relatively little snow in comparison with the rest of the province. This, coupled with the barrier the lake presents, means that wintering birds such as hawks and crows can be found here in numbers that are not usually encountered again until southern Ohio. Flocks of Snow Buntings and Horned Larks pick grit along the roadsides, and on the Point itself Yellow-rumped Warblers join the flocks of chickadees, nuthatches, and kinglets, and lingering sparrows root in the tangles.

Pelee's fame is as a place for migrants and rare wanderers. Its checklist includes 349 species, and on a good day in spring lists of well in excess of 100 species are usual. It is not particularly noted for special nesting species, however, and Rondeau to the east offers much more habitat for southerners that reach the limits of their ranges in southwestern Ontario. But for the sheer spectacle of migration in progress, Pelee is unparalleled.

OTHER FEATURES OF INTEREST IN SOUTHWESTERN ONTARIO

Southwestern Ontario is of great interest to Canadian naturalists because the flora, and to a lesser extent the fauna, is part of the Carolinian Forest Region of deciduous hardwoods, a community that occurs nowhere else in Canada. Pelee, Rondeau, and Wheatley provincial parks are all noteworthy botanically, and in Windsor a section of Ojibway Park protects an extensive stand of long-grass prairie—ironically, one of the finest in the country—which is at its best in early fall.

There is sport fishing and boating along this section of the Erie shoreline, and excellent beaches in the park itself. There are historic sites in Windsor and Amherstburg. Ontario was the terminus of the Underground Railroad for runaway slaves, and Amherstburg has the North American Black Historical Museum chronicling the history and heritage of black people (277 King St., open Wednesday to Sunday). The home and burial place of the Reverend Tom Henson is at the "Uncle Tom's Cabin" Historic Site 1 mile west of Dresden on Route 21, which in turn intersects with 401 some 50 miles east of the Route 77 junction. Niagara Falls, that tourist mecca, is some 220 miles away, and the Niagara River is a gull hot spot in the fall.

★   ★   ★   ★   ★

CHAPTER 5

HORICON MARSH, WISCONSIN: GEESE, GEESE, AND MORE GEESE

N FALL, WHEN THE FIRST FROSTS PAINT THE leaves red and yellow and the harvested fields lie gold under the bright autumn sunshine, the cooling, shortening days bring the geese south.

Even the confirmed urbanite can feel the lure of the goose migration. For the birder, just one flock can add spice to a quiet day, but the huge migrant concentrations of the big birds become objectives in themselves. Horicon National Wildlife Refuge is one of the biggest—and certainly one of the most famous—staging areas on the continent.

Canada Geese are the attraction at Horicon. Fall numbers range between one and two hundred thousand, or over a quarter of the total Canada Geese using the Mississippi Valley flyway. Such enormous numbers would overwhelm a smaller area, and indeed the concentrations can present some problems at Horicon as well, but with thirty-one thousand acres even these vast flocks can disperse quite effectively.

The approach to the Refuge is through rolling Wisconsin countryside, and there's little on the drive up from Milwaukee to suggest an approach to a major wetland. We turn west on Route 49, passing through rich farmland with well-fed cattle browsing contentedly and tall stands of corn in the midst of harvest. Here and there small flocks of Canadas are flying about, but there seems no particular direction or purpose to their movement. Then, as we crest a hill, a vast lowland spreads before us an enormous expanse of muted brown cattails, the uniformity broken only by small clumps of trees and shrubs. Horicon is reputed to be the largest cattail marsh in the United States: true or not, this is a formidable wetland.

We continue down the hill and soon find ourselves driving along with stands of cattails on either side. We're not the only ones here to see the geese. Little clusters of cars line the shoulders of the road, and knots of people stand looking out over the marshes. And here, in the pools and leads of the marsh, in tens and hundreds, are geese. As we continue westward there are more and more of them, flying over and feeding in the fields to the west.

The town of Waupun is the host to this extravaganza, and on mild days during the goose passage even the air of the town seems redolent of geese. Our motel is tucked down a quiet side street. The marsh itself lies in a vast glacial depression that runs south some twelve miles to the town of Horicon itself. The southern third of the wetland—10,991 acres—is owned by the state of Wisconsin and called the Horicon Marsh Wildlife Area. Horicon National Wildlife Refuge constitutes the northern two thirds of the marsh, 20,976 acres, and is administered by the U.S. Fish and Wildlife Service.

Toward evening we are back out again on Route 49 with the other vehicles on the shoulder, watching the foraging flocks return to the marsh for the night. It is an impressive sight. At times the entire sky seems filled with geese, some in long orderly V's and others in little groups of twos and threes, some high and others low, and everywhere the incessant clamor of the birds as they drop into the marsh to join the flocks already there.

Dawn is even more spectacular. The pools along the highway have almost vanished under the masses of geese, and flock after flock pass overhead; groups of birds fly low to feed on the neighboring fields, and higher up, long chevrons of birds etched against the clouds continue their flight south.

The best motel is in town, just off the main street:
Inn Town Motel—27 S. State St. (¼ mile west on Route 49—½ block south), Waupun, Wisconsin 53963. (414) 324-4211. Open all year. <u>Rooms</u>: 16 units, double and single rooms. <u>Amenities</u>: Television, air conditioning. <u>Terms</u>: Single $24, double $30–32. MC, VISA. The best place to eat is **Hardee's** (open 6 A.M.), at the east end of town.

For campers, the following is in a pleasant woodland just west of town:
Waupun County Park—C.T.H. MMM, (north on County Park Rd. from Route 49) Waupun, Wisconsin, 53963. (414) 324-2769. <u>Campsites</u>: Primitive area, 35 electrical/water. <u>Amenities</u>: Pool, picnic area, playground, trails, ball diamond, dump station, firewood. <u>Terms</u>: Primitive—$5; Electric and water—$8; Dump station— $2; Firewood—$1; Pool to $1.50.

Horicon has had a checkered history. The story of European settlement is a variation on an all too familiar theme. The first settlers dammed the marsh for a sawmill, and the waters rose nine feet to become a vast thirteen-mile-long lake. Steamboats plied the waters for years until the dam was finally removed. The marsh returned, but then the wildlife was hunted commercially and truckloads of birds were sent to market. This continued for decades, until in the 1900s the area was drained for farmland. The attempt proved unsuccessful, but the marsh was destroyed in the process.

Not until 1921 did an effort to restore the original wetlands commence, and a new dam was constructed. Since then the place has returned to something like the vast expanse of open water, cattails, and swampy tangles that it must have been prior to drainage.

To reach Horicon from Milwaukee, take Route 41 northwest to Route 49, and then west. The network of roads around the marsh are, starting from 49 on the east, Route Z south to Route Y, then at Kekoskee Route TW to Route 28, southwest to Horicon. Returning north, take Route E to Route 26, 26 north to Route 1, and then back to 49 just east of Waupun. There are maps at both the Refuge office on Route Z and the Wildlife Area outside Horicon.

There is a picnic area on Route 49 and toilets, and further toilets at the Refuge and Wildlife Area headquarters.

A useful reference is Daryl D. Tessen's *Wisconsin's Favorite Bird Haunts* (Wisconsin Society for Ornithology, 1976) and its 1979 supplement. The Wisconsin hotline is (414) 352-3857. You can bird the circumference of the marsh in a long day, but two or three might be better if birding is good, and more time will be needed if you visit the neighboring locations.

Geese have likely been a part of Horicon for thousands of years. Indian tribes hunted here, but the large flocks apparently date from the early days of the Refuge in the 1940s, when attempts were made to attract them by baiting. The geese came—more and more of them. First there were 2,000; in the 1950s numbers increased to more than 50,000. By the 1970s over 200,000 were staging here, almost half the birds in the Mississippi flyway, and maybe 10 percent of all the Canadas on the continent. They stayed for longer and longer periods, so it is now possible to see large flocks from mid-September until well into November.

Wildlife authorities were not particularly pleased with this development. It reduced hunting opportunities elsewhere, and—more serious—the birds caused substantial crop damage, as well as creating a danger of epidemics from huge numbers of birds remaining for such long periods.

The first attempts to encourage them to move on in the late 1960s proved disastrous: the birds simply dispersed to neighboring farmland with even more crop damage. More recently the flyway managers have had some success in attracting geese to other wetlands in Wisconsin, all with an eye to reducing the Horicon flock to about 100,000. But there are now more birds in the Mississippi Valley flock, and in 1987 the Horicon fall count was still 236,000.

Part of the current approach to managing the wetlands is to manipulate water levels to favor other waterbirds in addition to the geese. Indeed, Horicon is an outstanding venue for waterbirds from spring through fall. The Refuge checklist contains 216 species, with another 32 "accidentals."

In the breeding season the islands in the Wildlife area attract up to a thousand pairs of herons and egrets, the largest heronry in Wisconsin. Thousands of Redheads nest, together with as many as a dozen other species of duck. At this time Yellow-headed Blackbirds call from the cattails, over the open water graceful Forster's Terns hover and plunge, and Tree Swallows swirl around their nests in the holes in the dead stubs.

Even in fall, while the goose numbers eclipse everything else there are lots of other things to be seen. Shorebirds frequent muddy areas in the pools, and other waterfowl are here in numbers as well. Then there are the usual marsh birds. Occasionally we hear snatches of Swamp Sparrow and Marsh Wren song from the cattails, and a bittern flies low over the reed beds. Other herons are easier to see: Great Blues stand motionless in the still pools, and toward evening Black-crowned Night-Herons appear. In late afternoon thirty or so Great Egrets line the banks of the Rock River just west of the marsh itself.

Spring migration brings substantial numbers of geese and other waterfowl to Horicon and there are concentrations here from the middle of March through April, but the birds tend to move on more quickly and there are fewer than in fall. Later there are shorebirds, the other marsh dwellers, and landbirds moving through the trees and bush that surround the marshes.

Horicon is surrounded by a network of good roads. The stretch of marsh along Route 49 is the most rewarding, running as it does directly across the north end of the Refuge, with marshes and pools on either side and ample shoulders for stopping. A tour of the other areas yields more varied— and excellent—birding, and the foot trails located off Route 49 are a great way of getting out of the car and seeing both land and water birds.

We drive down to the Refuge headquarters situated along the eastern boundary of the marsh for brochures and a checklist. Here a good migrant flock of landbirds is crossing between a woodlot and the cornfields on the north of the entry road. Most are Dark-eyed Juncos and White-throated

Sparrows, but we find other species as well: a couple of Fox Sparrows, with Yellow-rumped and Palm warblers flitting around on the bare branches. Everywhere on the fields there are geese, and Northern Harriers quarter constantly low over the old fields and hedgerows.

Farther south, just west of the village of Kekoskee, a dike runs out across the marsh. You can drive or hike this if you visit before September 15, but it's closed once the hunting season opens. It is still worth a trip down to the water here: we find more juncos and warblers foraging in the shelter of the waterside shrubs, and a few coots swim away jerkily.

The state section of the marsh is open to hunting, and does not offer the same concentrations of birds as the areas farther north, and there is considerably more open water here. The state headquarters are set on a hill looking out over the marsh—actually one of a number of drumlins that form islands in it—and walks here lead out to the marsh and through the woods and old fields.

A new network of trails is being developed in the northwest part of the Refuge, radiating from the site of the proposed interpretive center. We walk some of these one evening, as flocks of blackbirds fly up from the cornfields and little groups of goldfinches bounce among the fruiting thistles. A snipe zigzags off from one of the pools, calling creakily, and Palm Warblers pump their tails in the goldenrod. In the woodlot a Downy Woodpecker and White-breasted Nuthatch keep company. Beyond lies the marsh—and the geese.

It's the geese you remember. On our last morning we sit at breakfast in the local Hardee's and look out on a sky of the softest blue, with scattered fleecy clouds painted a delicate pink. Across this canvas line after line of geese fly by, some low and near at hand, others little more than distant wisps of dark against the radiant sky. For half an hour we sit there, and for half an hour the geese pass; as we walk out to head across the marsh they are still coming, their numbers seemingly undiminished.

Not far from here are some other locations that can also

provide rewarding birding. To the east the Kettle Moraine State Forest area has a good mix of landbirds, and to the west Fox and Beaver Dam lakes also attract migrant waterfowl, while in spring the wet fields between these lakes and Route 151 attract both waterfowl—including swans—and a wide variety of shorebirds.

AND IF YOU GET FED UP WITH GEESE . . .

As the glaciers receded the Horicon basin formed a lake, and the islands in the Wildlife Area are really the tops of submerged drumlins. The area's geological significance has been recognized in its designation as an Ice Age National Scientific Reserve, an outstanding example of an extinct post-glacial lake. There are interpretive programs at the Area headquarters in spring and fall.

Waupun is noteworthy for sculpture as well as geese. The industrialist Clarence Shaler presented the city with a fine collection of statues. Two can be seen at Forest Mound Cemetery, where there is also a pleasant woodland and a small slough, and another is on the city hall terrace.

Milwaukee, some 60 miles to the southeast, has all the facilities of a large city. The Milwaukee County Zoo (10001W. Bluemound Rd., 771-3040, 9 A.M.–5 P.M., $3.50) is very good, and Milwaukee Public Museum (800 W. Wells St., 278-2702, 9 A.M.–5 P.M., $3) has natural history exhibits. Schlitz Audubon Center (1111 E. Brown Deer Rd., 352-2880, 9 A.M.–5 P.M., $1.50) has nature trails adjacent to Lake Michigan, and Whitnall Park (5879 S. 92nd St.) is a large municipal park which includes a botanical garden and a nature center.

★   ★   ★   ★   ★

CHAPTER 6

SOUTHEAST TEXAS: A LITTLE TOUCH OF MEXICO

FOR A BIRDER, TEXAS HAS IT ALL. THERE ARE rarities, spectacular migrations, and huge concentrations of wintering birds. In its southernmost corner are some species that do not belong to the United States at all: they are Mexican, for southern Texas relates more to the subtropical regions of Middle America than it does to the lands to the north. The search for these often elusive southerners draws birders to the valley of the Rio Grande year after year, and they're the reason that anyone who wishes to see all the birds that occur north of the Mexican border must one day visit Texas.

But even without these specialties southern Texas would still be one of the prime birding venues in North America, where huge numbers of waterfowl and shorebirds winter. In spring and fall there are times when this part of the state teems with migrants, sometimes forced down by bad weather, sometimes simply part of the huge river of southbound migrants, here visible and pressed into a flood as the landmass narrows and their numbers reach a peak.

Then there are the Whooping Cranes. Sooner or later every North American birder wants to see a Whooping Crane, and here is the best place to see them. The cranes are the glamour birds of the continent: even people who cannot tell a sparrow from an eagle go to look for them. You often meet such folk walking down the ramp from the viewing tower at Aransas National Wildlife Refuge in Texas. "Yup," they assure you, "a couple of 'em, right out in the marsh there."

The slender white birds they have seen usually turn out to be Great Egrets, but sometimes there are indeed Whooping Cranes to be seen from the tower. Aransas is the wintering grounds for most of the continent's whoopers, and at times a pair can be spotted, distant white specks over a sweeping vista of dark salt marsh. There are other places where you can hope to find whoopers, but the Texas wintering grounds are by far the most reliable destination for these magnificent birds, although ironically the loop road at Aransas is far from the best way to see them.

To get really close to the cranes, we take one of the regular boat tours that leave from the harbor in the town of Rockport and from the neighboring community of Fulton, both some miles south of Aransas. These boats sail north along the Intercoastal Waterway for views of the cranes along the shore.

They're not only much the best way of viewing Whooping Cranes, but we get wonderful views of the teeming wildlife along the Intercoastal Waterway as well. Dolphins play in the bow waves, gulls straggle behind, snapping up popcorn, shorebirds and herons forage in the shallows, and little flocks of duck jump up in alarm from the pools. White Pelicans, Double-crested Cormorants, and Roseate Spoonbills lounge on sandbars, and Forster's Terns cross and recross our wake, searching for fish in the turbulent water.

Most boats take two trips daily, usually 8 A.M. and 1 or 1:30 P.M. Reservations are advised, but some boats cancel if there are not enough passengers. Fares are $18–$25/person. One of the larger boats is the *M.V. Lucky Day*, which leaves from Mom's Bait Stand in Rockport Marina. Contact Capt. Harry Sloat at 1903 Glass St., Rockport, Texas 78382; toll-free 1-800-782-BIRD (daytime only). The *M.V. Skimmer* leaves from the Sandollar Marina in Fulton. Contact Capt. Ted Appell at Star Route 1, Box 225J, Rockport, Texas 78382, (512) 729-9589. This boat has no minimum requirement on its morning sailing, and is smaller, allowing it to get closer to shore than the bigger vessels.

Finally we arrive at the main foraging areas for the cranes. Out over the marsh in the distance loom two tall white shapes, much bigger than any egrets or herons—our first cranes, but too far away to see well. But we're not to be disappointed for long: ahead, two more appear in the pools close to the channel, and soon we're nearby. Tall white birds, dwarfing the nearby waterfowl, they move slowly, regally, as though aware of their importance. The red of their foreheads glows like the rubies in a crown; only their pale eyes have a wild, slightly hysterical look, as though the pressures of avoiding extinction have been almost too much to bear. On the boat the only sounds are the clicking of shutters and gurgles of delight. "Now," says someone nearby, "I can die happy."

We have seen as many as 27 cranes from one of these tour boats, and while some tours used to refund the fees if no cranes were seen, it takes poor conditions to miss them—only fog or very bad weather. The boats are not really steady enough for a telescope, but we have never seemed to need one anyway.

Rockport's attractions are by no means confined to the Whooping Crane tours. The town nestles comfortably on the peninsula that separates Aransas and Copano bays, and the tranquil bay waters teem with waterfowl. In fact, one of the very best birding spots is right in the middle of town, where a sheltered lagoon is winter home to flocks of Canvasback and coot, Marbled Godwits and dowitchers. It's designated the Connie Hagar Bird Sanctuary, in memory of the lady who did so much for birding here.

Rockport is on Route 35 some 32 miles north of Corpus Christi, and is contiguous with Fulton to the north. Both are relatively small communities, but there is ample accommodation. The following has the advantage of being over the road from the marina where the *M.V. Skimmer* is berthed:

Sandollar Resort—(Between Route 35 and Fulton Beach Rd.) HCR Box 30, Rockport, Texas 78382. (512) 729-2381. Open all year. <u>Rooms</u>: Double rooms, some with kitchenettes. <u>Amenities</u>: Restaurant, lounge, swimming pool, lighted fishing pier, marina, boat launching. <u>Terms</u>: Double $32, with kitchenette $38.

We have sometimes had difficulties with meal arrangements in this town, particularly for early breakfasts. At the Sandollar breakfast is at 7 A.M. in the marina. For fine seafood dining we favor **Charlotte Plummer's Sea Fare Restaurant**, at Fulton Beach Rd. and Cactus, just south of the Sandollar. Reservations are usually necessary: (512) 729-1185.

The road that runs past the sanctuary turns north to become the Fulton Beach Road, and is the scenic route to Fulton. Here the winds have pruned the dense live oaks smoothly upward at a 45-degree angle; the result would do justice to topiarist. A little way along, the Sandollar Resort nestles among the oaks.

Rockport is an excellent base to spend a few days before heading farther south. While Aransas National Wildlife Refuge itself is less than an hour's drive to the north, there are a host of good birding opportunities on the back roads right around the town. We usually find it most profitable to con-

---

Goose Island State Recreation Area—10 miles northeast from Rockport. From Route FM 3036 in Fulton drive north on Route 35 5.9 miles; then east on Park Rd. 13 1.4 miles, and south 1.2 miles. Star Route 1, Box 105, Rockport, Texas 78382. (512) 729-2858. Open all year. Campsites: 127 sites, 102 water and electricity, 25 no hookups. Amenities: Rest rooms, hot showers, boat ramp, fishing, swimming, beach, nature trails, dump station. Terms: Hookup $9, non-hookup $6. Park entry fee $2. 14-day limit.

---

centrate on this wonderful mix of woodlots, fields, and small ponds, and in drier areas there are some of the arid country birds that become more numerous farther south.

One of our own favorite places is Goose Island State Recreation Area, north of town. If you're a camper, this is the campground of choice. And what a choice it is! You can opt for a shell mound beside the bay, with flocks of Northern Pintail and Redheads feeding offshore and Long-billed Curlews wandering around off the campsites. The salt marshes behind have both Seaside and Sharp-tailed sparrows in the winter. When water levels are low—usually with northerly winds, as the winds rather than the tide seem to have most influence on these shallow waters—shorebirds abound, and Piping Plover join the commoner species on the shell bars on such days.

On the other hand, the shaded campgrounds are tucked into a delightful live oak woodland, and are surrounded by tangles of yaupon loaded with red berries. These thickets yield Northern Bobwhites and Carolina Wrens, as well as wintering landbirds such as Brown Thrashers and White-throated Sparrows. These are all birds you'll have trouble finding farther south. Set up a feeder and you'll get Tufted Titmice and maybe a towhee. There's a picnic area here too.

Corpus Christi is the major city in this section of the Texas coast. You can fly into here and it can form an excellent

On Route 35 south you join Route 181 northeast of Portland. This becomes the causeway across Corpus Christi Bay, and enters the city along the beach strip of Surfside. The hotel is on the east of the strip:

Best Western Sandy Shores Resort—3200 Surfside Blvd. (off Route 181), Corpus Christi, Texas 78403. (512) 883-7456. Open all year. Rooms: 252 units. Some rooms ocean view or oceanfront, some suites. Amenities: Restaurants, nightclub, swimming pool, whirlpool, sauna, gift shop, International Kite Museum. Terms: Single $43–85, double $53–95, suites $129–155. AMEX, CB, DINERS, MC, VISA.

The best campground is some 20 miles outside of the city on the Gulf of Mexico, but it's worth the drive:

Mustang Island State Park—Box 326, Port Aransas, Texas 78373. (512) 749-5246. Open all year. Campsites: 48 sites with water and electricity, as well as 200–300 primitive beach campsites with water, chemical toilets, and shade shelters nearby. Amenities: Rest rooms, hot showers, fishing, swimming, beach, nature trails, dump station. Terms: Water and electricity $9, no-hookup $4. Park entrance fee $2. 14-day limit.

Access from Route 181 is via Interstate 37 to the Crosstown Expressway (Route 286), then south to Padre Island Dr. (Route 358), and then east to the J. F. Kennedy Causeway (Route 22). Cross the causeway and continue to Park Rd. 53 and turn north on the barrier beach. There's excellent birding from the causeway on, with hawks likely on Mustang Island itself.

★

base, with both an abundance of facilities and many fine birding areas nearby. The Best Western is not only an excellent place to stay, with a fine beach and a beautiful view across the bay, it also provides easy access to the birding areas all along the causeway across Corpus Christi Bay.

We pass some of these on our route south through the town of Portland. As we head out across the long causeway there are vast expanses of sand flats, shell beaches, and open water on either side of the road. We have found the distinctive tawny Texas race of Clapper Rail in the small patches of salt marsh here, and a road leading into a small park on the east side of the bay gives a chance to explore these areas at more leisure.

The shallow water and flats are covered in shorebirds— dowitcher, Western Sandpipers, Sanderlings and Ruddy Turnstones; while on the drier areas of the shell beaches, revealing themselves only when they move and vanishing just as quickly, are Piping and Snowy plovers. Out on the shell bars American Oystercatchers feed, their improbable thick red bills looking vaguely unfinished, while out in the pools small flocks of American Avocets are resting and Black-necked Stilts with their slender red legs are picking daintily from side to side.

Suddenly the tranquil scene erupts into motion: the shorebirds rise in tight little flocks to perform intricate maneuvers over the flats. On every side there are calls of alarm, and the plover squat, trying to become even more invisible. Vanishing rapidly away over the flats is the cause of the tumult; the dark flash of a Peregrine Falcon. But soon all is as before; the avocets go back to sleep and the rest resume the serious business of probing for wriggly delights in the mud.

South of Corpus Christi the flat agricultural lands are gradually replaced by open range, until south of the town of Kingsville the road leaves communities, accommodations, gas stations, and side roads behind to become two strips of asphalt, running uninterrupted some 50 miles to the town of Raymondville. This is the legendary King Ranch, and to cover this fascinating area prompts an early start.

From Corpus Christi take Interstate 37 through town to Route 77 south. In Harlingen 77 is joined by Route 83 heading south to Brownsville. Six miles south of the city turn east on Route 100 to South Padre Island. At present the only rest area with washrooms is at Sarita.

The "coverage" here is all from the highway. It's not usually the recommended way of seeing birds, and this road in
particular is the main access route to the busy cities of the
Rio Grande Valley. Yet birding across the King Ranch can be
very, very exciting. We drive at a modest rate, and move off
to the shoulder of the road whenever we see something of
interest. (This is a half-day enterprise, and a good jogger
would soon leave us behind!)

The country is now open range. Sometimes there are yellow and gold vistas of long grass, interspersed with dark
mottes of live oak, low gray-green mounds that shelter turkey and deer. At other times mesquite dominates, its
twisted trunks and spiny branches leafless and gray in this
winter landscape. There are areas of sand dune, and from
time to time pools of fresh water, each with its own complement of birds. From one a group of shoveler jumps up in
alarm, on another wigeon wade in the shallows. And always
overhead there are the hawks and vultures, soaring endlessly, quartering, hovering, and sitting patiently in the tops
of the trees.

This is arid country. The cattle are scattered, and with
them are other things: often white-tailed deer, but sometimes some exotic African antelope, seemingly quite at
home in this dry landscape. We watch for Sandhill Cranes
over the open grassland and turkeys along the edges of the
woodlots, but it is the hawks, always the hawks, that turn an
hour's drive into a morning. The route becomes an education in the endless plumage variations of the Red-tailed
Hawk, but we find other species too—White-tailed, Harris',
and the occasional Ferruginous hawk, the specialties of this
corner of Texas.

Most of those soaring raptors, however, prove to be vultures. When we finally come to a row of them sitting on the
fencing beside the road it hardly seems worth another stop,
but just beyond lies a dead steer. Over the carcass Black
Vultures are quarreling and posturing, their only sounds low
hisses and the occasional clash of wings, their silence having an ominous quality. Suddenly there's a flash of white

and a pair of superb Crested Caracaras fly up into the trees. In the air caracaras often seem merely skinny, but on the ground they're impressive, with dramatic dark crests and massive bills.

There are rest areas dotted along the highway, the one south of Sarita an ambitious affair with washrooms, and picnic tables nestling under a grove of live oaks. This spot can be noteworthy later in the year when Tropical Parulas nest among the oaks, but now the only birds are a foraging group of Brewer's Blackbirds, and a Ruby-crowned Kinglet and Orange-crowned Warbler tagging along with a flock of Tufted Titmice. Such groups are now the common landbird fare. The other rest areas have yielded good birds in the past, but now that the highway has been widened their future quality is doubtful, for a while at least.

At Raymondville there is an abrupt contrast to the rangeland we have just crossed. The landscape is totally flat, and almost entirely plowed. This is the delta of the Rio Grande, one of the most intensively farmed places in the United States, and only the occasional roadside pond has much birdlife. As we proceed south through the city of Harlingen we begin to see orange groves, and skinny palms line the fields.

Some 15 miles to the east lies the Laguna Atascosa National Wildlife Refuge, although the idea of such an area in this manipulated countryside seems unlikely. South Padre Island, the community on the barrier beach just north of the mouth of the Rio Grande itself, is a good base for visiting the place. From the Holiday Inn here you can walk out onto the wide, pale, sandy beaches of the barrier island, and sometimes in winter you'll have only the Willets and the Laughing Gulls for company. Behind are the dunes, with picturesque tufts of beach grass and ghost crabs that materialize to scuttle away as you approach.

Port Isabel and South Padre Island are, in any event, well worth a visit. There are flats on either side of the causeway to the island where shorebirds forage and flocks of skimmers, terns, and gulls loiter. Generally the area offers a similar mix of waterbirds to those encountered near Corpus Christi, although here the white phase of the Reddish Egret seems commoner than elsewhere on the Texas coast.

Laguna Atascosa N.W.R. is located on the shores of the Laguna Madre, the waters between Padre Island and the mainland. It then runs inland, embracing a series of brackish and freshwater ponds, and areas of dense thorn scrub. Most of the landbird specialties of the Rio Grande can be found here, although they are usually easier to see in the

---

There are many hotels here, most rather expensive. The following is across from the end of the causeway, and an easy walk from the best birding areas:

Holiday Inn—100 Padre Blvd., South Padre Island, Texas 78597. (512) 761-5401. Open all year. Rooms: 227 units, standard with 2 double beds, king-size bed and sofa. Amenities: Restaurant (breakfast is at 7 A.M.), lounge, swimming pool, whirlpool, beach, tennis court. Restrictions: No pets. Terms: Single $87—112, double $95—120. AMEX, CB, DINERS, MC, VISA.

Camping on South Padre Island can be difficult, although there is primitive camping on the beach at the north end of Padre Boulevard. The following is just south of the causeway end, but in winter you must have reservations far in advance:

Isla Blanca Park (Cameron County Park)—Box 2106, South Padre Island, Texas 78597. From east end, Queen Isabella Causeway on South Padre Island: Park Rd. 100 south 0.8 mile. (512) 761-5493. On the Gulf of Mexico. Open all year. Campsites: 360 sites, 350 full hookups, 10 water and electricity. Amenities: Rest rooms, showers, recreation room, pavilion, swimming pool, saltwater swimming, boating, fishing, playground, laundry room, sewage disposal. Terms: Full hookup $10.

---

areas farther west. But the Refuge has a marvelous assortment of waterbirds, particularly in the late fall and early winter. It is a chance for a last look at the rich birdlife of the

Gulf Coast, and an introduction to the commoner landbirds that we can expect to see on the route ahead.

The first of these are evident as soon as we stop, and indeed the old mesquites and other taller trees immediately adjacent to headquarters are one of the better places for landbirds on the refuge. Here are the two common woodpeckers of the region, the Golden-fronted—looking like a pale edition of the Red-bellied—and Ladder-backed, which sounds rather like a Downy Woodpecker.

The 12-mile bayside motor tour runs first through dense thorn scrub. On a casual glance this is all quite uniform, but a closer look reveals many species of shrubs and small trees, known collectively as chaparral. One of the most attractive trees is huisache, covered in late winter with fuzzy golden balls of sweet-smelling blossoms covered in turn with bees. It's common in the Valley, and attracts birds as well as insects.

Finally the loop road winds its way to the Laguna Madre, and to gatherings of waterbirds that are spectacular even in the bird-rich Gulf Coast. Birds cover the flats, form straggling flocks on the offshore waters, and sit massed on the distant islands, challenging identification even with a 'scope. Here long flocks of pintail upend in the shallow water and the nasal whistles of wigeon drift in on the wind. Egrets and herons are everywhere dotted around, and tight little black bunches of coot dive clumsily for water weeds.

The shoreline here is low, a series of gray-green undulations against a vast sky. Dainty Black-shouldered Kites hover over the beach ridges, their wings held high over their backs—in supplication, perhaps, for more grasshoppers—

The Refuge is about 40 minutes from South Padre. Turn off Route 100 west onto Route 510 at Laguna Vista. The road signs now are not adequate, but you bear generally right, passing the side road to the airport, until you arrive at the headquarters, with washrooms and a picnic area. Entry fee is currently $2 per vehicle.

★

and as we drive south beside the water, flocks of sparrows fly up from the roadsides and mockingbirds and Logger-head Shrikes perch on the shrubs. Later in the year both Cassin's and Botteri's sparrows will perform skylarking songs along this road, but now we count ourselves lucky with just a glimpse of Cassin's, crouched motionless in the scrub.

Laguna Atascosa is a foretaste of birding along the Rio Grande. From here to Falcon Dam, almost 150 miles to the west, is the Valley, a huge, flat expanse of fertile land where broccoli is still being harvested in the middle of winter and fields of lettuce and cabbages alternate with sugarcane, pineapples, and citrus orchards. Here is a chain of bustling communities, and here too are acres of campers, RV parks that are the refuge for thousands of "snowbirds" escaping the hostile winters of the northern plains, and motels, and hotels and . . . There's not much room for birds, and indeed the views from the highway yield little but the straggling flocks of Great-tailed Grackles, chuckling and gurgling in a constant celebration of life itself.

But the birds are there to be found. Some, like the Mexican Crows at the Brownsville garbage dump, and the Red-crowned Parrots that fly in to roost every night in the gardens of McAllen, are at home even in this man-made environment. We can sometimes watch them in the evening from the hotel! For the rest, it's necessary to seek out the little pockets and islands of natural habitat that still remain, and even there they may elude you.

Santa Ana is a section of the original woodland which at one time must have occupied most of the lower valley of the Rio Grande. It is small as refuges go, roughly paralleling the road for a couple of miles and extending to the river itself, which here loops erratically up and down the southern boundary. Most of the refuge is covered in dense thorn woodland, with three "lakes" that are diked into sections to allow the Refuge managers to adjust water levels and simulate natural conditions.

Even a quick visit is worthwhile, and you can cover one of the best areas of the Refuge quite quickly. A short path that

The major center in the Valley is McAllen, some 60 miles west, reached from South Padre Island via Route 48 to Brownsville. This turns south from 100 just outside Port Isabel. McAllen is one of the cities along Route 83 west of Harlingen. We prefer Route 281, which parallels the Rio Grande closely and has none of the busy traffic of the main artery. Be sure to gas up at Brownsville.

There's an abundance of accommodation at McAllen, none of it in good birding areas. We favor the following, which has a 24-hour **Denny's** restaurant next door and an excellent **Luby's Cafeteria** opposite. The lines there move rapidly and the food is superb:

La Quinta Inn—1100 S. 10th St., McAllen, Texas 78501-5022 (On Route 336 1 block north of Route 83 and 10th St. intersection). (512) 687-1101. Open all year. Rooms: 122 doubles. Amenities: Swimming pool. Terms: Single $42–47, double $47–52. AMEX, CB, DINERS, MC, VISA.

For campers the following is the "must" choice. The serviced sites require advance reservations:

Bentsen—Rio Grande Valley State Park—From Loop 374, which is off Route 83 west of McAllen, turn left under the overpass and proceed to FM 2062, then south 2.6 miles to Park Rd. 43 south. Box 988, Mission, Texas 78572. (512) 585-1107. Open all year. Campsites: 142 sites, 77 full hookups, 65 no hookups. Amenities: Rest rooms, hot showers, boat ramp, fishing, nature trails, and dump station. Terms: Hookup $10, no-hookup $5. Park entrance fee $2. Limited stay 14 days. There's a picnic area here as well.

★

starts behind the visitor center leads to a footbridge over the irrigation canal and down the side of the levee, into another world. Here the path winds through tall chaparral, with the graceful, willowlike retama in the moister areas, and mesquite and the stubby huisache on the drier parts. As we move on the trees grow higher, festooned with long, gray tassels of Spanish moss. Abruptly the path ahead ends and a sign urges QUIET—DUCKS DOZING AND TURTLES SNOOZING. This is the Willow Lake, and almost anything can turn up here, but a hasty approach may yield nothing but a flurry of wings.

Even so, as we move out on to the observation deck an Olivaceous Cormorant takes off, seeming slimmer and longer than its Double-crested cousins, but luckily everything else stays put. This is a pleasantly small lake, ringed by trees and heavy cover. Ducks bob in and out of the tall, pale reed stems and from somewhere over to one side a Greater Yellowlegs calls. A pair of Blue-winged Teal anticipates spring with courtship display almost at our feet, and other ducks come and go: many shoveler, a Green-winged Teal or two, an American Wigeon.

To the back we can see the rich color of a Cinnamon Teal, and suddenly a flock of White-faced Ibis flies up briefly, a swirl of dark wings, only to vanish again. Meanwhile Great Kiskadees are arguing noisily about ownership rights, their vivid yellow breasts glowing in the sun. So many birds are packed into such a small space that it's hard to pin them all down—suddenly we're aware of two Least Grebes swimming in full view; were they there all along, we puzzle? No matter, we delight in these elusive creatures, often sought but not always found along the Rio Grande.

The next day we return very early and spend much of the day at the Refuge, following the trails from the Willow Lakes

---

Santa Ana is on Route 281 some 10 miles east of the junction of Route 336 south of McAllen. There are several hiking trails and a 7-mile loop drive, unfortunately closed to cars during much of the winter. During this period an interpretive bus runs regularly (fee), but while this may be a good way of seeing the Refuge, it is not much use for birding. There is no entry fee. Washrooms are outside the center.

★

across to the Pintail Lakes to the east, and birding under the huge old Texas ebonies that surround the old headquarters buildings. As we arrive at dawn an unearthly racket breaks out across the lake, and we're introduced to the local flock of Plain Chachalacas, long-tailed and turkeylike, rejoicing in the sunrise.

Santa Ana rarely disappoints: today we add a Green King-fisher at the Willow Lakes, as well as White-tipped Doves, Long-billed Thrasher, and Olive Sparrow, all regulars here in the Valley. We find time to admire the Green Jays, resplendent in exquisite greens offset by touches of yellow and blue. We find flocks of wintering warblers foraging in the delicate fresh green foliage of the ebonies, and discover a Buff-bellied Hummingbird among the shrubs and shrimp plants around the buildings.

Bentsen State Park is the other birding hot spot of the lower Valley. It too borders the river, but there the similarity to Santa Ana ends. There are no closed loop roads here, and indeed the campground is among the best winter birding spots along the Rio Grande. There are a couple of trails, and two resacas—old oxbows of the river—and everywhere is good for birds.

Wandering around the camping loop we quickly see more chachalacas and Green Jays, and glimpse our first Altamira Orioles, spectacular in vivid orange and black, visiting the feeders put out by the campers. At one campsite Clay-colored Robins have been visiting, the only place in North America where they occur regularly. A Mexican wanderer, a Blue Bunting, has been reported from another. Because access here is easy, any straggling birds are quickly located and there is a lively grapevine. We hear of Hook-billed Kites along the hiking trail, and finally locate one, deftly manipulating one of the tree snails upon which it feeds.

One more destination remains. To see some of the birds of the drier rangelands to the west we head out once again along the Rio Grande, leaving behind us the rich farmland of the delta and passing through the modest Chicano communities that make their livings from the arid country near

Falcon Dam. Our objective is Falcon State Recreation Area, located on the shores of the huge lake formed by the dam, which was erected to control the unpredictable flow of the Rio Grande.

The campground at Falcon, like that of Bentsen, is a great spot to bird. Many of the commoner birds of the Bentsen feeders can be seen here too, but the more usual visitors include Scaled Quail, Pyrrhuloxias and Curve-billed Thrashers. The atmosphere is wholly different: where Bentsen is situated in shady riverside woodlands, this is on the top of a hill in low thorn scrub. The vista here is of grays and sage greens and the ground is gravelly, with plants more widely spread. It's close to being desert, and the desert birds are here to be found: a roadrunner wanders from site to site

You can commute to Falcon from McAllen, but it makes for a long day. The following is a beautiful restored hotel built about 1895 and located in Rio Grande City, some 25 miles east of Falcon. Its restaurant does not serve breakfast, but there are fast-food places to the east:

The LaBorde House—601 E. Main St., Rio Grande City, Texas 78582. (512) 487-5101. Open all year. Rooms: 8 historical and 9 modern rooms. Amenities: Dining room, cocktail lounge. Terms: Modern rooms $40, historical rooms $59.

Falcon State Recreation Area—(From McAllen, head west on Route 83 some 65 miles to FM 2098. Turn left here and head northwest 3.2 miles to Park Rd. 46). Box 2, Falcon Heights, Texas 78545. (512) 848-5327. Open all year. Campsites: 117 sites, 31 full hookups, 31 water and electricity, 55 no hookups. Amenities: Rest rooms, hot showers, boat ramp, fishing, swimming, beach, nature trails, dump station. Terms: Full hookup $10, water and electricity $9. Non-hookup $6. Park entrance fee $2. 14-day limit. There are a couple of picnic areas.

★

scrounging bacon scraps, Cactus Wrens churr and chuckle, and dapper Black-throated Sparrows perch up above the scrub to sing silvery little songs. The flocks of blackbirds that descend on the more open feeders often include a Bronzed Cowbird or two.

A Falcon highlight is the morning drive down the side road that overlooks the foot of the dam. Here Black Vultures sit hunched along the cement walls, and a Great Horned Owl roosts above the floodgates. Far below, the river is placid, dotted with reed beds. We 'scope the tranquil waters and the riverside trees, and are rewarded with a Ringed Kingfisher sitting on one of the snags above the water. Only along the Rio Grande is this big cousin of our kingfisher at home.

All of the state park areas have bird checklists, as do the National Wildlife Refuges. There are three finding guides which are useful: James A. Lane's *A Birder's Guide to the Rio Grande Valley of Texas* (1978) and his (with J. L. Tveten) *A Birder's Guide to the Texas Coast* (1980). Both L&P Press, they are the basic guides for this area, while Edward A. Kutac's *Texas Birds: Where They Are and How to Find Them* (Lone Star Books, 1982), is relevant to the state as a whole. There are several hotlines: for Texas statewide (713) 821-2846; for Sinton and the Rockport area, (512) 364-3634; and for the lower Rio Grande Valley, (512) 565-6773.

If this is your first visit to Texas and you've never been to the Southwest or Mexico you can expect to add some 20–30 species to your life list on this route. You'll also get a multitude of wintering species; trip lists for this route could range between 150 and 200 species or even higher, depending how energetic and lucky you are.

In winter you should always be prepared for cold, even when it is hot. We have scraped ice off our vehicle in Bentsen, and a "norther" can drop the temperature dramatically in a couple of hours.

★

Texas is a place to return to at different times and seasons. The Whooping Cranes themselves arrive fairly late—October—and usually leave in early April. This is before the waves of spring landbirds move north, and too late for their southbound flight. But it is in time for the flocks of waterfowl, and late fall through early spring can yield these birds, as well as many of the Mexican specialties, year-round. The route described can be comfortably covered in winter in ten days, but we have known folk to turn it into a month's winter holiday.

OTHER THINGS OF INTEREST

There's lots to interest a naturalist in southern Texas. Even in late winter a few days of warm weather and some rain will paint the roadsides with wildflowers, plants with evocative names like baby blue eyes, scrambled eggs, and Indian blanket. When you reach Santa Ana the problem may be putting a name on your finds at all—many of the species there occur only in the Valley, and you'll have trouble finding them in a guide.

Other animals can be seen too. Javelinas are widespread in chaparral, and we have seen bobcats in both Santa Ana and Bentsen. Reptiles and amphibians tend to like the warmer weather, and then they abound. The region boasts twenty or so lizards and an even larger number of snakes, although most of these go unnoticed except to the trained eye.

The Gulf beaches have their own attractions, and it's impossible for card-carrying beachcombers like us to pass up all that wonderful wave-washed sand. But even the Gulf can be cool in the winter, so if your interest in beaches is of a more passive nature, you'll probably prefer a later visit. Whenever the trip, the beaches are there—miles of them, with all the usual beach sights and razzmatazz if you want them. You'll have to work a little harder for solitude, but it's there too.

If you're a history buff, the route we follow—part of the Texas Tropical Trail of the travel brochures—has memories

of Spanish colonial days and the Mexican war, with historic buildings in Brownsville and in Fulton, where the Fulton Mansion State Historic Structure—(512) 729-0386. Wed.– Sun. and holidays, $2—is on Fulton Beach Rd. just south of the Sandollar. The tiny, free La Lomito mission near the town of Mission is between Bentsen and McAllen, 3 miles south on FM 1016 and 0.25 miles west. It's one of the oldest Texas missions still in use, and nearby Anzalduas County Park has good birds. At Kingsville is the headquarters of the King Ranch—west off Route 141, (512) 592-6411—and you can take a 12-mile loop tour of the ranch free, complete with cassette-recorded commentary (Tape and cassette $3). It's not only fascinating in itself—the ranch dates from 1853 and is the largest in the continental United States—but it can be fair birding. The *Texas Tropical Trail* map issued by the State Department of Highways is full of other information on the communities along the route.

The coast also abounds in fishing opportunities, from lighted fishing piers to offshore charters. Most of Texas seems to fish! A lot of the winter visitors fish too, and because they're mostly retirees this area caters to the other recreational needs you would expect in such a group. So such things as marinas and golf courses are many, and increasing, around Brownsville, Harlingen, and McAllen. And it states the obvious to note that Mexico is only a bridge away along the Rio Grande, and the Mexican towns of Matamoros and Reynosa, among others, welcome North American tourists.

★   ★   ★   ★   ★

AT DAWN RUGGED HEADLANDS LOOM TO THE north. Last night's heavy swell has subsided and the sea is calm and silvery, with long strands of mist. Everywhere there are seabirds. Lines of murres fly between the boat and the distant shoreline, gulls circle and mill around, and vast flocks of Greater and Sooty shearwaters sit quietly on the still waters, flopping heavily along the surface to take off as the boat approaches. Here and there Parasitic Jaegers dash and twist, bank and dive, chasing one another and everything else indiscriminately. A Great Skua approaches, dark and powerful with flashing white wing patches; it inspects the boat briefly before heading on.

The overnight ferry from North Sydney, Nova Scotia, to Argentia is not the fastest way of getting to Newfoundland—

we will have been at sea eighteen hours when we dock—
but it certainly can be the most exciting. Not that every voyage will yield such a bonanza of pelagics, the birds of the
open ocean, and we have been lucky. Sometimes you can
make this crossing and see nothing; sometimes the voyage
can be rough, and unless you're a good sailor you don't really care whether you see anything or not. But sometimes
you can hit the jackpot, and today we have.

Newfoundland is the place to see seabirds. They nest in
enormous numbers on its cliffs and islands, and they ply its
offshore waters in thousands. Many can be seen right from
shore, while for others a boat trip is better. For the true pelagics the ferries are probably best, but on any trip the
chances of seeing pelagic birds are unpredictable.

The shorter ferry route to the "Rock" runs from North Sydney to Port-aux-Basques at the other end of the island, and
it occupies only a half day. From it too, you can see pelagic
birds, and on one unforgettable occasion a Black-browed
Albatross flew across our bow, but usually the birding is not

Ferries are operated by Marine Atlantic, and advance
reservations are necessary. Phone (902) 794-7203; toll-
free U.S. 1-800-341-7981; Maine 1-800-432-7344;
Ont./P.Q. 1-800-565-9411; N.B., N.S., and P.E.I. 1-800-
565-9470. As of 1990 there is a new boat on the Argentia route. It operates June 15—Sept. 15, leaving
9 A.M. and arriving 9 P.M., going to Newfoundland on
Tuesdays and Fridays and returning Wednesdays and
Saturdays. $38.50/adults, $93.25/autos. You probably
should now aim for the return sailing, as birding is best
in the morning, and at the Argentia end. It is advisable
to reconfirm these schedules when going.

The first-time visitor should contact the Newfoundland Dept. of Development and Tourism—toll-free
1-800-563-6353—for copies of their free booklets,
which have much useful information both on the Island
and on visiting Canada generally.

★

of this quality. Most of the folk who take their cars across choose to go one way and return the other.

Alternatively one can fly into St. John's, an option that has much merit in terms of speed. Newfoundland is a deceptively large island. If you follow the Trans-Canada Highway from St. John's to Port-aux-Basques you will have driven almost six hundred miles. If you follow any of the long, winding roads that head out along the many peninsulas and to the coastlines of Newfoundland you could add many more miles. Unfortunately—or fortunately, because this can be a breathtakingly beautiful place—some of the best birding areas are at opposite ends.

The highway down the west side of the Avalon Peninsula is a good introduction to Newfoundland. It rises and falls like a roller coaster, climbing steep headlands only to drop down again to tiny villages nestled in hidden coves. The houses are simple, brightly painted, and dotted around haphazardly in the small communities. Boats are drawn out along the rocky shoreline, and in the little fields there's maybe a horse, or perhaps a cow or two. Many homes sit empty: this is not a prosperous part of the world. All along the road are neat, wind-trimmed forests of spruce, forests that commence knee-high at the shoreline and taper up smoothly until, with luck, they are almost head-high farther back. These low, tangled trees are the tuckamore or simply "tuck," and we soon discover that they are virtually impenetrable.

Occasionally a deeper valley or a more sheltered area supports trees of a more familiar size, but over much of the vista there are none, only open expanses of rock and low grass, especially along the narrow gravel road to Cape St. Mary's Bird Sanctuary. It heads south from St. Bride's, where our motel overlooks the sea and the grassy, rocky slopes around the scattered houses that constitute the village.

It turns out to be sheep that keep the grass cut—we soon encounter them on the road, and have to persuade them to get out of the way. The Newfoundland approach to free-ranging stock is relaxed; there's lots of free range, relatively few roads, and little traffic. The animals simply wander around. Not all are dull, domesticated creatures, for later in the trip we are to see a herd of caribou straggling across the road west of Trepassey.

The headquarters for the Bird Sanctuary is at the end, in one of the buildings associated with the lighthouse at the

---

St. Bride's is accessible via Route 100 south from both Argentia and St. John's. The 8-mile gravel road to the Cape is well marked on the right at the far end of town. The only accommodation in the area is:

Bird Island Motel—St. Bride's, General Delivery, Placentia Bay, Newfoundland, A0B 2Z0. (709) 337-2450. Open all year. Rooms: 9 housekeeping cottages: 3 with 2 rooms, each with double bed, sofa in living area; 4 with 2 single beds, 2 with 1 double bed; overlook Placentia Bay. Amenities: All units have kitchen, bathroom, and shower. Laundry, mini golf course (9 hole); convenience store nearby and restaurant in St. Bride's. Terms: (And below, all C$) Single $40, double $50, VISA.

There's a small picnic area and privy at the lighthouse. The nearest formal campground is **Fitzgerald's Pond Provincial Park**—Route 100 (12 miles off Route 1, 16 miles from Argentia). Open May 15–September 15. Campsites: 24 sites, no hookups. Amenities: Swimming, hiking, picnic tables, fire pits, pit toilets, drinking water. Terms: $6; park entrance fee $2.

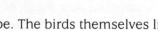

Cape. The birds themselves line the cliffs a mile or so to the east. It's an enchanting walk, full of anticipation, the distant green headlands jutting out into the sea sparkling far below, while overhead American Pipits glide downward with cascades of song. Underfoot the turf is springy and resilient, dotted with the tiny pinkish spikes of alpine bistort and low clumps of blue iris. Occasional sheep stand and glare, their eyes malevolent, cold like porcelain.

Soon the colonies are in full view, high cliffs lined with murres—both species nest here—and kittiwakes. Then, as we walk down to the tip of the headland, ahead is a vast pinnacle entirely covered in nesting gannets; from the viewpoint at cliff edge we could easily toss a rock into the colony. The big white birds with their rich yellow-cream heads and light blue eyes are even more striking here at close quarters. They totally disregard us, busy dueling with neighbors, stealing nesting material, and constantly coming and going. One bird with an eye for color has incorporated a mass of bright blue plastic netting into its nest.

It's some time before we get around to the multitude of birds passing the headland and sitting on the waters below. There are a few impeccably groomed Razorbills, and dark little Black Guillemots bob up and down waving coral-red feet. Farther out Great and Double-crested cormorants fly past, birds that nest farther up on the peninsula. Search as we may, it would be naïve to think we hadn't missed anything—there are just too many birds and too much activity; the scene is overwhelming.

St. John's, our next destination, is both the capital of Newfoundland and one of the oldest and most delightful cities on the continent. Its famous harbor is among the finest in the world, and the city sits on the hills around it, dominated by the twin towers of the Basilica of St. John the Baptist. The town is a colorful array of joyously painted old wooden houses around a port bustling with shipping from all over the world. To the east lie the green grassy heights of Signal Hill National Historic Park, its historic batteries looking down over the harbor. St. John's residents still head up here to sit looking out over the ocean, watching the boats coming and going through the narrow strait below, much as they must have done for generations.

Tucked below the batteries is the Battery Hotel, with superb views of the harbor and ready access to the birdy areas around the park. Wilson's Warblers flit nervously in the brushy patches up the hill, and the ponds there attract unusual gulls.

The city's largest area of natural open space, C. A. Pippy Park, lies inland and it too has some small lakes that attract waterbirds, and wooded sections that have a good mixture

From Argentia use Routes 100 and 1 east to St. John's. The latter becomes Kenmount Rd. in the city, and the downtown area is reached via Freshwater Rd. There is an abundance of facilities and accommodation; the following recommended for its superb views and situation:

Stel Battery—100 Signal Hill Rd., St. John's, Newfoundland A1A 1B3. (709) 576-0040; toll-free 1-800-267-7835. Open all year. Rooms: 151 units with king, queen, or twin double beds. Amenities: Dining room, lounge, gift shop, indoor swimming pool, whirlpool, and sauna. Terms: January–March $49, April–December $85. AMEX, DINERS, MC, VISA.

Campers should head for:

Pippy Park Trailer Park—P.O. Box 8861, St. John's, Newfoundland, A1B 3T2. (709) 737-3669. From junction of Route 1 (Kenmount Rd.) and Prince Philip Dr.: go 1.5 miles northeast on Prince Philip Dr., then ⅓ mile northwest on Allandale Rd. to Nagle's Place. Open May 1–October 31. Campsites: 156 sites, 94 full hookups, 38 no hookups, 24 tenting. Amenities: Recreation hall, heated swimming pool (June 5–September 7), playground, rowboat rental, fishing, shoreshoes, hiking trails, store, flush toilets, hot showers, sewage disposal. Terms: Full hookups $14, no hookups $10, overflow and tents $5.

★

of the more common Newfoundland landbirds. If you're camping you can sit in your campsite and watch Boreal Chickadees foraging in the low spruces and listen to Fox Sparrows singing!

Cape Spear, a few miles out of town, is the easternmost point of North America. On the day we visit there's a Humpbacked Whale cavorting just off the viewing platform, and Greater Shearwaters are circling nearby. Even if you miss out on such goodies, this is a delightful spot. Clumps of interrupted fern and blue iris grow around the old batteries, and after all, this is the last place an errant eastern landbird can end up west of Ireland!

To reach Cape Spear from downtown, take Water St. to Leslie St., turn left across the bridge and continue on this road. For Bay Bulls use Water St. and Pitts Memorial Dr. to the Bay Bulls Rd. (Route 10).

Loyola O'Brian runs Bird Island Charters—(709) 753-4850 or 334-2355—from the Bay Bulls dock. Trips are at 10 A.M., 2 and 5 P.M., and take 2—2.5 hours. Cost is about $20.

St. John's doesn't immediately spring to mind as a destination for winter birding, but some of North America's most sought-after birds are regulars here. Dovekies, white-winged gulls, Snowy Owls, and Gyrfalcons are just some of the species that can be found at that time. The Christmas Bird Counts tell the story, and they reveal that in some years a most amazing mixture of birds can show up around the city. Here disoriented wanderers from elsewhere on the continent reach the end of the line, and storm-blown waifs from the Old World make their first landfall. These birds usually arrive in migration times, although they may go undetected until winter forces them to seek food and shelter at feeders. On occasion Newfoundland has played host to flocks of lapwings and Greater Golden-Plovers, scattered Redwings and Fieldfares, and others.

In the breeding season St. John's is a good base for visiting the huge seabird colonies on the east coast of Newfoundland. One morning we head south along the coast road to drive the twenty or so miles to Bay Bulls, there to join a boat tour sailing out to the nesting islands off Witless Bay. These islands are covered in thousands of seabirds, and although you can see these throngs in the distance from the shore, you can do much better from a boat. It is not possible to land, nor is it necessary. The spectacle is even more dramatic from the water.

Newfoundland has its own very distinctive accent, customs, and culture. Newfoundland folk delight in storytelling, and there's a wealth of infectious jigs and square dances. You cannot avoid these things on a visit to the island, and who would want to? They surface in the most unexpected places. Our boatman, Loyola O'Brian, proves to be a champion square dancer, and as the boat chugs smoothly out of the harbor he breaks spontaneously into a light and dexterous jig. Then, as the toe-tapping, lively music seems to demand a partner, my wife Joy is seized and whirled around, hiking boots and all, revealing a hitherto unsuspected talent!

But it's soon time to get down to the serious business of birding. While the numbers of birds at Cape St. Mary's were impressive, the numbers here seem astronomical—Witless Bay hosts one of the largest seabird colonies in the world. Not only are the islands covered in birds but the sky around them is full of birds, the water is dotted with birds, and their constant clamor drowns out the sound of the boat's engine. Razorbills, murres, Atlantic Puffins, Black Guillemots, Black-legged Kittiwakes, Great Black-backed and Herring gulls are all here. Little flocks of kittiwakes take off from the water ahead of us, and every few seconds a murre rockets over the boat on whirry stubby wings.

Yet the most abundant species of all is not to be seen. Gull Island is home to over half a million pairs of Leach's Storm-Petrels, but these birds are secure underground in their burrows or far out at sea, returning only at dusk to relieve their mates on the nests.

Three islands embrace the Witless Bay Bird Sanctuary, although most boat tours only visit the northernmost two. Gull Island is heavily wooded: most of the nesting gulls and the puffin burrows are dotted over the grassy areas and woodland edges, the petrels nest in the woods themselves, and kittiwakes occupy the cliffs below, together with murres and Razorbills. Further south is the smaller Green Island, with even larger numbers of murres, together with most of the other species. Great Island to the south is well separated from the two and has a smaller mix of species, but there are large numbers of puffins there and a few Northern Fulmars, while as many as a million pairs of petrels are reputed to breed in the wooded interior.

The Trans-Canada Highway was built long after Newfoundland was settled, and it passes through relatively few communities. The island's economy was based on the sea, which linked its fishing villages—the outports. The highways came later, and the Trans-Canada route passes only the fjordlike arms of the inlets, with smaller roads looping up and around the many peninsulas to join picturesque villages once linked only by coastal ferries.

One such village is Trinity, well worth the long detour up from Clarenville. This beautiful village is one of the oldest settlements in North America—it was founded in the 1500s—and its superb harbor was a focal point for naval activity, both French and British, in the tumultuous early days of the colony. Today it is a quiet place with historic buildings nestled into the many coves and Common Goldeneyes perched on the chimneypots. From the Village Inn whale-watching expeditions depart to search the waters of Trinity Bay. These trips are not primarily aimed at birds, but can nevertheless yield excellent birding.

To reach Trinity from Clarenville, take Route 230 (allow about 1.5 hours with some stops, one way). The following is the place to stay:

The Village Inn—P.O. Box 10, Trinity, Trinity Bay, Newfoundland A0C 2S0. (709) 464-3269. Rooms: 8 units, double bed or twins. Amenities: Dining room, lounge, central washrooms, whale-watching trips. Terms: Single $40, double $45. Meals additional. Whale- and bird-watching: 7-day expedition package $998 includes meals, accommodation, charters. 3-day expedition package $465 as above. Daily expeditions $80.

If seabirds are the draw that brings birders to Newfoundland, the landbirds will provide an exciting bonus on arrival. Land birding here seems topsy-turvy: the commoners elsewhere are rare, and the Rock's common birds are often rar-

ities everywhere else! Least Flycatchers are rare, but Yellow-
bellieds are common. Gray-cheeked Thrushes are usual in
the low spruce forests, but Wood Thrushes are no more than
scarce vagrants. Song Sparrows are rather uncommon but
Fox Sparrows appear in abundance, and among the warblers the commoner breeding species include Blackpoll,
Mourning, Palm, and Wilson's. And then there are Spruce
Grouse, Willow and—just perhaps—Rock Ptarmigan.

Heading north and west on the Trans-Canada, the stunted
vegetation of the Avalon Peninsula is soon replaced by the

Accommodation in the Terra Nova area is rather limited. There are picnic areas, washrooms, and two
campgrounds through the park, and checklists and information at the information center at the entrance. The
following is about 30 minutes from it, and has fair birding adjacent. It is a good base, although there are some
less expensive places closer:

Holiday Inn—(Route 1 at Clarenville) P.O. Box 967, Clarenville, Newfoundland A0E 1J0. (709) 466-7911. Open
all year. Rooms: 64 units. Amenities: Dining room
(breakfast at 7 A.M.), lounge, swimming pool, gift shop.
Terms: Singe $77–82, double $85–90. AMEX, CB, MC,
VISA.

Terra Nova National Park—Glovertown, Newfoundland A0G 2L0. (709) 533-2801:

Newman Sound Campground—Off Route 1. Open
May 23–October 8. Campsites: 380 sites, no hookups.
Amenities: Beach, swimming, canoe and bicycle rental,
fishing, 9-hole golf, nature trails, playground, kitchen
shelters, washrooms, showers, coin laundry, grocery
store, restaurant, sewage disposal. Terms: $8.50, 14-
day limit.

Malady Head Campground—On Route 310 (Eastport
Road). Open June 19–September 7. Campsites: 165
sites, no hookups. Amenities: Beach, swimming, boat
ramp, fishing, playground, nature trails, washrooms,
showers, sewage disposal. Terms: $7.50, 14-day limit.

★

dense boreal forests that occupy much of the island. Terra Nova National Park, just west of Clarenville, has particularly fine forests; a beautiful area of fjords and high wooded hills. It's home to a fine array of boreal forest birds: Black-backed Woodpeckers, Gray-cheeked Thrushes, and such finches as Pine Grosbeak, crossbills, and Pine Siskins. Stop at one of the picnic areas and you'll soon have Gray Jays for company. We find rich birding in the open alder thickets at Burnt Point, near our campground at Malady Head. There are Yellow-bellied Flycatchers and several species of warblers foraging here, and we soon find that, like the Newfoundland people, the birds have distinctive accents as well!

On the west shore of Newfoundland the Great Northern Peninsula stretches, rugged and remote, over two hundred miles north to L'Anse aux Meadows. In this isolated spot there are the remains of the ancient Viking settlements, relics of the first European settlements in the New World a thousand years ago. The peninsula attracts wandering birds as well, and is a migration route late in the year for such mouth-watering northerners as Gyrfalcons.

Two ferries link the peninsula with Labrador, an inaccessible and roadless region that is home to boreal and tundra birds. Both routes are of particular interest to the visiting birder who has not yet encountered pelagic species. The ferry from St. Anthony links all the small communities along the coast of Labrador; it is a major undertaking that few birders are willing to tackle. A much shorter commitment of time is required for the Strait of Belle Isle ferry, which runs from St. Barbe to Blanc Sablon, a 12-mile trip that is the shortest of Newfoundland's links with the mainland. Crossings on this boat do not yield the imposing numbers of birds that can be encountered on the longer ferry trips, but they can produce a good mixture of species including all three jaegers, Northern Fulmars, Greater, Sooty, and Manx shearwaters, phalaropes and alcids.

Gros Morne National Park, situated at the base of the peninsula less than twenty miles from the Trans-Canada, has some of the finest scenery and the best birding of the entire trip. Gros Morne itself is part of the Long Range Mountains, which form the backbone of the Great Northern Peninsula. It is an ancient range of low, flat-topped mountains molded by glaciation thousands of years ago; today they're a potent geology textbook with glacial striations, hanging valleys, raised deltas, and deep fjords. They dominate a flat coastal plain dotted with small lakes and bogs.

The Long Mountains are testimony to the fact that mountains do not need to be high to be dramatic. Here there are no giant waves crashing over rocky headlands, no lush forests or snow-capped peaks, but this is one of the most hauntingly beautiful places I know.

The highway follows the coastline north through the park. To the west, low tuckamore-covered cliffs skirt the pebbly bays along the Gulf of St. Lawrence, today tranquil with lu-

---

Turn off Route 1 at Deer Lake onto Route 430, which leads up through Gros Morne National Park. To reach the south section and Stornoway, turn onto Route 431 at Wiltondale at the park entrance. The village of Woody Point is a short distance off to the right as this highway curves toward Trout River. There are campgrounds, picnic areas, and toilets throughout the park; checklists and information are available at Wiltondale and (more reliably) the Center near Rocky Harbour.

---

minescent fog banks. Eastward lies a sweeping expanse of stunted spruce, small neat pools, and yellow-green bog, a vista of muted greens relieved here and there with the white speck of a nesting gull. Beyond lies the long, low line of mountains, their steep slopes etched in sharp relief in the hazy sunlight; here dark and forbidding, there a blend of rich blues and mauves. In places deep valleys gouge their way into the heights, with vast folded ramparts on either side.

The view from the windows of Stornoway Lodge is even more spectacular, with the Gros Morne dominating the skyline across the fjord and the red heights of the Tablelands brooding over the South Arm to the east. Below lie the picture-postcard villages of Norris Point and Neddy Harbour and the sparkling waters of Bonne Bay itself. It's a scene that is never the same twice: with the constant interplay of light and shadow it changes while you watch.

Gros Morne itself stands separate from the neighboring heights, its steep sides towering up over twenty-six hundred feet to its flat oval summit. This summit has a reputation as one of the most reliable places for finding Rock Ptarmigan in eastern North America: all you have to do is climb the mountain. A very steep trail crosses a scree of large boulders to reach the top, and those hiking acquaintances who have tried it say it is one of the most arduous climbs they have ever undertaken. Anyone planning to tackle this hike

---

Stornoway Lodge—Woody Point, Bonne Bay, Newfoundland, A0K 1P0. (709) 453-2282. Rooms: 10 motel units with washrooms and showers. Amenities: Dining room, coffee shop, lounge. Car ferry across Bonne Bay. Terms: Single $44, double $52.

Gros Morne National Park—P.O. Box 130, Rocky Harbour, Newfoundland, A0K 4N0. (709) 458-2417:

Berry Hill Campground—Off Route 430, 2.5 miles from Rocky Harbour. Open May 15—October 15. Campsites: 156 sites, no hookups. Amenities: Swimming, fishing, nature trails, playground, running water, washrooms, shower, kitchen shelters, sewage disposal. Terms: $9.50.

Lomond Campground—12 miles from Wiltondale, off Route 432. Campsites: 35 sites no hookups. Amenities: Boat launch, pit privies, running water, washrooms, outdoor rinsing showers, fireplaces, picnic tables, kitchen shelters. Terms: $5.

Greenpoint Campground—6.5 miles north of Rocky Harbour, on Route 430 overlooking Gulf of St. Lawrence. Campsites: 18 open unserviced sites. Amenities: Hiking, swimming, spring water, fireplaces, pit privies. Terms: $6.

★

should be in good physical condition, allocate an entire day to the task, and—above all—be prepared for hostile weather conditions. A warm sunny day here can quickly give way to heavy fog with a bitter wind, particularly at the summit. You are then faced with finding your way down again in the fog.

If you fail to find Rock Ptarmigan here—and they are by no means certain in spite of optimistic assurances you may receive—another place for them is on the Serpentine Tablelands on the south side of Bonne Bay. Together with Gros Morne itself the Tablelands are the major components in the dramatic scenery of the park. They are a gigantic mass of barren red-brown rock towering above the pleasant green lowlands below. The highway crosses this desolate place to

the fishing village of Trout River; and along here, at the head of the Green Gardens Hiking Trail that leads out to the coast, you can climb up in the opposite direction to the top of Table Mountain.

This ascent is much less precipitous than the one up Gros Morne, and lucky people have found Rock Ptarmigan here. The downside is that the plateau on top of Table Mountain is enormous, and your chances of finding the birds are correspondingly more remote. You should also observe the precautions mentioned above, because here it is even easier to get lost. Take a compass. And no, I didn't see any the day I went up.

Fortunately ptarmigan are not the only birds here. On the south side the woodlands around Lomond and Glenburnie are delightful places to bird. You can log a dozen species of warbler, Swainson's and Hermit thrushes are widespread, and small groups of Purple Finches and Pine Siskins roam through the conifers.

To the north, birds are less easy to find. Merlins hunt across the bogs, and Rusty Blackbirds and Lincoln's Sparrows appear among the alder thickets. Savannah Sparrows are widespread, the commonest small bird of more open habitats. Back in the woodlands Fox and White-throated Sparrows predominate, together with Ruby-crowned Kinglets, warblers, and the occasional juncos. Pine Grosbeaks, never very numerous, turn up in the low spruces along the edges of the bogs. Two particularly noteworthy nesting species are American Tree Sparrows and White-crowned Sparrows, which can be heard and seen on the lower slopes of Gros Morne.

The best shorebird habitat lies farther north in the park, on the sands off Belldowns Point and in the areas around Cow Head and the community of St. Paul's. Our June trip yields little here but Spotted Sandpipers and Greater Yellowlegs, both of which breed in the area, but in migration periods a much wider variety of shorebirds occur.

Western Newfoundland has a richer mix of breeding species than areas farther east, and the traveler heading for Port aux Basques will find some places farther south worth visiting. The St. George's River at Stephenville Crossing has wide shorebird flats, abundant Ospreys and Common Black-headed Gulls nesting nearby, while the Port au Port Peninsula has long promontories at either end that concentrate birds in migration. Farther south the Codroy Valley is a pleasant agricultural area, a striking contrast to the mile upon mile of forest you will have experienced across the Trans-Canada, and a haven for field species that you will not have encountered in the rest of the trip. You can even expect to add Red-winged Blackbirds to your Newfoundland list!

For the botanist, Newfoundland offers some species and varieties that are confined to these rugged northeastern coastlines. Boreal forest and open barrens dominate most of the province, and some plants that favor these habitats are particularly common here: never have I seen such a pro-

---

You should allow at least 10 to 14 days for a Newfoundland trip, exclusive of ferries. Your list is not likely to be large—maybe 80 to 100 species—but the quality of the birds on it should compensate for that!

---

fusion of butterwort, and the exquisite rhodora abounds. Gros Morne National Park is particularly interesting, with a rich array of orchids ranging from arethusa on the open bogs to lady's slippers and purple fringed orchids in more sheltered areas. The Tableland has a limited but most unusual flora including alpine campion and meadow-rue, yellow mountain saxifrage and a rare form of thrift, all—unlike ptarmigan—easy to find.

SOME OTHER THINGS TO DO IN NEWFOUNDLAND

While in Gros Morne the boat trip on Western Brook Pond— 2.5 hours; June 1–15, 1 P.M.; June 16–August 31, 10 A.M., 1 and 3 P.M.; $16; (709) 458-2730—should not be missed. You're not likely to add many birds, but the trip down the long fjord bounded by 1800-foot cliffs on either side is one of the most spectacular and dramatic anywhere.

The Newfoundland mammalian fauna is limited, but the presence of caribou and—during summer—whales is noteworthy, and the introduced moose abound. There are no skunks, or snakes or ragweed either for that matter! Fishing here is superb, whether in the many lakes and rivers for salmon and trout, or jigging for cod off St. John's.

Newfoundland has a particularly rich and colorful history, and this is displayed in the museums of many communities, and particularly in the National Historic Parks of Signal Hill and Cape Spear—(709) 772-5367; Castle Hill—(709) 227-2401 near Placentia; L'Anse aux Meadows (a Viking village and artifacts) and Port au Choix (an ancient Indian and Dorset Eskimo site) on the Northern Peninsula (709) 623-2601.

The island's distinctive culture is all-pervasive, and its difference from the mainland is revealed constantly in matters as varied as its own time zone—half an hour ahead of Atlantic Canada—its own small-gauge railway, and through speech and food. Seafood is a staple everywhere, with cod almost always on the menu—in fact, "fish" here means cod. All this provides the visitor with the opportunity for culinary (and other) adventures, trying such delicacies as cod's tongues, fish 'n' brewis, bakeapple berries, and partridge-berries.

★   ★   ★   ★   ★

CHAPTER 8

SOUTHERN BRITISH COLUMBIA:
BIRDS OF THE NORTHWEST COAST

BRITISH COLUMBIA IS A PLACE OF CONTRADIC-
tions. It's a rugged land with a gentle climate. Most of
its people live on the coast, but the long Pacific coastline itself is almost inaccessible by road. The province is
heavily forested with some of the last areas of untouched
wilderness left on the continent, but a birder will be drawn
to the busy cities for the waterbirds and shorebirds that can
be found nearby, and for a couple of introductions that don't
belong here at all!

You can see groups of loons and alcids swimming just
offshore, vast flocks of waterfowl, mud flats teeming with
shorebirds, as well as the characteristic landbirds of the
northwestern rain forests. We are in Victoria for all of these,
but the vista from our window in Dashwood Manor seems

an unlikely one for birding: rows of neat houses, their lawns carefully tended and gardens bright with flowers, boulevards lined with well-mown grass, paths full of joggers, sightseers, honeymoon couples, and kids flying kites. On the tranquil waters beyond ferries ply busily, cargo ships rendezvous with pilot boats, and on weekends there are throngs of yachts, fishermen, and power boats. Only the distant Olympic Mountains opposite add a dark counterpoint: snow-capped, somber, forbidding, usually as heavily mantled in black clouds as the scene nearby is bright with sunshine.

Yet out on the Strait of Juan de Fuca life continues much as it must have done before any city was here. Strings of cormorants fly past, flocks of gulls circle and mill around upwellings; stubby auklets crash-land at promising fishing sites, and in the distance tall triangular fins surface regularly above the water, a pod of killer whales moving to some mysterious destination farther east.

Victoria too is a place of contradictions. It is the capital of British Columbia, a province of mountains and massive forests, of lumbermen and fisherfolk. Yet here is a picture-postcard city that seems more English than the English themselves. Red double-decker buses with Union Jacks emblazoned on their sides carry sightseeing tours around town, white-flanneled cricketers play on meticulously tended greens, lampposts are festooned with pots of geraniums and lobelias, and you can order afternoon tea with scones and clotted cream at the Princess Hotel. It is a city on a human scale, a modern city built in an Old World image. It's loaded with birding spots.

Here and there the New World at its doorstep intrudes: the Trans-Canada Highway climbs the side of one of those mountains on its way out of town, and even some city parks boast conifers that turn the picnickers beneath into pygmies. In these woodlands live the elusive landbirds of the northwestern rain forests, but Victoria itself is sheltered from much of the rain, a sunny town with pleasant weather through much of the year. Its distinctive vegetation is a

Victoria is accessible by air or ferry from Vancouver (see below). In both cases the city is approached via Route 17 from Swartz Bay and Sidney. The Scenic Drive is usually well marked and it and the parks mentioned are shown on the free tourist maps of the city: there are too many streets involved to list them all here. The lagoon is west on Route 1A (Island Highway) to Ocean Blvd. (follow the signs to Fort Rodd), and then past the fort entrance down to Lagoon Rd.

There is a huge range of accommodation in Victoria, but little that directly overlooks the Strait. One very good place that does is also opposite Beacon Hill Park. It is:

Dashwood Seaside Manor — Bed and Breakfast Inn — 1 Cook St., Victoria, B.C. V8V 3W6. (604) 385-5517. Heritage mansion overlooking the Strait of Juan de Fuca and Beacon Hill Park. Open all year. Rooms: 14 units, queen and double beds, some suites with fireplaces. Amenities: Combination bath, fully equipped self-catering kitchens, laundry. Terms: (the following, and all below, C$) Double $85–140; includes supplies for full breakfast. MC, VISA.

A hotel close to the tourist centers of downtown and still reasonably close to the Strait is:

The Embassy Motor Inn — 520 Menzies St., Victoria, B.C. V8V 2H4. (604) 382-8161. Open all year. Rooms: 102 units, Harbor Wing overlooking the inner harbor, a new modern tower, some suites with kitchenettes, 12 efficiencies, 33 kitchens. Amenities: Restaurant and lounge, swimming pool, sauna, coin laundry. Terms: Single $58–87, double $68–116, suites $122–138. Kitchens extra, $10. AMEX, MC, VISA.

brushy forest of gnarled garry oaks, and madronas with shiny green leaves and pale bark peeling to reveal patches of cinnamon.

We're going to bird the waterfront, a lazy man's approach to birding. From the harbor downtown we follow the Scenic Drive, where there is a series of parking spots and pull-offs.

From each we view the beaches, the rocky coves, and the open water beyond.

One of the first is a rocky headland called Clover Point. At one time this spot marked a sewage outfall that attracted birds from miles around, but since that was cleaned up the place is not much better than anywhere else. At a glance things seem quiet: the motley array of gulls on the lawns are all Glaucous-winged, the common large gull of the Northwest, with more loitering on the rocks below. It takes a closer look to reveal the little groups of dark shorebirds probing the rock pools: Black Oystercatchers, ungainly birds with heavy red bills and red-rimmed eyes, looking as though they had too much to drink with their last oysters; little sparrow-sized jobs that prove to be Least Sandpipers; Black Turnstones probing under the kelp, and the flash of a white rump that reveals a Surfbird.

In the waters just offshore are little parties of Harlequin Ducks, and farther out Rhinoceros Auklets dive, appearing only to vanish again before we can move our binoculars. Double-crested Cormorants fly past, and in the far distance flocks of small, pale birds rise from the water, wings flashing white as they bank and turn in unison before dropping to the surface again, Red-necked Phalaropes on their way south.

Most of these birds are the basic stuff of birding this route, appearing again and again at each stop. There will be others—here a Wandering Tattler on a rocky knoll, there a couple of Pelagic Cormorants perched on a buoy. At Cattle Point the offshore islands teem with birds, and this can be the departure point for "mini-pelagic" boat trips. These visit the offshore colonies, with close looks at nesting gulls and auklets.

There are good landbirding spots along the Scenic Drive, one of them Cattle Point itself. The point forms the seaward end of Uplands Park, one of the best remaining areas of garry oak woodland in Victoria. Tangled clumps of low trees are interspersed with open grassy "balds" bright with flowers in spring. Bewick's Wrens and Rufous-sided Towhees are common residents here, and tiny flocks of Bushtits scurry through the vegetation in a perpetual game of follow-my-leader.

At the north end of town the Drive passes through Mount Douglas Park. Here you can picnic under the giant conifers along the shore, and then drive the steep climb to the summit for a wonderful view over North Victoria. At places on the drive up there are access points to foot trails, with opportunities to see forest birds on the slopes below.

Another landbird locale is next door to downtown. Beacon Hill Park is a typical large-city park with sports fields, gar-

---

The closest campground to the city is Goldstream, without hookups and set in heavy forest. The following is well to the north on the Saanich Peninsula, but overlooks the Cordova Channel and has fair birding:

KOA Victoria East Campground—Box 129, Saanichton, B.C. V0S 1M0. (604) 652-3232. (11 miles north on Route 17 to Mount Newton exit, then east 1.5 miles). Open all year. <u>Campsites</u>: 174 sites, 31 full hookup, 94 water and electricity, 59 no hookup. Shaded and open sites. <u>Amenities</u>: Recreation room, horseshoes, playground, coin laundry, store, sewage disposal. <u>Terms</u>: $15/2 adults, electricity $2, sewer $1.50. VISA.

Goldstream Provincial Park—(12.5 miles west on Route 1) Victoria, B.C. V0R 2P0. (604) 387-4363. Open April 1—October 31. <u>Campsites</u>: 159 sites, no hookups. <u>Amenities</u>: Nature trails, swimming, fishing, flush toilets, sewage disposal. <u>Terms</u>: $12.

★

dens, duck ponds, a small zoo, and crowds of people; but there's some oak woodland as well and, in the southeast corner, a patch of large conifers. Chestnut-backed Chickadees forage here and there's usually a covey of California Quail to be found somewhere around. In wintertime the waterfowl keep the grass trimmed.

There are other places around Victoria where it is possible to get a flavor of the West Coast forest and its giant trees. Goldstream Provincial Park is on the Trans-Canada Highway leaving the city as it starts to climb the long grade called the Malahat. The day use area is located near the mouth of the Goldstream River where you can watch the salmon running in later fall (usually some nine weeks from mid-October).

A useful reference to Victoria is *The Naturalist's Guide to the Victoria Region*, edited by Jim Weston and David Stirling (Victoria Natural History Society). If you plan to spend much time here, the Davenport map to *Greater Victoria and the Saanich Peninsula* is invaluable. For the Province as a whole David Mark's *Where to Find Birds In British Columbia* is valuable, but unfortunately out of print at the time of writing. The Victoria hotline is (604) 592-3381. A good source of books and information is **the field-naturalist**, 1241 Broad St., Victoria, B.C. V8W 2A4 (604) 388-4174, the same store as Swiftsure Tours.

★

Nearby stand enormous western red cedars that were a hundred years old when Christopher Columbus first set foot on the continent. Hiking trails at Goldstream not only climb to the steep heights above, but also follow the river. Dippers bob on the rocks, and with luck you can find such forest specialties as Blue Grouse, Steller's Jay, and Varied Thrush.

There are some excellent birding areas west of the city. Esquimalt Lagoon is a delightful spot where the road from Fort Rodd Hill National Historic Park crosses the sandbar of a tidal lagoon. On one side little flocks of Western and other sandpipers scuttle along the water's edge, and gull flocks dot the shore at regular intervals. Here the mix of birds may be quite varied. There can be a few California, Mew, or Ring-billed gulls in with the Glaucous-wingeds, and later in the season Heermann's Gull turns up, a Mexican breeder that disperses north along the coast in later summer.

Over on the lagoon itself Great Blue Herons hunch along the edge, and at the far end are some feral Mute Swans, together with an array of semidomesticated ducks of dubious parentage. Like this kind of assemblage everywhere, the birds are worth a second look, as wild birds will join them on occasion.

There is no one "best" time for visiting Victoria, or indeed coastal British Columbia as a whole. A late summer visit yields both earlier shorebird migrants and the local waterbirds still on their breeding grounds. A visit earlier in the year, say in May or early June, can be better for such landbirds as Blue Grouse or MacGillivray's Warbler, which are very difficult to locate later in the season. Winter has waterfowl concentrations and hard-to-get birds such as Rock Sandpiper and Ancient Murrelet.

None of British Columbia's large population centers are located directly on the Pacific Ocean. You arrive in Vancouver to be confronted by the Strait of Georgia and Vancouver Island looming in the west. You cross to the Island itself and arrive in Victoria only to find a view of Juan de Fuca Strait to the south. There is only one place on the entire coast where you can drive directly to view the open Pacific, and it is there, Pacific Rim National Park, our next destination.

The Pacific Rim Highway is the only major road across Vancouver Island, a distance of 100 miles or more. It starts modestly enough, leaving the Trans-Canada through second-growth woodlands outside Parksville. The first real taste of its scenic quality comes as it runs along the shore of Cameron Lake and then enters a stand of gigantic old Douglas firs, the Cathedral Grove of MacMillan Park, a remnant of the ancient forests towering silent and awe-inspiring on both sides of the highway.

For Pacific Rim, leave Victoria north on Route 1 (the Trans-Canada) to the Parksville bypass to Route 4 and continue west. There are good accommodations in the villages of Tofino and Ucluelet, but they are much in demand. The following has a good restaurant adjacent:

The Schooner Motel—315-321 Campbell St., Box 202, Tofino, Vancouver Island, B.C. V0R 2Z0. (604) 725-3478. Open all year. Overlooking Tofino Bay. Rooms: 16 units, double or queen beds, some with kitchenettes. Amenities: Schooner Restaurant and lounge adjacent. Terms: $56–76.

The national park campgrounds are ideal, but you may have to settle for a private campground until a space is available. One of the best is:

Bella Pacifica Resort and Campground—Tofino, Vancouver Island, B.C. V0R 2Z0. (604) 725-3400. On Mackenzie Beach. Campsites: 120 sites, including oceanfront and wilderness. Full and partial hookups. Amenities: Hot showers, flush toilets, beach access. Terms: $15–17/2 persons; $2 electricity, $1.50 sewer, $1 water.

Pacific Rim National Park—Green Point Campground—P.O. Box 280 Ucluelet, Vancouver Island, B.C. V0R 3A0. (604) 726-7721. (14 miles north of Ucluelet on Route 4.) Open all year but fully open March 31– October 15. Campsites: 94 sites, no hookups. Amenities: Boat launch, fishing, swimming beach, nature program, flush toilets, sewage disposal, no showers. Terms: $10.50 per day. 7-day limit.

After Port Alberni the road really gets down to business, twisting and winding through a series of steep mountain valleys before arriving at the sea. It would be even more beautiful if the industrial character of the forests on Vancouver Island were less obvious. As the side-rail graffiti opposite one particularly ravaged mountainside puts it, "Bye-bye Wilderness." Finally the forest becomes more stunted and the highway levels out, to end at a T-intersection. The road now follows the coast. One short spur runs south to the fishing village of Ucluelet, and the longer leg runs north through the park itself to the village of Tofino; there isn't anywhere else for it to go. It's a delightful little place, with our motel sitting handily right in the center.

This is not a park to view from the windows of a car. You really don't see the sea from the highway, which runs for most of its twenty or so miles through rather uniform coniferous forest. To savor the park's quality and the vast empty beaches of the Pacific, you must head for the parking areas and trailheads along the route and start walking. Near the shoreline the tangled, gnarled old trees are hardly higher than a man, and their taller branches rise bare as if in silent

supplication to a harsh Providence. But back from the shore in sheltered valleys the rain forest grows with an almost tropical exuberance; massive trees, dense understory, and mosses and lichens everywhere.

For the birder here there is much challenge, and some unusual rewards. This is a silent forest, and the Winter Wrens, creepers, and Varied Thrushes are difficult to find

The Wickaninnish Centre is part of the Pacific Rim National Park interpretive complex. It is situated 2½ miles off Route 4, and includes exhibits, a viewpoint overlooking Long Beach, and a restaurant. Admission is free. Opening hours vary, but phone (604) 726-4212 for more information.

even when they do choose to sing. Landbird variety is low, but some species are unusually common. Steller's Jays and Northwestern Crows hang around the picnic areas, thickets yield Wilson's Warblers and the dark coastal Fox Sparrows, so unlike the rusty birds farther east; kinglets and Townsend's Warblers sing from the tops of the conifers, and juncos and Orange-crowned Warblers forage in the more open areas.

Along the shoreline, birds abound. Walking out from the woods at Comber's Beach, we discover a vast sweep of wide sand stretching over five miles in both directions. Behind us the last low Sitka spruces barely rise above the tangles of tall beach grass, and at the back of the beach itself lies a broad windrow of gigantic logs bleached pale by the sun.

Offshore, bobbing flocks of waterbirds cover the ocean, extending well beyond the limits of even the best telescope. Dark little groups of scoters can be seen, and alcids of several species challenge identification. A Tufted Puffin flies past, and there are loosely scattered flocks of Common Loons, together with smaller numbers of Red-throated and Pacific loons. Out along the horizon fly long lines of cormorants, both Brandt's and Pelagic; and even farther out the occasional Sooty Shearwater planes low over the water. Along the beach itself are loitering groups of gulls, and tightly packed flocks of shorebirds feed busily along the water's edge.

Don't miss a visit to the Wickaninnish Centre and a meal at the restaurant there. The views are spectacular! You can sit at a window high above the water looking north along the full sweep of Long Beach and be served gourmet seafood in tasteful surroundings.

One of the opportunities that Pacific Rim offers is the chance to get offshore and see some oceanic birds at close quarters. A full-fledged pelagic trip from Ucluelet can yield such species as Black-footed Albatross, Northern Fulmar, Pink-footed Shearwater, and Leach's and Fork-tailed storm-petrels, all birds calculated to make a land-bound observer drool with envy.

The poor man's pelagic trips in southern B.C. are from one of the ferries that ply the Strait of Georgia between Vancouver and the Island. True pelagic birds occur much less frequently on these trips than off Pacific Rim, but a fascinating array of seabirds is possible, particularly in migration periods. The two major ferry routes link Vancouver Island and the mainland, one between Nanaimo and Horseshoe Bay in North Vancouver, and the second between Swartz Bay at the tip of the Saanich Peninsula, and Tsawwassen south of Vancouver.

The latter route is the more productive. The Saanich Peninsula extends north from Victoria, and the route has the added advantage that it passes close to Victoria airport. The short grass surrounding the runways here is probably the best place for seeing the introduced Eurasian Skylark. These birds have been long established in the Victoria area, but they are local and can be hard to find.

The first half of the ferry trip to Tsawwassen winds through the Gulf Islands, and it is here, and particularly in the narrow channel at the eastern end of this passage—Ac-

Information on the ferries can be obtained from BC Ferries, 1112 Fort St., Victoria, B.C. V8V 4V2 (604) 669-1211 in Vancouver, 386-3431 in Victoria. Boats on the two routes mentioned run hourly mid-May to early October, and every two hours the rest of the year. Reservations are not required. Fare $17 cars plus $4.75 per person each way.

★

Tsawwassen is south of Route 17 about 2 miles from the ferry. It is a good base for covering the Greater Vancouver area, although you must be prepared for a drive through the city to reach Stanley Park and Lion's Gate Bridge. There's rather limited accommodation here, however, of which the following is the best:

Best Western Tsawwassen Inn—1665 56th St., Tsawwassen, B.C., Canada V4L 2B2. (604) 943-8221; toll-free 1-800-528-1234. 3 miles from Tsawwassen ferry. Open all year. <u>Rooms</u>: 151 units, hotel tower and motel units, suites with mini bars, whirlpools, and kitchens, some water beds. <u>Amenities</u>: Dining room, lounge, indoor and outdoor swimming pools, whirlpool, sauna, gift shop. <u>Terms</u>: Single $58–95, double $63–100. AMEX, CB, DINERS, MC, VISA.

A campground in the same general area is:

Park Canada Recreational Vehicle Inns—Box 190, Delta, B.C., Canada V4K 3N6. (604) 932-5811. (4799 Highway 17 via 52nd Street.) Open all year. <u>Campsites</u>: 145 sites, full hookups. <u>Amenities</u>: Recreational lounge, laundry room, washrooms, showers, heated swimming pool. <u>Terms</u>: $12–16/2 persons.

tive Pass—that the largest numbers of birds occur. This is one of North America's Bald Eagle bonanzas. Eagles dot the tops of the evergreens beside the channel, sit on rocks along the shoreline, and soar idly above the boat. People with time to spare have counted forty or more eagles on this passage, but there are always too many other distractions for us to get a good count. Waterbirds skitter away from the boat or dive and swim along the shoreline, where sea lions bask on the rocks. Once we are out beyond the islands there's always the possible pelagic to watch for. Common Murres, Pigeon Guillemots, and Marbled Murrelets are regular on this route, and Parasitic Jaegers are possible in fall.

The ferry link between Victoria and Port Angeles in Washington State can be even more productive, particularly in later fall and winter. Many true pelagic birds have been reported at this time, and Cassin's Auklet is another possibility.

Tsawwassen lies on a peninsula that runs south to Point Roberts in Washington—itself a good birding site—and is a sharp contrast with Vancouver Island, and indeed with the rest of British Columbia. It's flat. This is part of the historic delta of the Fraser River and although most of the open country is now drained for agriculture, vast tidal flats remain. These are a magnet for waterbirds. Huge flocks of Snow Geese and ducks winter there; twenty to thirty thousand Brant can be seen in April and shorebirds occur in mind-boggling numbers in fall.

Our hotel is just inside town, but there are three outstanding birding spots in this area. The first, and most daunting due to its size, is Boundary Bay. This huge bay lies to the east of town, and extends almost 10 miles across to the

---

From Tsawwassen Route 17 is the main access to the rest of the mainland. For Crescent Beach drive to the Freeway (Route 99) and then right to the King George Highway intersection. Bear right on Crescent Rd. (not on the highway itself) and continue to keep right, following Crescent and then Sullivan to their end in Blackie's Spit. There is a beach area with washrooms nearby.

To reach the lagoons bear left on Route 99 and continue to Sea Island Way, following the signs to the airport and crossing the Sea Island bridge (if you're coming from the city be sure to use this bridge, not the main route to the airport across the Arthur Laing bridge). Then take the first right, and follow this road around to Ferguson Rd. Turn left and the road eventually ends up at the plant. Although private property, birders are allowed in after signing the book at the office door. There are no washrooms in this area.

For the Reifel Sanctuary turn left off Route 17 on Route 10, continuing west on River Rd. when 10 ends, to Westham Island Rd., and follow the signs. There's a pleasant picnic area and washrooms there (Sanctuary open 9 A.M.—4 P.M., $2.50, 946-6980).

★

---

town of Crescent Beach. You gain access to it from several roads that dead-end around its perimeter, and one of the better areas is near Crescent Beach itself. Here a narrow sandspit juts north, and you can walk out to view the tidal flats with their shorebirds and loitering flocks of gulls and terns. British Columbia's only Elegant Terns have occurred here but we have to be content with a Caspian, together with scattered Whimbrels probing the mud among the tiny "peep."

The real birding hot spot of these coastal lands, and indeed of much of the West Coast, is appropriately enough a sewage lagoon. The Iona Island lagoons are situated on a small island on the North Arm of the Fraser, north of Vancouver International Airport, itself located on another island. In fact you can sometimes see them from the plane as you land. Just across the river is the city, and the Vancouver Natural History Society has arranged access to the lagoons for birders.

They're not the easiest places to reach and are characteristically pungent, but they are well worth the effort. Sharp-tailed Sandpipers occur here regularly in September, and a star-studded list of other rarities have been found. This is one of the continent's shorebird hot spots. On our visit there are enormous numbers, massed in dense flocks. The aromatic goo teems with Western Sandpipers, together with the occasional Baird's and Semipalmated and small flocks of Long-billed Dowitchers.

The state of the tide is always an important factor in coastal watching. The time to visit these flats is when the tide is coming in, so that distant birds gradually move toward you. At the lagoons themselves the tide is even more important than elsewhere, and here the largest gatherings of birds occur at high tide, when the feeding areas elsewhere are submerged.

Shorebirds are far from the only feature of a trip to Iona. There are lagoons outside the fences of the plant as well, and all of these attract ducks and gulls, particularly as the area is relatively secluded. Hawks forage over the tidal flats and fields along the road, and trees and hedgerows there attract landbird migrants. In fact this area has yielded several of the Vancouver area's extreme rarities.

Of more interest to a visitor, perhaps, the first sections of the road around the bridge to the airport are one of the more reliable places in Vancouver for seeing the introduced Crested Mynah, which occurs nowhere else in North America. This is an urban species that behaves rather like a starling, and if you do not succeed in locating it here you will be reduced to crossing the Fraser River bridge to the north and driving around the residential areas looking for these birds sitting on wires or investigating garbage cans. The flying bird is very distinctive with rounded wings and striking white wing patches. On the ground, crest or no crest, it looks surprisingly like a starling.

Our third destination in the delta is the George C. Reifel Sanctuary, located on yet another island close to Tsawwassen itself. At this privately owned refuge, large numbers of resident waterfowl nest in the diked ponds and adjacent marshes. The water levels are manipulated to provide habitat succession, and Reifel too can yield good numbers of shorebirds when the tide is right, with a particularly good record for Sharp-tailed Sandpipers.

It's also a productive spot for landbirds, which nest and feed in the cover along the dikes. Appropriately enough, however, its main claim to fame relies on the waterfowl that are attracted to it. A summer visit is not ideal for these, but later in the year geese and ducks on the adjacent marshes and flats build up to huge numbers, and like Iona Island the open country around the refuge can be very good for hawks and open-country birds, especially in the winter.

One of the better birding areas in Vancouver itself is Stanley Park, a thousand-acre city park immediately adjacent to downtown. It's no place to visit on a Sunday afternoon, but at other times the loop drive that runs counter-clockwise around the perimeter of the park gives access to a wonderful variety of habitats. The waters of Burrard Inlet that surround the park yield gulls and other waterbirds, often including Western Grebes at Ferguson Point. The two freshwater lakes in the park, Beaver Lake and Lost Lagoon, attract an assortment of ducks, and the extensive natural woodlands can be good for woodland species.

In North Vancouver, across the Lion's Gate Bridge, Lighthouse Park sits on the north shore at the entrance to Burrard Inlet. It is much smaller than Stanley Park but the land birding can be better, and it is reputed to be a good place for locating Blue Grouse when they are booming in spring. Both these places attract Hammond's and Pacific-slope flycatchers, as well as Black-throated Gray Warblers, Western Tanagers, Black-headed Grosbeaks, and flocks of Red Crossbills in the tops of the conifers. Farther east are Cypress Bowl and Mount Seymour Provincial parks, both situated on the forested slopes above North Vancouver. Here you could add

---

Vancouver itself and the major parks mentioned are shown on the insets to the provincial roadmaps, but you should pick up a copy of the free *Visitors Map of Greater Vancouver,* which has more detail, including the roads in the more outlying areas.

In Vancouver *The Natural History of Stanley Park*, produced and distributed by the Vancouver Natural History Society, can be useful, and they also carry provincial checklists (Vancouver Natural History Society, Box 3021, Vancouver, B.C. V6B 3X5). The Vancouver hotline is (604) 876-9690.

First-time visitors to B.C. and Canada will find the province's travel and accommodation guides useful. Write Tourism British Columbia, Parliament Buildings, Victoria, B.C. V8V 1X4.

B.C. is not a place for big lists—landbirds can be elusive and big migratory waves are rare—but you may total 100–120 species for your trip, depending on the time of year. Included should be some species that you'll have difficulty finding elsewhere, a range of typical western birds that will be exciting for an eastern visitor, and there's always the possibility of something really rare in places like Iona lagoons.

★

birds that may have eluded you elsewhere; species such as Black Swift, Gray Jay, Red-breasted Sapsucker, Mountain Chickadee, and Hutton's Vireo.

THERE'S ACTUALLY MORE HERE THAN BIRDS TO CAPTURE YOUR INTEREST

Southwestern British Columbia abounds in attractions that could distract the most dedicated birder. Fine scenery and photogenic opportunities are everywhere on this trip, with Tofino getting my vote for the most scenic community. The west coast flora with its giant trees is fascinating, but the wealth of seashore life is perhaps the biggest natural attraction. The rock pools off the Victoria waterfront and Long Beach are so intriguing and full of life that hours can slip while you wander from rock to rock and probe under hunks of kelp.

Vancouver has all the usual big-city attractions, and although Victoria is much smaller it is a major tourist destination and has a multitude of things to see and do. My own favorite is the Royal British Columbia Museum—675 Belleville St., Victoria, 387-3701, 9.30 A.M.–7 P.M., $5—which has an exceptionally fine collection of exhibits covering not only natural history but the very rich cultures of the West Coast Indians with their elaborate ceremonies and magnificent art. Totem poles, one of the characteristic features of these cultures, can be seen in nearby Thunderbird Park, and there are large poles in Beacon Hill Park and in Vancouver's Stanley Park.

Anyone who delights in gardens will find Victoria as a whole enchanting, and there are attractive public gardens in the major parks, but a visit to Butchart Gardens—15 miles north on Route 17 at Brentwood, 652-4422, 9 A.M.–9 P.M., $8.50—is a must. This privately operated garden in an old quarry is a jewel of its kind. Vancouver abounds in gardens too, with the best-known probably being the Bloedel Conservatory in Queen Elizabeth Park—872-5513, 10 A.M.–9 P.M., $2.20—but my own favorite is the Van Dusen Botanical Gardens—5251 Oak St., 226-7194, 10 A.M.–dusk, $3.35—

nearby. These are laid out by country of origin: if you are a botanist they are fascinating, and if you are not they are beautiful anyway. The University of British Columbia also has an attractive and interesting Botanical Garden.

The Vancouver Aquarium in Stanley Park—682-1118, 9.30 A.M.–9 P.M., $5.50—is justly renowned. Among the other Vancouver attractions is the 137-meter-long Capilano suspension bridge; and the fish hatchery farther up the road is worth a visit as well. If shopping interests you, Victoria is likely the best bet, with a host of antique and other gift shops.

★   ★   ★   ★   ★

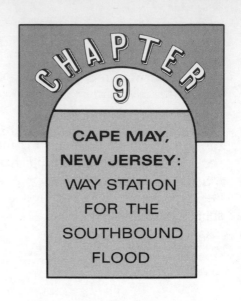

CHAPTER 9

CAPE MAY, NEW JERSEY: WAY STATION FOR THE SOUTHBOUND FLOOD

HEN THE DAYS BEGIN TO SHORTEN AND summer commences its long, gradual slide into autumn, the migrants start to move south. At first it's a trickle, but by September millions of birds are flooding southward to escape the cold of the northern winter. It's a movement we can only sample, for much of it occurs at night, and on a scale we can scarcely comprehend let alone see. The best most of us can hope for is the opportunity to see a few of the travelers as they pause to rest and refuel. Yet even such fragmentary glimpses can yield the highlights of a birding year—long anticipated, keenly savored in the event, and the stuff of cherished memories for years afterward.

There are a few special places where a birder can hope for more than this pittance. They're places of refuge, sought by desperate birds faced with vast expanses of ocean or hostile terrain; way stations where exhausted or disoriented migrants can pause and regroup before pressing on once more. Typically they're all oases of a kind—not just trees and water in the desert, but grassy openings in dense forest, and everywhere islands and headlands along major water bodies and along the coastlines themselves.

Points and headlands can yield some of the most dramatic concentrations: birds moving along them suddenly meet an open and hostile expanse of water and halt uncertainly at the tip, or find themselves drifting out over the water during their migration and head for the nearest land.

Cape May is one of the very best and the most famous of such places in North America. In fall, nocturnal migrants moving with the northwest winds of a cold air mass find themselves being blown out into the Atlantic, and turn down along the New Jersey coast. They finally arrive at a point where water lies ahead in all directions, and with dawn approaching they dive into the nearest woodlands for shelter. Those woodlands are part of Cape May. Not only is it a place where huge numbers of birds can be seen, but it is also a place where the rare becomes regular, and the unexpected is always possible.

We arrive at Cape May at lunchtime. The day is warm and humid, not exactly the sort of weather that encourages migrants to hasten south, and we decide to check into the campground and eat before heading out to start birding. We locate a campsite shaded by tall oak trees and with a satisfying surround of shrubbery, a good spot tomorrow morning, we hope, when we'll be birding in earnest.

Lunch is hardly under way before we spot movements in the bushes. And it turns out to be a long meal. A couple of hours later we are still at it, but by now we have a list of several Black-throated Blue Warblers, the males pictures of restrained elegance in dark blue, black, and white; a Veery rooting in the dead leaves; Scarlet Tanagers in their muted fall colors picking berries from the understory; and a rarity for us, a Worm-eating Warbler, a symphony of soft fawns and warm beiges. Then there is an assortment of other fall warblers—twelve species in all—working their way through the heavy vegetation, together with a constant parade of Blue Jays and visits by the local White-eyed Vireo and chickadees. Such is a quiet afternoon's break during fall migration at Cape May.

On the map Cape May is a county, a town, or even a collection of small communities located at the southernmost

---

To reach Cape May, take the Garden State Parkway south to its end. Here you can continue straight ahead into the town, or bear right (west) on Route 109 to reach the main birding areas. Drive to Route 9, and continue west on 9, following the signs for the Lewes (Delaware) ferry, for 0.5 miles to the first light. This is Route 626, or Seashore Rd. (poorly marked), and you turn left here, to head south over the Intercoastal canal. The better birding areas lie to the right of this road. Just across the bridge, Route 641 (New England Rd.) runs west to end in Higbee Beach. About 1.5 miles farther, in the western outskirts of Cape May (Seashore Rd. changes to Broadway as you enter town), Route 606 (Sunset Blvd.) runs west to Sunset Beach, with views over the bay. The other main birding areas are south of this road.

There is a wide range of accommodation in Cape May itself, with most of the hotels overlooking the ocean along Beach Avenue, which runs east from the foot of Broadway. Many are closed between October and May, and others are converting to condominiums, so it is advisable to reserve in advance. One motel on the front with an ocean view and with restaurants nearby is:

Periwinkle Inn—1039 Beach Ave. (P.O. Box 220), Cape May, N.J. 08204. (609) 884-9200. Open April 15 to October 31. <u>Rooms</u>: 50 units, 14 efficiencies. <u>Amenities</u>: Refrigerators, pool. <u>Restrictions</u>: no pets. 3-day minimum stay in season. <u>Terms</u>: 2 persons, 2 beds: $50—$106.

There are two campgrounds on the "Island." Both have many long-term lease sites. The best for birding and the one we have used is:

Cold Springs Campground—0.7 miles west on New England Rd. (609) 884-8717. Open May 1 to October 15. <u>Campsites</u>: 100 mainly wooded sites, 45 full hookups, 55 water and electric, tenting. <u>Amenities</u>: hot showers, sewage disposal. <u>Terms</u>: $13.50/2 persons.

The following, closer to town, is more open and has more facilities:

The Depot Travel Park—0.8 miles south on Seashore Rd. (609) 884-2533. Open May 15 to September 30. <u>Campsites</u>: 135 sites, 100 full hookups, 35 water and electric. <u>Amenities</u>: hot showers, sewage disposal. <u>Terms</u>: $15.50–$16/4 persons.

tip of New Jersey; an island formed by the Atlantic Ocean and Delaware Bay, together with the canal of the Intercoastal Waterway to the north. The town of Cape May itself occupies the eastern section of the island, but to the west lies an area of fields, woodlots, and small communities—the birder's Cape May. Like many concentration points it is not much to look at: a few marshy fields, some ponds and areas of low, tangled woodland; a patchwork of old homes set amid overgrown gardens and hit-or-miss agriculture, all interspersed by a network of small roads.

Dawn finds us standing on a dike at the westernmost end of all this, at Higbee Beach, looking south over the treetops. Behind us to the north is an expanse of fill dredged from the canal, and beyond again is the canal itself, with the Cape May-Lewes ferry dock visible in the distance. To the east a hazy sun edges above the trees, and we stand and wait expectantly as the expanse of dark canopy ahead gradually resolves itself into individual trees, and the leaves of the vine tangles that seem to cover everything gradually take shape. It's a dense canopy: what the trees' own leaves do not conceal, the vine tangles do. We search the opaque blanket for some suggestion of movement, for some glimmer of life.

Quite suddenly we have it. A few small birds shoot out into the sky above the dike, and just as abruptly dive back into the heavy cover. One lands into the reeds along the dike below us, momentarily revealing itself as a female Indigo Bunting before vanishing again. Next comes a small exodus from the trees: a dozen or more warblers again shoot out over our heads, and now head off erratically over the open flats toward the canal. It's a pattern that is to repeat itself

---

At the end of New England Rd. is a small parking lot serving Higbee Beach. Trails lead down to the beach itself and both north and south, while the road itself curves north toward the canal. The dike lies on the right a short walk along this road, just as it leaves the woods. All the trails and the road itself can yield excellent birding.

---

again and again as we stand here; one of our fellow observers looks after the disappearing throng and speculates that somewhere, to the north, there must be a grove of trees that will yield spectacular birding. For the sharp-eyed and the lucky, several species are already identified: a Black-throated Green Warbler, an American Redstart, a Yellow-rumped, all sufficiently distinctive even in fall, even with these fleeting glimpses, to allow identification. For the rest we stand, hoping for some birds to appear that are not in quite such a hurry.

One by one they do. A Northern Oriole tops one of the shrubs with a splash of orange. Lower down a Great Crested Flycatcher flashes russet and yellow as it darts after insects above the canopy. A Palm Warbler emerges briefly, tail wagging endlessly, and a Magnolia Warbler displays a brief flash of yellow. Soon more warblers are flitting in and out of the bushes. Not the vivid array of spring migrants, these, but birds in muted browns and greens, challenging the skill of many of the watchers on the dike. If only they would stay still for a moment! If only they would stay in view!

Somebody says that this is almost a waste of time, and indeed maybe only one bird in ten or so can be identified. But there are many birds, and even the few that are well seen add up to exciting birding. Dawn on the dike is something of a Cape May tradition as the viewing here is better, in spite of the hosts that pass unidentified. At ground level the birds are even more difficult to see in the dense cover.

But there is more to Cape May than the heavy woodlands of Higbee Beach. We leave for the "meadows," an area of wet, sandy grassland and open pools backing the sand dunes along the shoreline a few miles farther east. The whole is preserved by the Nature Conservancy, as it represents a habitat that has now become rare along a coastline under the pressure of constant development. Well-marked trails lead through the meadows and they can yield excellent birding, with good views of birds in the marshy areas. This is a place for open-country species, and as we head out we watch for hawks overhead and occasionally hear the clear whistles of Greater Yellowlegs somewhere in the distance.

The path is bordered with the glowing pinks of gerardias, punctuated by the occasional rich blue of mist flower. Soon we are distracted by Ospreys. In many places even one Osprey is cause for excitement, but here they are constantly visible, and now we are privileged to see one of the special delights of Cape May: a dozen of these magnificent birds

---

Both the meadows and the state park lie south of Sunset Blvd. (Route 606). The small parking lot for the former is on the south just past the T-intersection with Bayshore Rd. (Route 607), which runs north to connect with New England Rd. Please stay on the marked trails. About 1 mile farther, Route 629 runs south to the state park, easily identified by the lighthouse, passing Lily Lake and the headquarters of the Observatory on the west. Entry is free at the state park, where there are public washrooms and a picnic area.

★

circling slowly overhead, long wings held in their characteristic crook, white heads shining in the sun.

The walk yields steady birding, one of those very satisfying paths where there is always something to look at and
always something new appearing. Here a Baird's Sandpiper
on a wet sandflat, with that slightly flattened look that
Baird's Sandpipers always have, as though someone had sat
on them by mistake; there a group of stubby dowitchers
probing the water vigorously, their heads almost immersed
in the water. Out on the beach a flock of terns periodically
swirls out over the ocean in a flurry of motion before returning to their resting places again. The challenge is to find
something different in this crew, but they are all Commons
apart from a couple of Royal Terns standing off to one side,
distinctive with their large size and striking orange bills. As
we head back onto the meadows again we find more terns
over the pools, this time a mixture of Common and Forster's, twisting and turning in graceful arcs across the open
water.

In the afternoon we head for Cape May State Park, just
west of the meadows. It includes Cape May's most familiar
landmark, the old lighthouse. Just beyond the parking lot
here a low platform overlooks a marsh, the site of the fall
hawk count. It is manned continuously during that period
by members of the Cape May Bird Observatory. They maintain a count of the steady succession of raptors passing over,
because Cape May is also one of the East's major observation points for thousands of migrating falcons and accipiters. The platform is the place to find what is around, to see
and be seen, for the "regulars" to meet friends and renew
acquaintances.

It's warm and hazy when we arrive, and we quickly discover that one of the main constituents of the Cape May
passage is American Kestrels. The sky high above seems to
be full of the dainty little falcons, some flying steadily southward over the point and others circling around uncertainly
on light, fluttery wings. Periodically Sharp-shinned Hawks
appear lower down, flying steadily before they too are ar-

Cape May Bird Observatory maintains a small office nearby opposite a productive large pond called the Lily Lake. The observatory is run by the New Jersey Audubon Society, and is a "must" visit to find out what special birds are around and to pick up local checklists and other information. (609) 884-2736; the hotline is 884-2626.

A useful reference to birding sites in New Jersey is William J. Boyle, Jr.'s *A Guide to Bird Finding in New Jersey*, 1986, Rutgers University Press. A two-volume work of great historic interest is Witmer Stone's *Bird Studies at Old Cape May* (1937, republished in 1965 by Dover Publications Inc.).

rested by the expanse of water ahead and circle backward while deciding what to do next. Occasionally a Merlin appears, a small, dark, powerful falcon dashing impatiently to some appointment far to the south. At one point two larger birds are suddenly crisscrossing the wetlands, striking terror among local gulls and pigeons alike: Peregrine Falcons, pausing for a moment of light entertainment before heading purposefully out across the bay.

It seems a little ironic that here, bounded on three sides by ocean, the main emphasis should be on landbirds. In practice, of course, this is not really the case as most paths lead eventually to the sea, and on each the open water is scanned for waterfowl and seabirds offshore. The marshes themselves also attract the rich abundance of the herons, egrets, and shorebirds characteristic of the coastline; but it is true that Cape May is more noteworthy as a concentration point for landbirds than for viewing oceanic species. This changes in the late fall and through winter when such species as eiders and scoters, and perhaps even an alcid or two, can be seen bobbing in the waves offshore, and the elusive shapes of jaegers and Northern Gannets come and go in the distance.

A visit to any of the coastal marshes in the earlier fall will introduce you to the green-headed fly, whose fiendish bites can make life miserable. Unfortunately repellents do not seem to work very well for this beast, but long-sleeved shirts and a hat can at least minimize the target areas.

It is primarily the fall migration that has made Cape May famous. From August through October a constant flow of birds passes the Island, with each day bringing its own particular assortment of birds, each part of the season its own distinctive mix. In early fall the shorebirds and the earlier warblers and flycatchers arrive; in September the hawks start to move in earnest and every Tree Swallow in the world seems to be decorating the wires and low shrubs near the waterfront; while in October the later hawks and shorebirds pass, and sparrows dominate the passerine flocks.

But other seasons are special here as well. Spring migration brings some species, such as Mississippi Kite, that are very rare in fall, even though the numbers and variety of species as a whole are less spectacular. Summer is likely the quietest time, but even then there is a fair mixture of more southern-nesting species such as Chuck-will's-widow and Blue Grosbeak, and on the beaches Piping Plover and Least Terns breed.

To imply that the fall passage is literally constant is to mislead. Like all such places, Cape May has its off-days— and weeks! I once spent a September week here with overpowering heat and steady south winds. The migrants didn't like it any better than I did, but fortunately such episodes are the exception. It's always the anticipation of change, the wondering what tomorrow will bring, that is part of the fascination.

To get a better flavor of coastal birding we head north on the Garden State Parkway to view the salt marshes that back the barrier beaches north of the Point. It's a windy day when we set out for Stone Harbor, one of the chain of small communities that occupy the barrier beaches along the coast. As we drive along the parkway the trees open in places to reveal the wide expanses of salt marsh to the east, and when we turn off on the Stone Harbor causeway we find marsh bordering the road on either side.

Most of it is a rich green carpet of cord grass evenly dotted with the white figures of Great Egrets, each standing motionless, neck poised upright, watching for its next meal. The overall effect is of an exceptionally lush green lawn dotted with exceptionally elegant lawn ornaments. Here and there little groups of Snowy Egrets huddle, hunched conspiratorially as though plotting a takeover of the marsh, and occasionally individuals prance out to embark on a grotesque chase of some unfortunate small fish, wings fanning wildly and neck waving from side to side.

To reach Stone Harbor, drive north from Cape May on the Garden State Parkway to the light at Mile 10. Turn right and cross the causeway to the town of Stone Harbor. Turn right on Third Ave. and continue south for about a mile until the woods of the heronry appear on your left. You can also walk or drive around to Second Ave. at the rear, and this street continues south to a parking area from which you can walk out along the beach to the Point. To drive out across Nummy Island (toll 50¢) you must return to Third Ave. and continue south. It's tempting to continue south from here through the Wildwoods back to Cape May, but the route is very slow and rather unproductive.

There are shyer inhabitants of these marshes too, and a patient watch can reveal the gray shape of a Clapper Rail moving along the edge of the grass. Earlier in the year Sharp-tailed and Seaside sparrows sing sizzly little songs, but now they must be coaxed out unpredictably by "pishing"—making those squeaky noises that sometimes intrigue a bird enough to make it come to investigate. At low tide shorebirds scatter over the mud flats of the receding pools, scuttling about and probing busily for the rich abundance of food.

Most of the herons originate from a heronry that has occupied a woodlot in Stone Harbor since the late 1930s. Now it sits incongruously surrounded by housing with a paved parking lot, and if you do not have your own binoculars, you can pop a coin into one of the viewing scopes that are mounted along the fence. Incongruous or not, Stone Harbor is justifiably proud of its heronry, and is to be commended for protecting the place.

There are birds to be seen here even at mid-day, but the real spectacle is at dusk when the diurnal species—Great, Snowy, and Cattle egrets, Little Blue and Tricolored herons, and Glossy Ibis—come back to the trees to roost, while the Black and Yellow-crowned night-herons depart for their evening's fishing. Pick a clear evening—the setting sun glows pink and apricot on the white plumage of the egrets, an unforgettable sight.

Just south of Stone Harbor the road heads out again over the salt marshes, across Nummy Island, and this is often a better area for viewing salt marsh species. Before crossing the causeway, however, we continue south on the barrier island itself. It is possible to walk out on the sandspit of Stone Harbor Point, where there are loitering flocks of gulls, often associated with American Oystercatcher and plover feeding along the shoreline, while Black Skimmers forage up and down the channels of open water. Careful searches along these open beaches can yield Piping Plover.

Some forty miles north of Cape May, but only a little north of Atlantic City and hence easily accessible from the main access roads to the Point, is Brigantine Wildlife Refuge, an area of fresh- and salt-water pools that has an outstanding reputation as one of the finest concentration points for water and shorebirds on the East Coast; it provides a visit to the Cape May area with a spectacular complement.

Our own arrival at Brigantine—more properly the Brigantine Unit of the Edwin B. Forsythe National Wildlife Refuge, and affectionately known to New Jersey birders as "the Brig"—comes shortly after dawn. As we start out along the dike the sun bathes the wetland in silver and gold, and flocks of waterfowl are silhouetted black against the glistening water. On our right we look down over the rich green of the salt marsh, dotted with the inevitable egrets, with Laughing Gulls and terns patrolling the channels among the vegetation. Ahead of us sparrows dive into the weed tangles along the road and spooky little groups of duck jump up at our approach. Flocks of Tree Swallows cross and recross the pools, gradually making their way south to replenish the hosts at Cape May itself.

This is a place for leisurely scanning. Every few yards we stop the vehicle and carefully look over the pools and

---

To reach Brigantine from the Garden State Parkway, enter the service area located between exits 40 and 44. At the north end of this is a small road signed to Jim Leeds Rd. Proceed down this to the light (Jim Leeds Rd. itself) and turn right. In about 0.5 miles there is a Y-fork, where Jim Leeds Rd. bears slightly right. Bear left here onto Great Creek Rd. (but unmarked). This continues east, eventually crossing Route 9 and then curving around to enter the Refuge.

The Refuge is open from dawn to dusk, and the tour road is all-weather good gravel surface. The entry fee is $3, paid at a self-registration station. There are washrooms here, and a sightings book. The headquarters building across the road has a few displays, and bird checklists.

I have assumed Brigantine will be covered in conjunction with Cape May, but there are ample accommodations of all kinds in Atlantic City if required. Campgrounds are fewer: one nearby is:

Shady Pines Campground — south on Route 9 to Route 30, 1.6 miles west on 30 and then 1.5 miles north on Sixth Ave. (609) 652-1516. Open March 1—November 1. Campsites: 100 sites, 40 full hookups, 55 water and electricity, tenting. Amenities: Flush toilets, hot showers, swimming pool, sewage disposal. Terms: $18/2 persons.

★

marshes. Every few yards reveals a different vista with different birds, or inlets that must be investigated and mud banks that might conceal shorebirds. Even in late September, long before the enormous flocks of geese and ducks that will stage here later have arrived, the numbers of waterfowl are formidable. Everywhere there are Canada Geese and flocks of Mallards and American Black Ducks. And there are other species as well: wigeon, teal, pintail, and shoveler.

We climb the viewing tower and scan the open waters of West Pool to the north, and beyond the salt marshes to the south. Cormorants are visible in the distance here, hunched black shapes on the pilings out in the channel, and dainty

---

Cape May's bird checklist has 404 species, Brigantine's 289, with a strong weighting toward water and shorebirds, where almost anything may turn up. Like concentration points everywhere, Cape May is outstanding for numbers and rarities, rather than particular species.

---

groups of yellowlegs feed on distant tidal pools. Farther on we pass a cross dike and look out at the tower where the local pair of Peregrine Falcons sit, idling away the morning.

The East Pool beyond has much more vegetation and even larger numbers of waterfowl, and as we turn the corner to drive north, viewing becomes easier as the sun gradually moves behind us. In one area a huge flock of sandpipers feeds and reveals an early Dunlin and a White-rumped Sandpiper among the throngs of Semipalmateds. On another flat a mixed flock of gulls and skimmers rests while nearby a few Snow Geese, harbingers of the hosts to come, are grazing among the marsh grasses. Finally our circuit is almost over, and we leave the open water behind to head through the old fields and woodlands that occupy the western section of the reserve. But there are still birds to be seen: landbird migrants move through the trees and the ringing songs of Carolina Wrens punctuate our passing. Farther on again we pass the more overgrown pools near the entrance road and add Wood Ducks to our list.

The morning has yielded no great rarities, but it has been birding at its best: superb atmosphere, abundant birdlife, and always something new around the next corner.

OTHER THINGS TO DO WHILE AT THE SEASIDE

The general naturalist will find the wide diversity of habitats around Cape May fascinating. There are echoes here of the Pine Barrens of New Jersey to the north, and the deciduous woodlands, salt marshes, dunes, and meadows all have their own appeal. Rock hounds seek tide-worn quartz pebbles along the beaches of the Point.

The town of Cape May itself is one of the oldest seaside resorts on the entire coast, and if gingerbread houses are your thing there are lots here; the entire town is outstanding for its abundance of historic buildings. Regular sightseeing tours are available: for information contact the welcome center at 405 Lafayette St., (609) 884-5404. There's also excellent boating and fishing.

★   ★   ★   ★   ★

CHAPTER 10

SOUTHERN CALIFORNIA: SEACOAST TO MOUNTAIN, FOREST TO DESERT

RECENTLY READ AN ARTICLE BY A CALIFOR-nian who speculated that sooner or later all the bird species in North America would be found somewhere in the state. There are times when this doesn't seem as im-probable as it sounds. California abounds with both birds and bird-watchers, and even eastern warblers stray to the desert oases and the headlands of the Pacific. The search for such waifs occupies the time of many of the state's bird-ers, but the visitor is more likely to find the wonderful array of native species more fun. California has an exceptional wealth of habitats, ranging from desert to seacoast and dry chaparral to mountaintops. They're easy to get to and con-veniently close to one another. And each has its character-istic birds.

The southern part of the state is the most productive for the visiting birder looking for new species, and the choice of when to visit can be difficult. Winters are mild and there are large populations of waterbirds and shorebirds to be seen. In spring, as these are leaving, the migrants pour north to flood into the migrant traps of deserts and along the coast; and fall migration can bring vagrant shorebirds and other rarities from the north and east. But I prefer early spring, when the desert heat is less daunting to a Northerner, and we can hope for a little of everything: some lingering wintering species, the returning migrants crowding into desert oases, and the residents already busy with household duties.

Coastal California, from San Diego to Los Angeles and north through Santa Barbara, together with the mountain ranges behind and the Colorado Desert to the southeast, offers a bewildering array of birding opportunities, together with some of the most formidable conurbations in the United States. Los Angeles, indeed, is a good base for exploring the region but for its sheer size and heavy traffic. Even if they don't dissuade you, the enormous amounts of time they can waste might. Our trip starts in the beautiful city of San Diego, and our route can, if we wish, avoid Los Angeles completely. This certainly doesn't assure an absence of crowds and heavy traffic, but with some luck there is more solitude to be found in this burgeoning state than anyone has a right to expect.

San Diego is not only one of the most attractive cities in the United States, but it abounds with good birding opportunities. The first comes along the Mexican border in the small valley of the Tijuana River. It is not a pretty place, a kind of grab bag of dumps, market gardens, horse farms, stock pens, abandoned land, and new housing developments all jostling uncomfortably together. The border patrol plays hide-and-seek with would-be Mexican emigrants, and aircraft from the nearby base drone constantly overhead.

But it's good for birds. The Tijuana Valley is one of

All the areas described for San Diego are readily accessible from Interstate 5. The exit for the Tijuana Valley is Dairy Mart Rd., just before the border crossing. Follow this road south, and you can then cover the network of small roads to the west. The valley has neither public toilets nor formal picnic areas.

Our route in California lacks accommodations in "birdy" locations. The hotels in San Ysidro are less expensive than in San Diego itself, and are well situated to cover the valley. The following is comfortable, and has a **Coco's Restaurant** (open 6 A.M.) adjacent:

Travelodge—Mexican Gateway—701 East San Ysidro Blvd. (take last U.S. exit from I-5 and I-805), San Ysidro, California 92073. (619) 428-2251; toll-free 1-800-255-3050. Open all year. Rooms: 34 units, some suites. Amenities: Swimming pool. Restrictions: No pets. Terms: Single $40, double $45. AMEX, DINERS, MC, VISA.

Camping is rather limited. We found the following satisfactory but noisy:

Border Gate RV Resort—1010 San Ysidro Blvd. (from I-5 via Dairymart exit, 1 block on Dairymart Rd. and then 1 block north on San Ysidro Blvd.), San Ysidro, California 92173. (619) 428-4411. Open all year, accepts overnight guests. Campsites: 179 sites, full hookups. Amenities: Recreation room, playground, heated swimming pool, whirlpool, coin laundry, store, showers, flush toilets. Restrictions: No tents. Terms: 2 adults $22—25.

Campers who are wholly self-contained, however, should head for **Silver Strand State Beach**—4½ miles south of Coronado on Route 75. (619) 435-5184. Campsites: 122 sites, no hookups, 2 handicapped sites; gates to the campground are locked at night, time depending on day length. Amenities: Beach, flush toilets, cold showers. Restrictions: Dogs must be kept on leash at all times and are not allowed on the beach. No second vehicles allowed in the camping area after gates are closed. Terms: $10, dogs $1 extra.

★

Southern California's birding hot spots, with a long list of rarities to its credit. We find nothing exotic, unless you count the spectacular Magpie Jay that nearly lands us in the ditch as it flies across the Mexican border, likely someone's escaped pet. Still, there are Black-shouldered Kites and Lesser Goldfinches, special to us. On the wet fields Marbled Godwits and White-faced Ibis jostle in the lush grasses, and hawks perch on the fence posts. Flocks of sparrows forage along the roadside weed patches and migrant warblers in the groves of trees. There's even some beauty: at Border Field State Park a Black-necked Stilt is feeding, black-and-white plumage and slender red legs mirrored vividly in the amber pool, framed exquisitely by a golden-yellow carpet of hatpins.

Palm Ave. westbound from I-5 finally bears north to become Silver Strand Blvd. There are turnouts on the east of the road. The state beach is some 3 miles north of Palm on the left, and the park road runs to a series of paved parking lots on the beach (washrooms). You can view the ocean from here and then walk through the underpass below the road to view the bay side, where there are picnic areas. San Diego can be a confusing city to a stranger: a city road map is a good investment.

For a wonderful array of waterbirds we head north on the Silver Strand Boulevard up the west side of San Diego Bay. The bay and dikes here are alive with birds: small groups of Brant swim buoyantly just offshore near a jumble of power boats and a miniature galleon; cormorants fly low across the still water and mixed flocks of duck dive and surface in unison, as if by order. Out over the mud flats hosts of shorebirds are feeding feverishly, anticipating the return of the tide. Black Skimmers fly past, and on one shell bar a small group of Elegant Terns quarrel, streamlined with long, narrow crests and slender orange bills. On the dry upper beaches of the state park Snowy Plovers glide like ghosts across the pale sand, while out in the surf of the Pacific loons are diving. Later in the year endangered Least Terns nest along here, but we're too early for them.

Not all of the San Diego waterfront is open sandy beach. To the north, at Point Loma and beyond, the ground rises high above the water, dropping steeply to a rocky shoreline. At Sunset Cliffs, and at La Jolla well to the north, the road runs along the cliff top with frequent parking areas overlooking the ocean. Here are wonderful opportunities to view the birds of these rocky headlands.

On our visit the day is rather foggy, a bonus in spite of the poor visibility; the cool mist discourages the usual horde of joggers and sightseers, and seabirds approach shore more readily. In the mist just offshore whales feed, churning the calm water into roiling eddies, with gulls in greedy, screaming masses. From time to time flocks of Black-vented Shearwaters loom suddenly out of the mist, banking and gliding low over the surface, only to disappear again as quickly.

Among the loitering gull flocks we find Heermann's Gulls mixed among the ever-present Westerns and Ring-billeds, the young birds dark, almost black, and the adults exquisite

---

To reach Sunset Cliffs take Interstate 8 (Ocean Beach Freeway) west from Interstate 5 to its end; then bear right on Sunset Cliffs Blvd. which finally runs along the cliff edge, with numerous turnouts. The road then turns inland as Hill St., and while in the area it would be a mistake not to follow this to Catalina Blvd. and turn right to visit the Cabrillo National Monument (fee). We have never found the birding there very exciting, but the view over San Diego is sensational, and sea otters play in the surf offshore.

La Jolla is farther north again. Exit Interstate 5 at Ardath Rd. and bear left at the bottom of the hill on Torrey Pines Rd. Watch for Prospect St. and bear right again, continuing right to emerge along the cliffs on S. Coast Blvd. Street parking, washrooms, and picnic tables.

★

with their striking red bills and white heads contrasting with the delicate gray of their bodies. Just below us a small group of Black Turnstones is resting, spruce in formal brown-black plumage, but other birds prove more difficult to find. Finally we locate a Wandering Tattler and Surfbirds working along the edges of the rock pools. On one rocky pinnacle groups of cormorants are sitting, each species carefully segregated from the rest: Double-cresteds are spread evenly across the top, Brandt's sitting on the seaward side as though poised for instant takeoff, and Pelagic relegated to the cliff face itself.

Torrey Pines State Reserve is located at the extreme northern end of San Diego, and one of its main functions is to preserve the tree after which it is named, endemic to Santa Rosa Island and this one spot on the mainland. The entry road makes a short, steep climb up through an open grove of the pines to parking areas surrounded by dense thickets of aromatic sage. In early spring these steep, shrub-covered hills are a flower garden, with owl clovers, shooting stars, Mexican poppy, and a host of daisy species coating the ground in yellows, whites, and gold.

It's a good place to meet the birds of the coastal chaparral, the shrub community that covers much of coastal California. Everywhere Wrentits sing their bouncy little songs, to an eastern ear vaguely reminiscent of Field Sparrows, and

---

You can reach Torrey Pines Reserve from La Jolla by simply returning to Torrey Pines Rd. and driving north. From Interstate 5 exit on Genesee Ave. west (S21) and continue north. Turn onto the park road at the bottom of the hill where the highway curves to run alongside the beach.

Checklists are available here at the delightful old museum. Sometimes a nominal park entry fee is charged. There are washrooms but no picnic area; however, there are rather limited facilities in the park area below, along the river on the other side of the highway.

★

pop out unexpectedly to view the trespasser with pale, hostile eyes. Scrub Jays, so much brighter than their eastern cousins, hop around looking for handouts, and small coveys of California Quail scuttle through the undergrowth. California Thrashers and Towhees scratch among the dead leaves and White-throated Swifts rocket low overhead.

It is impossible to spend long in Southern California without being aware of the mountains, even if they're often hidden behind a dirty yellow blanket of smog. In warm weather their green forests promise cool and shade, and in winter the snows on their summits are a reminder that the cold and ice are not far away. They are both an attraction and a challenge. Go east and you must cross them, and so it is that Interstate 8, as it starts its journey to the deserts of Arizona, winds up into the pine-covered Laguna Mountains.

They're not very high by the standards of the Rockies and the Sierra Nevadas, but they're enough to trap the rain. Their eastern slopes lie stark and barren under the perpetual sun, with tall agaves rearing candelabras of yellow blossoms from clumps of fleshy, spiny leaves, and red rocks and contorted pinnacles and jumbled screes and long-forgotten shacks. Farther east again, we descend out onto a vast, wide expanse of pebbly, sandy soil softened by a carpet of neat, evenly spaced small bushes, a delicate blending of olive greens, grays, and silver. We have arrived in the Colorado Desert, one of the driest places in North America.

Yet as we continue east the desert gives way to a broad agricultural plain, with orange groves and a neat network of side roads crisscrossing diked fields of rich cropland. The desert here is no greener than anywhere else; an enormous irrigation network creates this lush countryside. This is the Imperial Valley, and we're now below sea level—in fact nearby Calipatria, 183 feet below, bills itself as home of the world's largest flagpole—the flag itself flies just above sea level! To the north, hidden behind the fields and the haze, surrounded by a desert where only sparse creosote bush and baccharis grow, is the Salton Sea.

Such arid surroundings seem an unlikely sort of place for

a large body of water, but then Salton Sea is unlikely from many points of view. It was formed accidentally, by a diversion of the Colorado River. It is now considerably saltier than the ocean, and is growing more so every year as the streams that feed it are heavily loaded with pollutants. The fertilizers, pesticides, and salt-laden runoff from this cornucopia of farmland are gradually killing its life. Yet it is still full of exotic tropical fish species, though the fish are gradually succumbing to the increasing salinity, resulting in huge die-offs. The stench can be overwhelming. And it really is huge: over thirty miles long and some fifteen wide at its southern end. In summer it is incredibly hot.

None of this sounds very enchanting, but it's also an incredible place for birds.

First you have to get there, and in this case getting there is very much part of the fun, as there are other places of interest in the Imperial Valley. In Brawley an isolated colony of Gila Woodpeckers can be found along the road that runs down beside the hospital. A few miles farther north, where Rutherford Road runs eastward, the stock farms can yield huge flocks of blackbirds and Common Ground-Doves. Crissal Thrashers skulk in the low thickets along the creek here, to be coaxed out by vigorous "pishing." Nearby are Ramer and Finney lakes, where there is a colony of Yellow-headed Blackbirds and good birding generally.

Heading north from Calipatria through the flat expanse of lush green fields it's even harder to remember we're in the middle of the desert! Finally we turn onto the side road to the headquarters of the Salton Sea National Wildlife Refuge. The fields along here merit more than a casual glance, as Mountain Plover and other shorebirds can be found in the wintertime, and Burrowing Owls sit sleepily in their holes along the edges of the levees.

The Refuge headquarters, at least in the winter months, has a bird feeder that attracts an assortment of sparrows and blackbirds. These are worth careful examination: in spite of its alleged rarity on the checklist, we have never failed to find a Green-tailed Towhee here in early spring.

Exit Interstate 8 at Route 86 north. Head through El Centro to Brawley, then jog right to continue north on Route 111, which follows the east side of Salton Sea to Indio.

The Finney-Ramer Unit of the Imperial Wildlife Area is well marked some 5 miles north of Rutherford Rd. (Route 26S) and 1 mile south of Calipatria on the east of Route 111. The hospital in Brawley is south of town west of Route 86. The woodpeckers may be in the hospital grounds or farther along the dirt road. They like eucalpytus trees!

To the south the widest range of accommodations is in El Centro. The following is close to Interstate 8 and has a campground associated with it and its own restaurant:

Vacation Inn—Travelodge—2000 Cottonwood Circle (I-8 to Imperial Ave., exit left to Ocotillo Dr., turn left to Cottonwood Circle), El Centro, California 92243. (619) 352-9523; 1-800-255-3050. Open all year. Rooms: 189 units, some suites and kitchenettes. Amenities: Restaurant, lounge, therapy pool, swimming pool, laundry. Restrictions: No pets. Terms: Single $42–45, double $45–52. AMEX, DINERS, MC, VISA.

Vacation Inn—Travelodge RV Park—Open all year. Campsites: 31 full hookup sites and concrete pad. Amenities: Swimming pool, whirlpool, laundry, full toilets, hot showers. Restrictions: No tents. Terms: $14/2 adults, pets $1 extra.

A more pleasant camping area is at Wiest Lake, east of Route 111 on Rutherford Rd.: **Wiest Lake County Park** (Imperial County)—From Brawley: go 4 miles north on Route 111, then 2 miles east on Route 26 S. (619) 344-3712. Open all year. Campsites: 40–50 sites, 20 electricity. Amenities: Recreation hall, lake swimming, boating, ramp dock, fishing, flush toilets, showers. Terms: Electricity $8, no hookup $5.

★

One feature of the Refuge is the enormous flocks of wintering Snow Geese that often feed in the fields nearby. At their peak upward of 50,000 birds have been counted.

Salton Sea teems with birds. The duck populations have been estimated at half a million. In winter huge squadrons of American White Pelicans and Double-crested Cormorants fly up and down the Sea, silhouetted against a mauve backdrop of distant mountains. The surface of the water is dotted with thousands of Eared Grebes, with small groups of Clark's Grebes and a wonderful array of other waterfowl. Seabirds that find themselves dead-ended in the Gulf of Cal-

ifornia sometimes drift northward, and the sea has a long list of oceanic strays, with such rare vagrants as Brown and Blue-footed boobies and frigatebirds turning up in the early fall. Migration can yield huge flights of swallows and groundings of other landbirds.

One of the best access points to the water is Garth Road near the headquarters. Here there are flocks of shorebirds, gulls, and ducks on both sides, and it is one of the more reliable areas for Yellow-footed Gulls later in the year. An-

Salton Sea NWR headquarters (No fee; checklists, picnic area, washrooms) is at the west end of Sinclair Rd., some 4 miles north of Calipatria, and Garst Rd. is the first side road running north to the east of the head-quarters. The Wister Unit is well marked on Route 111 about 8 miles farther north again. There is a rather charmless primitive camping area on the latter. Do not drive the dirt roads in this area when they are wet.

other good area is the Wister Unit of the Imperial Wildlife Area, where a network of dirt roads and levees leads out to the water, and the impoundments themselves attract ducks and waterfowl. Somewhere on one of these roads you'll be standing on the San Andreas Fault.

We stop at the entrance to bird the salt cedars around the maintenance areas, and are quickly rewarded with Verdins and a Black-tailed Gnatcatcher flitting through the filigree of leaves, while more searching turns up an Abert's Towhee and Pyrrhuloxias rooting around in the root tangles. At first we pass dry fields where dignified Long-billed Curlews pace. We select one of the more passable crossroads and drive down toward the shore with a vanguard of landbirds flitting through the shrubs ahead. In one pool a group of Cinnamon Teal are feeding, in another there are Black-necked Stilts, and in an area of deeper water Canvasback, Redhead, and Ruddy Duck.

Finally we arrive at the shore, a luminous vista of pale flats were avocets and Willets rest. Farther out white skele-tons of trees are dotted with the snakelike silhouettes of cor-morants, dark counterpoints of reality in a surreal world. Beyond, the silver water merges imperceptibly into the faint pinkish glow of the sky, and white pelicans sit suspended as though in midair.

At the north end of the Sea the desert seems to be fighting a losing battle with development and groves of tall date palms. This is probably the only place in North America where you can buy dates fresh-picked from the trees, and could well be the only place in the world where date milk-shakes are for sale.

By Indio the development seems to have won, but a road-runner still stalks across the scruffy bit of desert beside the Best Western Date Tree Motor Hotel, and Cactus Wrens decorate the telephone wires. In the hotel garden—a tiny oasis of tranquillity as much from the bustling highways and busy railroad as from the desert itself—a Verdin nests in the columnar cacti and a pair of Abert's Towhees dash in and out of the oleander hedge, using the trash bin as a handy lookout.

Finding the desert birds is not always so easy. They're at once more widespread and more elusive; being everywhere, they can sometimes seem to be nowhere. They have a way of adding themselves to the list one by one. But a visit to a location like Cottonwood Springs oasis in the Joshua Tree National Monument may add several, although even here timing is crucial: come early in the morning and there is life everywhere, but later in the day the birds will have vanished.

The road to the Springs climbs slowly through desert accented by tall spindly wands of ocotillo. After early spring rains each is tipped by a vivid tuft of scarlet blossoms, and hummingbirds zip from one to another, sampling the nectar. The oasis nestles below a towering jumble of red rocks, a clump of tall fan palms rising from a wet ledge. Formerly a substantial stream flowed here, but now there is little water to be seen, only the tangles of shrubbery and a few tiny pools lower down marking its course.

But the birds know it's here. At one tiny pool the unlikely duo of a Summer Tanager and Lawrence's Goldfinch are bathing, the tanager resplendent in rose-red and the goldfinch nattily decked out in gray, accented by blacks and golds. Warblers flit among the surrounding bushes, and high above echoes the sweet cascade of a Canyon Wren. Farther up the slopes a covey of Gambel's Quail is foraging under the shrubs, and out on the tip of a slender branch a sudden flash of violet iridescence reveals a Costa's Hummingbird. It's not long before we've added Rock Wren,

Accommodation in the desert tends to be expensive, particularly in the cooler months and around Palm Springs. Indio is more reasonable:

Best Western Date Tree Motor Hotel—81-909 Indio Blvd. (eastbound I-10 to Indio Blvd.), Indio, California 92201. (619) 347-3421; toll-free 1-800-292-5599. Open all year. Rooms: 113 units, queen- and king-sized beds, some suites with private spa and kitchen. Amenities: Restaurant and lounge adjacent, swimming pool, whirlpool, coin laundry. Terms: Free continental breakfast. Single $42–64, double $48–70, suites $98–112. AMEX, DINERS, MC, VISA.

Campers will find acres of developed RV parks full of refugees from winter. The following is more pleasant; there are few waterbirds here, but desert species occur:

Lake Cahuilla County Park Campground—(Riverside County; south of Indio at the junction of Jefferson and 58th St., nine miles south of Route 111), P.O. Box 3507 Rubidoux, California 92519. (619) 564-4712. Open all year. Campsites: 140 sites, 60 water and electricity, tent sites. Amenities: Fishing, boating, swimming, hiking trails, equestrian trails, store, flush toilets, hot showers, disposal station, no drinking water. Terms: Electricity $10, no hookups $7, pets $1 extra. 14-day limit.

The Cottonwood Springs campground is even better, but a little out of the way for the rest of the route unless you plan to go to Twentynine Palms:

Joshua Tree National Monument–Cottonwood Spring Campground—74485 National Monument Dr., Twentynine Palms, California 92277. (619) 367-7511 (26 miles east of Indio on I-10, then 7 miles north). Open all year. Campsites: 62 sites, no hookups. Amenities: Hiking trails, flush toilets, disposal station, no showers. Restrictions: 32-foot maximum RV length. Terms: $6.00. 14-day limit.

★

Route 111 continues northwest through Mecca to Indio, where it intersects with Interstate 10. This runs east with an exit at the Joshua Tree National Monument, although an unnumbered road from Mecca (starting in town as Ave. 66) cuts off the corner.

If you plan to visit Cottonwood Springs you have a choice of continuing on north from there through Joshua Tree National Monument to Twentynine Palms, and then west on Route 62. This can be a long, hot, and dusty drive and not very birdy; however, it is both scenic and interesting. Entry to the Monument is free. A visitor center is adjacent to the Cottonwood Springs campground, with brochures and checklists (nominal fee), and there are picnic areas and washrooms nearby.

The areas below are accessible from the Interstate westbound, Big Morongo Reserve via Route 62 north to Morongo Valley, where it is right on East Drive at the far end of town, some 10.5 miles from the Interstate. There is a checklist, and picnic areas and washrooms in adjacent Covington Park.

Phainopepla, and Black-throated Sparrow, all visitors to the little canyon.

Every desert oasis has its own character. Some may be no more than a cluster of greener, denser vegetation in a rocky crevice, but some have clear cascading streams, broadening into areas of marsh with cattails and willow, islands of lush greenery set improbably in a muted landscape of reds, browns, and grays.

Big Morongo Reserve is such a place, and its rich vegetation is a magnet to birds for miles around; a haven for migrants, a home for species that are alien to the surrounding desert, and reliable source of food and shelter for wintering flocks. It's another place for unlikely mixtures: on one side of the road Gambel's Quail feed in the arid scrub while a Cactus Wren churrs. Opposite, a Red Crossbill feeds in a pine tree and flocks of Red-winged Blackbirds squabble in the bushes. High overhead a tiny spiraling ball of vivid red reveals a Vermilion Flycatcher in its display flight.

Once into the heavy cover of the oasis itself it's easy to forget the desert surroundings: the chorus of frogs, Song Sparrow songs and goldfinch calls and the fresh green of the willows could place you in a spring marsh anywhere on the continent. On the right day these willows can teem with migrant warblers and other transients.

As we continue northwest through the Coachella Valley, the desert becomes more and more arid. Finally the valley narrows as we approach the pass through the mountains. Here Palm Springs nestles under the mountains to the right, its golf courses almost indecently green—geometrical oases with little white balls for birds. Between it and the road stretches a bare expanse of sand, one of the driest places in the entire desert. Little lives here, although it is the only

---

There is accommodation at both Banning and Beaumont. The following is comfortable and the restaurant opens at 6 A.M., although you may prefer the nearby **Denny's** for dinner:

Best Western El Rancho—550 Beaumont Ave. (I-10 exit Beaumont Ave., north 1 block), Beaumont, California 92223. (714) 845-2176; toll-free 1-800-528-1234. Open all year. <u>Rooms</u>: 52 units, 4 2-bedroom units. <u>Amenities</u>: Restaurant and lounge adjacent, swimming pool, indoor whirlpool, therapeutic spa, fitness room. <u>Restrictions</u>: No pets. <u>Terms</u>: Single $37—43, Double $40—46. AMEX, CB, DINERS, MC, VISA.

There's a campground on the San Jacinto road, and you may see a few open-country species there:

Banning Travel Park—(On Route 243, 1¼ miles south of junction I-10). 1455 S. San Gorgonio Ave., Banning, California 92220. (714) 849-7513. Open all year. <u>Campsites</u>: 115 sites, 63 full hookups, 37 water and electricity, 15 no hookups, separate tenting area. <u>Amenities</u>: Recreation room, volleyball, playground, horseshoes, heated swimming pool, laundry, grocery store, flush toilets, hot showers, sewage disposal. <u>Terms</u>: $9.50—14.50/2 adults.

★

home of the endangered Coachella fringe-toed lizard. All around sprouts a forest of giant windmills like enormous tree trunks, a testament to the force of the winds.

Now, closing in on both sides, are the mountains. To the north towers the huge mass of San Gorgonio and the San Bernadinos, and to the south the imposing peak of San Jacinto soars above its sisters. The character of the countryside changes rapidly, and when we arrive at Beaumont we're leaving both the pass and the desert, and entering a dry rangeland where wintering hawks decorate the powerlines.

From Beaumont a road winds steeply upward into the San Jacintos, starting from the dry range and quickly climbing into dense chaparral. This is the road to the mountain village of Idyllwild, and it climbs to over 6,000 feet before descending to join the Palms to Pines highway that crosses the mountains to the south.

As we start the long climb we are heading both upward and, effectively, northward. Above us winters last longer and summers are pleasantly cool, even when the cities below

---

The Idyllwild road is Route 243. To reach Humber Park, turn left on N. Circle Dr. and continue on Fern Valley Rd. There are picknicking and washrooms at Fulmor Lake and in Idyllwild itself.

Route 243 continues through town and down to join Route 74. From here you have a choice. If you plan to visit Los Angeles, return to Beaumont and the city lies ahead on Interstate 10. A left on 74 takes you back into the desert at Palm Desert. If you wish to return to San Diego without visiting Los Angeles, you can turn right on 74 and drive down to Hemet and on to Interstate 15, which is the fastest route back.

If you have more time you can continue on Route 74 up over the Elsinore escarpment and down to Interstate 5 on the coast. Route 74 can yield good birding, notably Tricolored Blackbirds around stock pens. The Ronald W. Caspers Wilderness Park, 7.5 miles from Interstate 5, has excellent birds.

★

Remember that weather in the mountains is unpredictable, and a cool, cloudy winter day lower down can prove bitterly cold higher up, with fog and ice. At such times negotiating the hairpin turns on the road can be an interesting experience, and chains are often mandatory. By the same token there is camping at Idyllwild, but it is not recommended in the wintertime. Interstate 8 over the Lagunas can also present difficulties in periods of severe winter weather.

It's difficult to drive in California and avoid steep hills and winding roads. On the route described, however, only the road up San Jacinto entails a major mountain drive, although Route 74 over the escarpment has its moments. You can reach Hemet without driving up the mountain by using Route 79 west of Banning.

A useful birding reference is James A. Lane's *A Birder's Guide to Southern California* (L&P Press, rev. by Harold Holt, 1985). The relevant hotlines are: San Diego (613) 435-6761 and (619) 479-3400; Los Angeles (213) 874-1318. You can cover the route described quite quickly or spin it out into two weeks or more. Expect a trip list of around 200 species; 30 or more could be new to you if you have never visited the Southwest before.

are sweltering. Plant and animal life both change, and on the exposed heights the birdlife is the same as that in the forests of British Columbia.

The chaparral is home to much the same species that we encountered in Torrey Pines, and when we stop at a turnout we can hear the bouncy songs of Wrentits from the shrubs below. The view here is spectacular, with the mass of San Gorgonio dominating the skyline on the other side of the valley to the north, and traffic winding antlike along the highway far below.

As we climb still higher, the road suddenly levels out and we find ourselves in shady groves of live oaks. Here Plain Titmice and Hutton's Vireos hide in the gray-green leaves, and Acorn Woodpeckers argue noisily and chase each other and peer at us around branches with knowing, clownlike faces. Soon we begin to encounter conifers: yellow pine, and Coulter pines with their enormous cones. The Scrub Jays of the chaparral are replaced by dark Steller's Jays, and we hear Mountain Quail calling from the slopes above. At the beautiful little Fulmor Lake there are thickets of manzanitas, their startling maroon bark contrasting with shiny dark green leaves. As we wander around in the crisp air, so refreshing after the heat of the desert, Mountain Chickadees flit among the tall conifers and a busy little group of Pygmy Nuthatches hustles by, working over the pine needles and peeping happily to one another.

The highest point accessible by road is the trailhead at Humber Park, a short distance above town. From here a nine-mile trail leads to the summit of Mount San Jacinto at 10,786 feet, in the Boreal life zone. Clark's Nutcrackers, Townsend's Solitaires, and Red-breasted Nuthatches are among the species to be looked for there. In the wintertime many of the high-country species range lower. We have had White-headed Woodpeckers and solitaires down below 5,000 feet, with wintering flocks of juncos and finches.

THERE'S A BEWILDERING ARRAY OF OTHER THINGS TO DO

Plant and reptile enthusiasts will find Southern California every bit as fascinating as the birder, and considerably more bewildering. The flora in particular is not only incredibly diverse, but is supplemented by an abundance of showy and conspicuous species that have been introduced and are now wild. In some areas it is not unusual to find that all the more conspicuous plants come from somewhere else, but I guess the same can be said about the people.

Joshua Tree National Monument—(619) 367-7511—is worthwhile for both the plants and the scenery. You pass from the low Colorado Desert into the higher Mojave Desert, and you can watch the flora change as you progress—fascinating! The cactus "garden" of teddy-bear cholla is wonderfully photogenic. Desert flowering tends to be rather unpredictable, but the end of March and early April seem to be generally good times for spring wildflowers.

California seashore life is rich with interesting rock pools in places like Point Loma, while offshore gray whales migrate in January and again in late March, and a number of other whale species can be seen on offshore boat trips (pelagics out of Los Angeles and San Diego can often yield these as well as excellent seabirds). California sea lions regularly sprawl on the rocks of La Jolla.

California's historical features seem to get lost in the other things for which it is noteworthy, but there is a chain of old Spanish missions up the coast, and indeed the Spanish influence is widespread everywhere. One attractive mission that is easily visited on our route is San Luis Rey, inland from Oceanside (On Route 76, open 10 A.M.–4 P.M. $2). Others include California's first at San Diego, Mission San Diego de Alcala (10818 San Diego Mission Rd., open 9 A.M.–5 P.M., $1).

There are so many other attractions in Southern California that it's quite beyond our scope to list them. In San Diego the Zoo (Open 9 A.M.–4 P.M., $8.50; 234-3153) and the Wild Animal Park (6 miles east on Route 78; open 9 A.M.–4 P.M., $12.95; 234-6541) are exceptionally good, and are the last locations for the California Condor! Sea World—Daily 9 A.M.–dusk, $19.95; 226-3901—is a major Oceanarium. The Old Town San Diego State Historic Park—237-6770—commemorates the first settlement and has many old buildings.

Southern California's beaches are better known for things other than birding, and there is an enormous choice of water-based activities on the coast, while inland water areas such as Salton Sea also provide boating and fishing. Golf courses abound, there is skiing in the San Bernadinos, and the mountains have hiking and climbing opportunities.

★   ★   ★   ★   ★

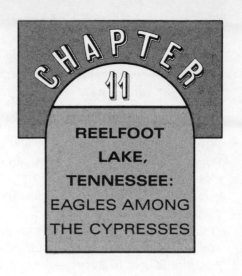

CHAPTER 11

REELFOOT LAKE, TENNESSEE: EAGLES AMONG THE CYPRESSES

REELFOOT LAKE LIES IN THE FERTILE BOT-
tomlands of northwestern Tennessee, surrounded by
flat fields of cotton, just a short flight for a foraging
heron over to the banks of the Mississippi. Heading down
the highway from Union City there's little to suggest a wetland: just a long line of heavy woodlands in the distance,
exceptional perhaps for their extent but with no hint of the
real quality beyond. Finally the trees thin out and there's a
vista of open water dotted with low clumps of cypress, sitting squat on heavy dark bases. More bald cypresses ring
the shoreline, tall and elegant, their open feathery foliage
rising in orderly, symmetrical tiers like the trees in a Chi-
nese woodcut.

It's startling to find a typical southern swamp here in northern Tennessee, and surprising too to find a major wetland that does not owe its origin to man's intervention. This lake began with an earthquake, the giant New Madrid quake of 1811. It was one of the most violent earthquakes ever in North America, but in those days western Tennessee was a remote region and there were few witnesses. The large depression that resulted gradually filled with water and Reelfoot was formed.

It's a large lake, over 8 miles long, but so dissected by promontories and headlands that it is almost four separate lakes in one. The shallow bays are full of stumps and snags, and secluded swampy backwaters hiding ducks and herons. Reelfoot is full of surprises, from the southern birds that nest here in the summer to the concentrations of Bald Ea-

To reach Reelfoot from the Purchase Parkway in Kentucky, continue southwest on Route 51 to Union City and turn west on Route 22. This runs down the east side of the lake to join Route 21, running west along the south end. At Tiptonville Route 78 intersects, and runs north parallel to the west shoreline.

gles that make it a birding destination in the winter as well. There are waterfowl in thousands, and elusive southern rarities more typical of Louisiana than Tennessee. There are wintering landbirds and flocks of migrant shorebirds. It's one of those places that can yield exciting birding no matter when you visit it.

Our destination is the Airpark Inn, an ideal base for a few days of exploration in this fascinating place. The Inn is built out into the lake itself, and its rooms are linked by boardwalk to the main lodge. You can sit at the broad windows in your room and watch egrets and Ospreys flying among the low cypresses out on the lake, and Red-bellied Woodpeckers and Common Yellowthroats foraging among the tall cypresses and heavy vegetation along the swampy edge. As we walk out to the end of the boardwalk a few coots swim away jerkily, and at nightfall we're serenaded by a duet between Barred and Great Horned owls.

The morning dawns foggy—not the dense fog that defeats all vision, but one of those luminous mornings when the hazy sun turns the cobwebs into cloth of gold and ghostly waterfowl float on invisible water. Sparrow flocks feed below the graceful gumtrees of the lakeshore—White-crowned, White-throated, a junco or two, rummaging among the red leaves and the withered cattails at the water's edge. On the bare gray branches overhead, bejeweled

---

The ideal accommodation is at the Airpark Inn:
Airpark Inn—Reelfoot Lake State Resort Park—Box 296, Route 1, Tiptonville, Tennessee 38079. (901) 253-7756. Open all year except Christmas season. Rooms: 20 units; 12 double, 8 accommodating up to 6 persons. Amenities: Dining room, lounge, exercise room, swimming pool, tennis, fishing. Terms: Single $34–38, double $34–49, suites $60.

The campgrounds at the Airpark are quite open and have no views of the lake. They are, however, secluded and birdy, and you can hear the owls at night. The south-end campground is right on the lakeshore with excellent birding, but is closed at the end of October:
Reelfoot Lake State Resort Park—address and phone as above. Campsites: 120 water and electricity. Amenities: Rest rooms with showers, dump station, swimming, fishing, boating, tennis, daily tours to see Bald Eagles December–March, special weekend and summer interpretive program, scenic boat tours. Restrictions: 14-day limit.
Airpark Campground—eight miles north of Tiptonville on Route 78, east 3 miles on Route 213. Open all year. Terms: $6.50/2 persons, primitive $3.25.
Southend Campground—4 miles east of Tiptonville on Route 21 & 22. Open April 1–October 31. Terms: $9/2 persons.

★

with droplets of water, a couple of titmice pause briefly before flying off calling wheezily. On the lake, black little squadrons of coot lend counterpoint to the silvery surface, and the stubby little cypresses rear delicate, insubstantial branches in the mist. Herons and cormorants come and go; finally a massive black bulk looms out of the mist as a young eagle flies past on ponderous wings, startling the waterfowl briefly before vanishing once more.

The Airpark Inn is one of the better places for seeing the eagles once they start to arrive in late November. By midwinter eagle numbers on the lake build up to as many as 200 birds. At that time the state park organizes eagle-spotting tours around the lake, and indeed the big birds are surprisingly accessible. The adults sit in the cypresses along

the shore, glaring around regally with their fierce yellow eyes and massive bills, while the young birds sit hunched like huge dark protuberances on the cypress boughs, ungainly adolescents that seem to have grown too quickly.

Bald Eagles are far from the only birds to be seen at Reelfoot in the wintertime. The shallow waters of the lake attract thousands of waterfowl, and flocks of wintering landbirds

are everywhere in the heavy woodlands. In summertime
this array is replaced by egrets feeding among the cypress
roots and Prothonotary and Yellow-throated warblers nesting in the woodlands. Swainson's Warblers can be found
here too in the cane thickets, and Least Terns hover over the
lake in search of small fish. Over the treetops Mississippi
Kites soar gracefully.

Our route takes us north toward the heavily forested areas
of the National Wildlife Refuge. On our way out to the highway huge flocks of blackbirds and little parties of meadowlarks fly up from the harvested fields. Earlier we might have
encountered shorebirds along here; for now we have to be
content with strings of Canada Geese heading over to the
lake, and a solitary Snow Goose tagging along at the end of
one of the lines.

Soon we're in Kentucky, and turning to cross the north
end of the refuge. A Loggerhead Shrike wire-hops ahead of
us, and in the nearby fields a group of diminutive crows
announce themselves as Fish Crows. They're regular, if
rather uncommon, here.

Walnut Log Road is one of the best birding spots on the
entire lake. The gravel road runs through rich swamp woodlands, surprising for their abundant birdlife even in winter.
We drive past dark pools where Wood Ducks jump up with
creaky cries of alarm, and still late in the season Carolina
Wrens seem to be practicing their rollicking songs from
every thicket. Constantly we encounter small foraging flocks
of Carolina Chickadees and titmice, together with Yellow-
rumped Warblers and kinglets, and the occasional creeper
or nuthatch. There's an amazing variety of woodpeckers.

Cross the north end of the lake via Road 1282, which
is on the right just north of the Kentucky line, to Route
311 south. There is a loop drive near the corner of
Routes 78 (Kentucky 94) and 1282, but it is usually
closed in winter. Route 311 becomes 157 when it enters Tennessee again, and eventually ends at Route 22.

★

Walnut Log Rd. is a small side road signposted to Walnut Log Baptist Church. It is the first surfaced road on the west south of the 1282 intersection, and is 1.25 miles north of the National Wildlife Refuge Headquarters, itself 1 mile north of the junction of Routes 22 and 157. Be sure to pick up a bird checklist at the National Wildlife Headquarters, and a copy of their folder which shows the route to Lake Isom N.W.R. as well. Walnut Log Rd. may also be closed at the end of the pavement in winter or in poor weather, but can always be walked.

Flickers, Downy and Hairy, Yellow-bellied Sapsuckers and Red-bellieds seem to be everywhere, and occasionally we glimpse the dark bulk of a Pileated Woodpecker working over one of the taller snags. Robin flocks fly out in shrill panic from thickets of holly, and here and there a towhee roots around among the dead leaves or a Winter Wren pokes in and out of a deadfall.

At the end of the road there is a short boardwalk to an observation tower looking out over the marshy areas in the northern part of the lake. There is a group of panhandling Mallards here, but the real waterfowl are farther out, and in no time at all we log fifteen species. There are Mallards, American Black Ducks and Gadwall, American Wigeon with their clear, piping whistles, busy little flocks of Green-winged Teal, and Redhead, Ring-necked Duck, and Canvas-

Access points on the east side of the lake are easily visible from Route 22: the first is the Kirby Pocket, a small section of the state park, and there are other spots where you can view the water from the side roads in the village of Samburg. Picnic areas and washrooms are at the state park locations. The state park offices have a useful auto tour map of Reelfoot which is excellent for bird-finding.

back diving out on the more open water areas. Somewhere from the cypresses on the other side we can hear the shouting of a Red-shouldered Hawk, and near at hand a Great Blue Heron rises from the shallows to flop away on heavy wings.

Walnut Log Road is a great place to bird at any time. In summer it is one of the best spots to find Swainson's Warblers, and a good array of other southern bottomland species—Acadian Flycatcher, Kentucky Warbler and Summer Tanager. It's one of the better places for Mississippi Kites as well.

The viewing areas at the south end of the lake are more open, and the marsh turns to wide stretches of open water. Diving duck are prominent here, with small groups of Bufflehead and goldeneye, and flotillas of coots. Most numerous of all, however, are Ruddy Ducks. They are everywhere, scattered all over the surface of the water, dumpy little birds with jauntily cocked tails, looking like a vast convention of well-used bathtub ducks.

An ideal way of seeing Reelfoot is to rent one of the flat-bottomed Reelfoot boats. These are equipped with small gasoline engines, but also have "Reelfoot oars," which are hinged so that they work backward, allowing the rower to see where he is going—an absolute necessity in this shallow wetland full of snags and cypress roots. The boats can be rented at the camps and parks all around Reelfoot, and are particularly useful in the upper part of the lake where road access is limited.

There are many access points to the south end of Reelfoot along Route 21. The Southend Campground is the easternmost of these, followed in sequence by the Spillway area, the Kiwanis Park, the Blue Bank picnic area, the C. Donaldson Hall and Museum with a short nature trail at the back, and finally, as the highway curves away from the shore, another picnic area. Along the west shoreline the best places are in the area of the Airpark itself off Route 78.

★

Five miles south of Reelfoot is Lake Isom National Wildlife Refuge, established as a reserve for migrant waterfowl and similar to Reelfoot but much smaller. Access here is quite limited but it is another good birding location that can readily be visited while in the vicinity.

For a taste of a totally different kind of wetland, as well as a wonderful array of the oak-hickory woodlands and other diverse habitats typical of Kentucky and Tennessee, a visit to the Land Between the Lakes is a must. This area is about a hundred miles east of Reelfoot and is as artificial as the latter is natural. The lakes are formed by two large dams erected on the Tennessee and Cumberland rivers by the Tennessee Valley Authority. Between them is a broad strip of land, some 170,000 acres in all, which is managed as "a national demonstration area in recreation, environmental education and resources management." What this means to a birder is that there are thousands of acres of upland hardwood forest, conifers, fields, and lakeshore, all available for exploration, all with their characteristic birds.

The lakes themselves—Lake Barkley to the east and Kentucky Lake to the west—have fluctuating water levels and are not as attractive to waterbirds as Reelfoot, but diving duck congregate, shorebirds and gulls loiter on any open bars, and there are eagles here too. The two dams, east and west of Lake City in Kentucky, can be very interesting as well with gulls milling around below the dam and diving ducks,

---

A useful reference to this area and elsewhere in Tennessee is Michael Lee Bierly's *Bird Finding in Tennessee* (1980, available from the author at 3825 Bedford Ave., Nashville, Tennessee 37215). The Tennessee hotline is (615) 356-7636.

There are 255 species on the Reelfoot checklist, and 248 listed for Land Between the Lakes. You could cover both Reelfoot and Land Between the Lakes in a couple of days each, but easily spend a week of leisurely birdwatching between the two.

★

Land Between the Lakes is east of the Purchase Parkway, with its bottom third in Tennessee and the rest in Kentucky. Take Route 80 east from the Purchase Parkway at Mayfield and continue east to Aurora, which is a small resort community serving Kentucky Lake. Accommodation is here if desired although there are TVA-operated campgrounds in the Land Between the Lakes itself. Reservations for the Energy Lake Campground are available at (502) 924-5602.

Continue east to the exit for the Golden Pond Visitor Center and the Trace, which is the road running north and south up the length of the area. Be sure to pick up a map and checklist (50¢) at the Visitor Center while you are there. From this point the Environmental Education Area is north on the Trace to the east of the road, and the dams themselves are immediately north of the Land Between the Lakes, where the Trace intersects with Route 62. There are several picnic areas.

The spillway of the Barkley Dam is east on Route 62, and accessible by a short side road just west of the bridge over the river. For the Kentucky Dam go west on Route 62 and then bear right on Route 282 west, to the point it jogs left at the entrance to the campground. Turn right here and drive down to the spillway.

cormorants, and gulls gathering in the waters above and visible from the viewpoints along the shoreline.

Our favorites are the woodlands in the Environmental Education Area, and particularly the trail around Hematite Lake. This runs through delightful oak-hickory woodlands, and there are Ring-necked Ducks and Hooded Mergansers on the lake itself. We chance on a small flock of Eastern Bluebirds bathing in a rain puddle with a group of goldfinches and other species, and spend an hour or so delighting in the constant movement at the tiny wetland. Yellow-rumped Warblers, cardinals, a towhee, and three species of sparrow all join the busy group from time to time. But it's the bluebirds that steal the scene, with that incredible blue

shimmering through the sparkling cascades of water droplets, or glowing intensely as the birds sit quietly in the
branches above.

OTHER THINGS TO DO AROUND REELFOOT

Reelfoot Lake is a noteworthy area for fishing, and scenic
boat cruises run daily from the state park during the summer (weather permitting: 9 A.M., 3½ hours. $4 plus $2 lake
preservation permit).

There is a wide range of recreational opportunities at
Land Between the Lakes with more than 200 miles of hiking
trails and boating and fishing here as well. The Golden Pond
Visitor Center has a multimedia presentation on the region,
hourly, 10 A.M.–4 P.M., $1. (502) 924-5602. The Environmen-
tal Education Area also has a center with a few exhibits and
a farm, and the Homeplace—south of Route 80; 9 A.M.–5
P.M. Mar.–Nov. $2.50. (502) 924-5602—is a living history
farm re-creating the lifestyle of the 1850s. There's also a
buffalo paddock nearby.

★   ★   ★   ★   ★

CHAPTER
12
ENGLAND AND WALES: WHERE IT ALL STARTED

NOWHERE IN THE WORLD DOES BIRDLIFE RE-ceive quite as much loving attention as in Britain. Birders abound, and their interest and energy are mirrored in a host of vigorous clubs and organizations catering to every facet of birding interest, and an incomparable network of reserves. In a very real way the British Isles were the birthplace of bird-watching—people were watching birds systematically there at least two centuries ago—although the competitive sport of birding, or "twitching" as the British call it, is probably a North American offshoot.

The British tend to be modest about their birds—one naturalist I met seemed astonished that a North American would visit England to bird—and it's true that some of the continental European species are missing, but that's more than balanced by the wonderful abundance of birdlife, including some of the finest and most accessible seabird colonies anywhere. Then there is the happy abundance of information to help you find your way around, helpful natives who speak approximately the same language, and a road network that seems to poke into every tiny corner of the British Isles. Anyone who imagines that you go to England just to visit cathedrals, castles, and fine old homes and to soak up the cultural life is making a serious mistake.

One of Britain's surprises is the enormous variety of landscapes tucked into a relatively small island. They range from desolate mountaintops and densely forested valleys to flat fertile farmland and huge industrial conurbations. Another surprise is the rich abundance of songbirds, especially in the parks and gardens. Most of these birds are exclusively residents of the Old World, and if you have never crossed the Atlantic before you can expect to add 90 to 100 birds to your life list, out of a total of maybe 120–130 species over the course of a couple of weeks.

Although lots are new to the visitor from North America, some birds are familiar and others are at least species that you will have heard of on the other side of the Atlantic, even though they may be rare there. So the first bird we see on arrival at Heathrow in London—as has been the case on all previous visits—is a Common Black-headed Gull flying overhead.

Welcome now to the Official Name Labyrinth, Transatlantic Edition. The Black-headed Gull of Europe is called the Common Black-headed Gull in North America, where it is rare. In the U.K. the European race of the Mew Gull is called the Common Gull, but—you guessed it—it's not the really common gull at all. The Black-headed (sorry, Common Black-headed in North America) Gull is the common gull in Britain. Got that? Now you're ready to cope with the differences between the official names, here and over there. Good luck!

Once away from the city, newcomers start to show up. Robinlike birds appear on the lawns, some jet-black and others dark brown; Blackbirds of both sexes, as familiar here as our robins are at home. More conventional-looking thrushes with speckled breasts turn out to be Song Thrushes, but the English Robin itself proves harder to spot. Finally, perched on the top of a wall is a bright-eyed little brown bird with a brick-red breast, much smaller and daintier than its American namesakes. The parks and gardens also yield Great and Blue tits, Chaffinches, and Greenfinches, and we spot the familiar form of a Wren—our Winter Wren—vanishing into some shrubbery.

The British skies tend to be rather empty of larger birds. Raptors are scarce here, but there is an abundance of crow species. In the evenings long lines of Rooks, ungainly creatures with heavy whitish bills, straggle back to their rookeries in the treetops of the country churchyards, where their contented cawing is one of the most familiar and best-loved sounds of the English countryside. Around the chimney tops Jackdaws squabble, small neat crows with gray pates and pale, knowing eyes. The Carrion Crow itself is common enough, and in the hill country and the North ravens are widespread.

The low country of East Anglia bordering the southeast coast must once have been covered in vast areas of forest, marsh, and swamp. Later it was to become the dynamic center of a rich woolen trade, and the rich merchants of the day erected monumental churches and fine mansions to the glory of God and their own prosperity. Today it is a quiet, gentle landscape, a patchwork of neat green fields and mossy woodlands, of small villages with the graceful towers and spires of the ancient churches rising above the clustered trees. It is the home of some of the country's finest bird reserves, and along this coastline the heaviest concentrations of migrants occur.

Our destination on this flat, featureless coast is the town of Aldeburgh, with its four-hundred-year-old Moot Hall and even more ancient church. At the south end of town, just where the brightly painted houses end and the high dikes hold the sea back from the low, fertile fields, is the Brudenell Hotel. Its windows overlook the seawall and the shingle beach beyond, and maybe a passing flock of Sandwich Terns, their yellow-tipped bills pointed purposefully at the water below. Swifts scream around the chimney tops and House Martins flash their white rumps under the eaves of the house next door. There's good birding right outside the main entrance here, but above all the Brundenell is a fine base for visiting the outstanding birding areas close by.

Our first destination is Havergate Island, an area of diked lowland accessible only by boat from the village of Orford. The narrow, winding road from Aldeburgh is bounded by tall hedgerows of hawthorn, and the lush countryside is interspersed with dark plantations of conifers. In places open, grassy areas—heaths—are covered with impenetrable spiny thickets of dark green gorse, in spring a riot of golden yellow blossoms. Our route is dotted with neat little hamlets with tidy brick houses and thatched cottages, and gardens ablaze with the red and orange of wallflowers.

Finally the road ends at the water's edge. To the east, a hazy gray line through the morning mist, lies the dike marking the coast. At our feet is the River Ore, here a channel of

---

To reach Aldeburgh take Route A12 from London northeast up the coast, following the bypasses around Colchester and Ipswich, to the A1094, which leads directly into town.

The Brudenell—Trusthouse Forte Hotel—The Parade, Aldeburgh, Suffolk, England IP 15 5BU. (0728) 452071, U.S.A. & Canada 1-800-225-5843. Open all year. Rooms: 47 units. Amenities: Dining room, lounge, elevator, beachfront, fishing and golfing nearby. Terms: Single from £49, double from £69. AMEX, CB, DINERS, MC, VISA.

★

Orford is south of Aldeburgh, on secondary roads. Take the A1094 west to the village of Snape, and then left on the B1069 as far as the hamlet of Tunstall, and then left again on the B1078. This runs generally eastward, later merging with the B1084, and dead-ending at the dock in Orford.

Minsmere lies off the B1122, which runs north from Aldeburgh through Leiston, then bears right to the village of Eastbridge and thence into the reserve, which is well marked. Wolves Wood is west of Ipswich to the south of Aldeburgh, on the north side of the A1071 about 3 miles east of the town of Hadleigh.

muddy water bordered by low, glistening banks of mud and backed by flat emerald expanses of salt marsh. Black-headed Gulls wander around listlessly and a scruffy young Herring Gull tugs at something revolting out over the flats. Behind us lies the village, and over the green water meadows on a rise to the west towers the bulk of the old castle, half hidden behind the trees.

We're waiting for Havergate's warden to pick us up, together with the others who have arranged to visit on this day. Then we set off down the river and shortly the tip of the island looms in sight, another line of low dikes in a place where dikes seem to terminate every vista. We are helped ashore along an impromptu boardwalk over the mud flats, and then cross the grassy dike to a reception area bounded, inevitably, by more dikes.

The history of Havergate Island is in part the history of the Royal Society for the Protection of Birds—the RSPB—itself. The English have been no kinder to their wetlands than their cousins over the Atlantic. And they have had more opportunity to destroy habitats: the cumulative impact of centuries of drainage resulted in the almost total elimination of all the larger marshes. The flat, marshy country of the southeast coast was made to order for such treatment, and so most of it was drained for agriculture. Birds such as the Bittern, Avocet, Marsh Harrier, and Ruff vanished—seemingly forever.

Then during World War II the dikes of one of the islands in the River Ore were damaged, and to everyone's surprise it was discovered that Avocets, long absent from Britain as breeding birds, had colonized the brackish flats that developed after the breach in the dike. To protect this fledging colony the island was purchased by the RSPB, and it set the Society on a successful course of reserve acquisition that continues to this day. At present they manage 114 reserves—there'll be even more by the time you read this—covering over 170,000 acres in the United Kingdom, ranging from remote seabird colonies, through reedbeds and marshes, to heath and woodland.

Management of these reserves is dynamic. Thorough inventories are taken of the animals and plants present, and careful plans made to maintain and increase the numbers of the rarer species, and generally to improve the diversity of habitat. At Havergate such management includes manipulation of the water levels in the various sections of the reserve, together with a program to actively discourage the colonies of Common Black-headed Gulls that would overwhelm the area if left undisturbed.

Because visiting arrangements at RSPB reserves vary from place to place I suggest writing to The Royal Society for the Protection of Birds, The Lodge, Sandy, Bedfordshire SG19 2DL for the current copy of their RSPB Reserves Visiting brochure, which lists fees (generally nominal), opening days, and the addresses of all the reserves. They also have for sale a book, *RSPB Reserves Visiting*, which gives summary details of each reserve, together with location maps. It is worthwhile if you plan to visit several reserves—some of the best birding sites in Britain—during your visit.

★

The birding here is from blinds. Our group of visitors is split into two and we are directed to the blinds at the south end; after lunch we will change places with the others and view the areas to the north. We head along a grassy path on a shoreline dotted with the tiny mauve flowers of sea spurrey; the banks of the dike, now rising enticingly on one side, sheltering unknown riches. Finally we arrive at the first blind. It's a large wooden structure, with its entrance along a boardwalk hidden from the areas beyond by a screen of dried rushes.

Inside we find ourselves looking out over an expanse of mud flats, crisscrossed by channels of shallow water and surrounded with more dikes. The whole area is covered in birds. Everywhere are Common Black-headed Gulls in various stages of nesting: some birds sitting quietly, others displaying, with much flying around and calling. Here and there are Avocets, some apparently on nests, and others moving daintily along the shallows, feeding with distinctive side-to-side sweeps of their bills. The European Avocet shares its smart black-and-white plumage and slender blue legs with the American species, but differs in its equally elegant black crown and hind neck.

The avocets and gulls are by no means the only birds present. Pairs of Eurasian Wigeon are scattered along the dikes and—familiar yet incongruous to North American eyes—a pair of Canada Geese stands alert. Common Ringed Plovers pick daintily on the drier parts of the flat, and a few Dunlin are probing vigorously, surprisingly small to someone accustomed to the larger North American race. A pair of Shelduck, striking large black-and-white birds with bold patches of chestnut, are wading in the shallows while a Eurasian Kestrel sits quietly on a post nearby.

Other blinds provide different views, both of this area and of other cells, each one varying in the amount of water present, the extent of vegetation on the flats, and the birds we can see. As we sit having our lunch outside the reception center, Curlews call, a wonderful liquid, bubbling note that somehow captures the quality of these lonely open places.

Common Terns hawk back and forth on the river, and among them is a Little Tern, once lumped with the North American Least, but now considered a separate species.

Possibly the most famous of the RSPB reserves is Minsmere. It lies a few miles north of Aldeburgh, separated from the ocean by a belt of sand dunes. It's the place for rare wanderers and for some of the nation's rarest breeding birds. In the more inaccessible parts of the reserve there are fields managed to provide habitat for the shy and declining Stone Curlew, and the reserve's coastal location, together with the great diversity of habitats, means that you never really quite know what may turn up. It is a very popular place; all England's birders seem to want to visit Minsmere!

Here again there are pools, the water level in each controlled to produce a variety of habitats. In one, the Scrape, there is much mud flat to attract shorebirds, and small islands have nesting gulls and Sandwich Terns. Other pools are deeper, and support extensive reed beds. These are the home of Bearded Reedlings and the increasingly rare European Bittern, as well as such commoner marsh birds as the showy Reed Bunting, as visible as the Bittern is retiring.

We straggle along the path, getting good looks at the ubiquitous Dunnocks and Linnets, while purposeful British birders stride past with no more than a passing glance, intent on finding the rarities that are doubtless visible from the blinds ahead. From one, a Temminck's Stint—looking to us like a muddy Least Sandpiper—is giving a procession of watchers some satisfaction as at least a minor notable.

For us the best bird of the day comes much later. We're in a blind overlooking a broad reedbed. Only a few shoveler

---

Britain is agreeably free of hazards, but there is one mildly venomous snake—the adder—and chiggers are present in the South. Paths can be extremely muddy; bring rubber boots or the equivalent and—of course—rain gear!

and teal are visible when a large hawk flies across in front of us. It has rich brown underparts and a buffy head, shading to the palest of gray tail and flight feathers, these in turn contrasting with black-tipped primaries. This graceful and attractive bird is a male Marsh Harrier, both bigger and heavier than the other harriers and more beautiful than any of them. Minsmere is the main home of Britain's very few breeding pairs, and an eye-level flypast is an experience to be savored and remembered.

One of the trails winds through an open oak woodland, decked in the fresh yellow-green of spring. The oaks are gnarled old trees, evenly spaced with broadly spreading crowns, and below them the clustered stems of hazels form an open shrub layer. The ground beneath is a haze of bluebells, a rich carpet of deep blue, shimmering silver in the patches of sunlight and darkening almost to purple in the heavier shade. The woods have their complement of landbirds too, and ring with the melancholy songs of Robins and the rich warbling of Blackcaps. Little groups of tits—six species are possible—and a Treecreeper forage among the trees, and we hear the wheezy calls of Greenfinches overhead.

The British landscape is almost wholly man-made. Maybe there are a few places that are still pristine, but they're limited to coastal cliffs and mountaintops. There's no such thing as virgin wilderness here; the plant and animal communities have evolved with man over centuries. But man-made does not mean tame. The austere hill country and the open sweeps of moorland are wild and uncompromising. That they were once forested does not make them less remote; that sheep may be a vital element in their natural communities does little to alter their wild character.

The oak woodlands are extraordinarily attractive—nature at its most delightful. Yet these wonderful areas are the direct product of management. For generations such woods have been used to produce not only oak timber (which matures very slowly), but poles that were used for a wide variety of purposes. The technique is called coppicing, and consists of cutting the shrub understory back to its roots at periodic intervals, stimulating the growth of the slender, straight poles. An open canopy is achieved by spacing the oaks evenly and quite widely.

Highly manipulated or not, these woodlands are rich in both birds and wildflowers. Indeed, some plants such as the yellow archangel—a showy member of the mint family— and the early purple orchis are intimately associated with this kind of forest. At one stage in the succession the shrubby cover becomes very dense and provides habitat for such birds as the Nightingale, while at another the woods are very open, encouraging the rich abundance of woodland wildflowers.

Today these communities are endangered, as there is no longer much demand for hazel poles. It is more economical to clear them completely or replant with introduced conifers. The RSPB is making an effort to protect and preserve some of them, and we have the opportunity to visit one nearby the next day.

In Wolves Wood our trail winds through a wonderful broad-leaved woodland of oak, ash, birch, and hornbeam. One of our first impressions is of the sheer volume of birdsong. Some of Britain's commonest birds, the Blackbird, Song Thrush and Robin, are all exceptional songsters, and here their chorus is joined by the rich songs of Blackcap and Garden Warbler. There are less ambitious efforts as well: the rhythmic calls of Great Tits, the limpid cascades of Willow Warblers and monotonous chanting of Chiffchaffs. But the thickets ring with the song of that virtuoso of the bird world, the Nightingale, and we manage to glimpse a couple of the birds, looking like small Hermit Thrushes as they vanish into the thicket.

Do Nightingales really justify all the poetical eulogies as the world's finest songster? They're certainly one of the most famous, and their efforts are impressive even in the middle of the day, when they do not have the entire stage to themselves. Like Northern Mockingbird songs, there's much individual variation, but a slow rising crescendo sequence is, at its best, one of the most remarkable bird utterances anywhere.

Nightingales are among a group of species that nest only in the South. As we head north we leave them behind, and the character of the countryside itself changes gradually. Hedgerows are replaced by dry stone walls, brick and thatch by gray limestone and slate. The villages now have an austere quality, and rocky pastures with sheep become more common as we approach the Scottish border. Overhead Skylarks sing incessantly, a silvery torrent of ecstatic notes that

The fastest routes around Britain are the M-class motorways, which are controlled-access highways. Unfortunately these provide links between the main urban centers, and are not always conveniently accessible. The A-class highways are generally wider than B-class, and the designation T, as in A1(T), denotes a trunk route designed for heavier traffic. Many good highways head north, but off the motorways travel in Britain is slow and two days would probably be required to reach Northumberland. The beautiful city of York offers an attractive midpoint.

From Aldeburgh the best route would probably be west off the A12 onto the A1120 to Stowmarket, and then continue west on the A45 past Cambridge, and then on the A604 to connect with the A1, which runs north, bypassing York to the west. The A64 and A1036 then lead directly into York itself.

The following is one of the most pleasantly situated hotels, within the old walled town and overlooking the Minster, York's famed cathedral:

Dean Court Hotel—Best Western—Duncombe Place, York (10 miles from A1 along A64), North Yorkshire YO1 2EF. (0904) 625082; U.S.A. 1-800-528-1234; Can. (416) 674-0555. Open all year. Rooms: 41 units, double and twin. Amenities: Dining room, lounge, elevator. Restrictions: No pets. Terms: Single from £50, double from £85, full breakfast included. AMEX, DINERS, MC, VISA.

★

are the constant accompaniment to all other sounds in the spring fields.

Just south of the Scottish border on the North Sea lies the county of Northumberland, where the ruins of ancient fortifications punctuate the coast, mute testimony to more turbulent times. Our destination is Berwick-upon-Tweed, perched on the border itself, a pleasant town with its small estuary—and birds—an easy walk from our hotel.

This is one of England's most beautiful coastlines, a place where rugged cliffs alternate with high, rolling dunes and vast tidal flats. Offshore lies a group of rocky islands, the Farnes, which are home to huge numbers of seabirds. The Farnes are owned by the National Trust, a body that also maintains many of the fine old buildings in the United Kingdom. Like Havergate, the islands can be reached only by boat; unlike Havergate, the boat must cross two miles of often stormy ocean. You may arrange to visit the Farnes, but the weather will decide if your arrangements are to bear fruit.

We are lucky. On the day of our visit it is foggy and the ocean choppy but the passage possible. There are really two groups of islands, the Inner and Outer Farnes, located about a mile apart, and our first destination is Staple Island in the Outer group. As we approach the rocky shoreline the fog gradually lifts, and in a moment of wonderful luminescence

The fastest route north from York is A19, which merges with the A1 in the conurbation of Newcastle upon Tyne and then continues north from there. For a much more attractive route for the first section of this drive, return to the A64 heading northeast to the town of Malton and then take the A169 over the north Yorkshire moors to connect with the A171 outside the seaside village of Whitby, and then head west again to join the A19 outside Middlesbrough. The area between Middlesbrough and Newcastle is heavily industrialized and you should allow ample time for delays here.

★

the rugged cliffs emerge, ethereal in the shimmering haze. Around us the skies are filled with a screaming tumult of Black-legged Kittiwakes and terns, and ahead every ledge, every cranny is filled with birds. Suddenly we are aware that there are landbirds here as well: incredibly, on the wave-washed seaweed of the dark rocks around us are small passerines, migrating warblers disoriented by the mist.

Anyone who thinks that the North American fall warblers are confusing should leave the Old World warblers to another day. We are faced with an array of little brownish and greenish jobs all looking more or less alike, but at the same time differing enough in minutiae that they just could be something different. Often voice and habitat can help, but in this improbable environment, viewed while bobbing about in a boat, we have only the look of the birds themselves to go by.

We have more or less concluded that they are all either Willow Warblers or Chiffchaffs and are about to get on with more interesting things when we spot a perky brown bird with a bright blue throat patch and orange in its tail. Bluethroats do not nest in England, but they do occur in migration—occasionally—and to our delight we're now looking at one.

By now the boat is moving into shore, if that's an appropriate name for the rocky shelf upon which we are to land.

Berwick-upon-Tweed is on the A1 itself, although the main highway now loops around it. The following is pleasantly situated:

King's Arms Hotel—Hide Hill (Take A1167 for Berwick town center), Berwick-upon-Tweed, Northumberland, England TD15 1EJ. (0289) 307454. Open all year. Rooms: 36 units (double, twin, single, suite, eleven with four-poster beds). Amenities: Dining room, lounge, snooker club, golf. Restrictions: No pets. Terms: Single £39.50—44.50, double £59—69, full breakfast included. AMEX, DINERS, MC, VISA.

★

Finally everyone is safely disembarked and given strict instructions to be back at the "dock" at an appointed time, and we are free to disperse over the rocks as we choose.

This is birding the way it always ought to be. Within a few feet of the path dark, glossy greenish Shags sit on their nests and display to one another, their snakelike necks swaying in unison. The rocks below are lined with immaculate kittiwakes and Common Murres—here called guillemots—and Razorbills are massed on rocky pinnacles. On one of the grassy sections toward the higher part of the island puffins stand around with an air of faint bewilderment, as though they had forgotten something. Close by, a pair of Northern Fulmars sit placidly in the lee of an old building, one of the birds incubating.

On the boat's return we head out around some of the smaller islands to view other bird colonies from the sea, while the long, sloping heads of gray seals bob around us in the surf. Then, under sunny skies and across a sea flecked with whitecaps, we turn back toward the inner group of islands to land on the largest, called Inner Farne. It is a flat, grassy island with a lighthouse and an ancient tower and

The locations mentioned are all south of Berwick-upon-Tweed and east off the A1. The Farne Islands are reached from the harbor at Seahouses on the B1340. Take the B1342 east from the A1 about 15 miles south of Berwick-upon-Tweed and continue to the village of Bamburgh. The road then joins the B1340 to continue south along the coast. The side road to Lindisfarne is an unnumbered road signposted to the village of Beal, about halfway between the B1342 intersection and Berwick-upon-Tweed itself.

For reservations to visit the Farne Islands write the boatman at Seahouses: Mr. Billy Shiel, 4 Southfield Ave., Seahouses, Northumberland NE 68 7YT. Boat fees for an all-day trip leaving at 10 A.M. (weather permitting) are currently £7 plus £2.40 admission to land on the Islands.

★

chapel, the remains of a small monastery built here in the thirteenth century and occupied for three hundred years.

Today most people come to see the birds, and a popular destination it is. The grassy sward is covered with Arctic Tern nests, together with some Common, a few Sandwich and—if you can find it—the odd Roseate. Interspersed among them are Common Eiders, the showy males often snuggled up to their mates, wholly ruining any concealment the females might achieve. But it's a lost cause here anyway: greensward is a poor choice for a bird all decked out in intricately scalloped browns. Eiders are notoriously tame birds and these are no exception. There are nests beside the footpaths, nests outside the door to the chapel, nests alongside the rocky wall where we sit to have lunch, nests everywhere. The terns are less confiding, but they too sit just a short telephoto focus off the paths.

On the cliffs at the far end are more of the species we encountered on Staple Island—all almost old hat by now—together with Herring and Lesser Black-backed gulls and some Great Cormorants. Jaunty black-and-white European Oystercatchers are foraging over the wave-swept rocks below, and a careful search reveals a group of Purple Sandpipers, dark shorebirds against a mass of darker kelp.

While a boat trip is necessary to see these seabird colonies, there is superb birding along the coast as well. Fulmars nest below the walls of the castle at Bamburgh, and farther north the island of Lindisfarne—also known as Holy Isle, and a location of great historical significance as the birthplace of Christianity in Britain—is an island only at high tide. At other times it sits amid huge expanses of tidal flats, connected to the mainland by a road with tide tables posted at both ends. If your watch is wrong you may be marooned for six hours! The flats themselves are covered during migration and in winter with masses of shorebirds. Thousands of Bar-tailed Godwits, Red Knots, and Dunlin winter here, together with vast flocks of waterfowl; mostly Eurasian Wigeon but the area also has large flocks of Whooper Swans, Brant, and Greylag Geese. A few of the shorebirds linger well into May.

Some of Britain's most enchanting scenery is in Wales. We're headed for Snowdonia, a mountainous region of deep wooded valleys, of clear hill streams and narrow winding roads. Our route south bypasses the Lake District, itself an area of outstanding beauty, and the wide tidal flats of Morecambe Bay, one of Britain's premier shorebird wintering grounds.

These are low mountains by North American standards— Snowdon itself, the highest, is a little over 3,500 feet—but they have their own drama and austere beauty. Their forbidding heights are covered with heather and tight sheep-cropped turf, interspersed with a multitude of rocks and boulders. They're crisscrossed with trails and produce challenging hill walking, with uncertain weather, dense fogs, and dangerous terrain. Meadow Pipits make little song flights over these slopes and Wheatears flash their white rumps, but birds are scarce here—often only the occasional raven over the higher tops.

The valleys are delightful. We stop to watch Buzzards soaring over the tiny, stone-walled fields, and drive through forests of oaks still glowing with the delicate soft greens of spring. In one pasture an attractive little black-and-white bird flits around in one of the trees—a Pied Flycatcher, characteristic of this hill country. Later we find one of the small gems of British birdlife, a Redstart, sitting on a post. Vivid

Heading west from Berwick-upon-Tweed, take the A698 to Hawick to join the A7, which continues southwest to Carlisle. Here it is possible to take the M6 south through the industrial western part of northern England to the M56 southwest of Manchester. Then continue westward on the A550, which connects with the A55 running westward paralleling the north coast of Wales. From here there are a variety of roads south, although perhaps the most direct is to continue past Colwyn Bay to the A470, which follows the Vale of Conwy south to Betws-y-Coed.

★

orange underparts contrast with black bib and dark gray back, and a white forehead provides accent. Then it flicks its tail and wings nervously, to reveal a rusty rump and tail. It all sounds gaudy, but the bird itself seems to epitomize refined elegance.

We're staying at Betws-y-Coed. To my ear, it's pronounced "Bet us ay coyd," with a lilting upward inflection at the end, but we find it difficult to handle the Welsh pronunciations. Fortunately the hospitable Welsh don't seem to mind, and their musical lilt is carried over into their English words as well. The village has an idyllic setting along a gentle stream called the Afon Llugwy; the Royal Oak overlooks one of its more open stretches. Later in the day the place teems with tourists, but it's easy to get away from the throngs into the quiet countryside.

Just up the road from the hotel, a public footpath follows the stream. The trail meanders through green pastures dotted with sheep, and the woodlands ring with the calls of titmice. On the boulders in the stream Gray Wagtails bob, long-tailed and elegant, flirting their yellow breasts in the water. At one point a Dipper whizzes past, dark chocolate-brown and white, to vanish under an overhang along the bank.

At first light a walk here reveals a Tawny Owl sitting sleepily in its hole, its soft dark eyes gazing at an excited flock of titmice. Nearby we hear the clear piping of a Nuthatch, while overhead there is the distinctive two-part song of a Wood Warbler, sounding as though it originates from two quite separate birds. A pink-and-blue Jay glides by silently, only to scream a few times when safely out of sight.

The Royal Oak Hotel—Holyhead Road, Betws-y-Coed, Gwynedd, North Wales LL24 0AY. (06902) 219. Open all year except December 25 and 26. Rooms: 27 units (9 double, 13 twin). Amenities: Dining room, lounge; fishing and golfing nearby. Restrictions: No dogs. Terms: £30–60, breakfast included. AMEX, DINERS, MC, VISA.

★

There are many places to walk in Snowdonia, and much excellent birding both here and elsewhere in Wales. It's also home to one of Britain's rarest birds, the Red Kite, and with luck you may encounter one. The center of their range is south of Snowdonia, and in fact we have found them at the dump at Tywyn, not exactly a glamour spot, but the town also is an excellent base to explore the attractive Dysynni Valley.

The British Isles as a whole are, in fact, exceptionally easy for the visiting birder to cover alone. Even if you confined yourself to RSPB reserves you could have an exceptionally fine vacation, with far more material than you would ever have time to cover. In this sense the areas we have visited here, although some of the very best, are no more than a sampling of the rich array of destinations available.

Even the vast city of London can yield excellent birding. As in all big cities, islands of greenery and patches of open water attract birds. Once I even saw a Razorbill sitting among the model yachts and paddling children on the Round Pond in Kensington Gardens! But the large reservoirs around the city are particularly outstanding sites (Staines and King George VI are adjacent to Heathrow Airport). They have large wintering waterfowl populations, and can be good in migration times. Hampstead Heath in the north and Wimbledon Common to the southwest both have good populations of breeding birds, while farther out of town Epping

The most direct return to London is via the A5 to Shrewsbury and thence to the M54 and M6 to the M1. A much pleasanter route is south on the A470 to Llandrindod Wells and then southeast through Hereford, Gloucester, and Swindon (using the A438, 417, and 419) to connect with the M4. To visit Tywyn, detour west from the A470 at Dolgellau on the A493, returning via the A489 from Machynlleth.

Forest to the northeast and Windsor Great Park (southwest of Heathrow) are fine birding spots, with Virginia Water in the latter the stronghold for the showy, introduced Mandarin duck.

There are bird-finding guides for almost every county—in fact the problem is more one of making a selection from the abundance available. We have found *The New Where to Watch Birds* by John Gooders (1986 André Deutsch) and *Birdwatching in Britain: A Site by Site Guide* by Nigel Redman and Simon Harrap (1987 Christopher Helm) both to be very good, with the latter having much more detail but lacking some of the sites mentioned in Gooders. If you like walking, *Birdwatcher's Britain* (John Parslow, ed.; 1983 Pan Books) is keyed to the excellent series of 1:25,000 and 1:50,000 Ordnance Survey Landranger Maps and is very detailed for the sites it does cover.

Britain is equally blessed with excellent bird field guides. I prefer *A Field Guide to the Birds of Britain and Europe* by Peterson, Mountfort, and Hollom (1984 Collins), but the *Hamlyn Guide to Birds of Britain and Europe* by Bruun, Delin, and Svensson (1989 Hamlyn) is also excellent, and *The Shell Guide to the Birds of Britain and Ireland* by Ferguson-Lees, Willis, and Sharrock (1983 Michael Joseph) has also received enthusiastic reviews.

Britain caters exceptionally well not only to birders, but to naturalists generally. Almost every branch of natural science has good illustrated field guides available; and the RSPB re-

---

The majority of transatlantic flights land at Heathrow Airport just west of London, and this is probably the most satisfactory jumping-off point for any tour of Britain, although it is possible to incorporate a flight back via Glasgow Airport as well. London's excellent subway network (the "tube") has a link to Heathrow, and is a better way of getting around the city than trying to drive by car.

For travel alone, a rental car is probably the best way to go. There is an abundance of good roads in Britain and a wide range of car rental agencies are available at Heathrow. If you do propose to rent a car it may be less expensive to arrange the rental through the travel agent with whom you are booking your flight rather than to wait until you arrive. Note that the British drive on the left-hand side of the road, that English traffic can be very heavy, and the roads, frequently with no shoulders, are extremely narrow by North American standards. A copy of the latest *Ordnance Survey Motoring Atlas of Great Britain* is invaluable for finding your way around.

There is an equal abundance of accommodation of all kinds, ranging from modest farmhouses and other bed-and-breakfast establishments (some are excellent) to first-class hotels. The more independent traveler should obtain copies of the current AA listings of *Hotels and Restaurants in Britain* and *Guesthouses, Farmhouses and Inns in Britain* (the Automobile Association, Fanum House, Basingstoke, Hampshire RG 21 2EA). Remember that for many smaller places, shared or central washrooms are usual (but not in the case of the hotels mentioned below), and elevators (''lifts'') are exceptional. Dress in the hotels is a little more formal than in North America, but generally neat and tidy attire is acceptable, although some hotels may require jacket and tie. Camping is possible, and would-be campers should obtain the AA *Camping and Caravanning in Britain*.

serves, while acquired with birds in mind, also protect the other flora and fauna, and embrace some of the finest natural habitats in the country.

AND IF YOU WISH TO BEHAVE LIKE A CONVENTIONAL TOURIST . . .

Most tourists, of course, do visit England for its cultural and historical interest, and unless you are very single-minded or

have been there before to do your sightseeing, you'll likely want to visit some of these places yourself. The major routes connecting the locations we have visited pass close to several noteworthy cities: apart from London itself, the East Anglia leg is close to Cambridge, with the magnificent old buildings associated with the university, notably King's College Chapel; and the trip north passes sufficiently close to the fine old cathedral cities of York and Durham, where it is possible to visit or indeed to stay as part of the trip. Elegant old mansions, Gothic churches, and ancient castles abound, with exceptionally fine old churches in East Anglia, and castles in the north and east. Any attempt to cover these places thoroughly would demand several holidays doing little else.

For those whose interests are more archaeological, there are many Roman remains in Britain. Hadrian's Wall runs west of Newcastle on the route north to Northumberland, with the town of Greenhead being close to one of the best-preserved sections. Persons wishing to visit the Stone Age monuments at Avebury can do so with only a relatively small detour south from the M4 south of Swindon, on the way back to London from Wales; and Stonehenge is a little farther south, west of Andover.

Among the many fine buildings in London, we are particularly fond of the beautiful Henry VII Chapel in Westminster Abbey (not Westminster Cathedral, which is quite different) opposite the Houses of Parliament. Saint Paul's Cathedral and the numerous fine Christopher Wren churches are outstanding. For those interested in art, the National Gallery and the Tate Gallery are a must.

The museum of most interest to a naturalist is, naturally enough, the Natural History Museum, and the adjacent Victoria and Albert and Science museums have their fascinations as well. The most outstanding public gardens are the Royal Botanical Gardens at Kew, on the outskirts of London (there are good birds there as well), and the keen botanist might also wish to arrange a visit to the Chelsea Physic Gardens.

A general caveat about visiting any of the public places in the U.K. is that they usually have opening hours that are rather limited in North American terms. Check locally before you visit.

★   ★   ★   ★   ★

CHAPTER 13

STILLWATER, NEVADA: SALTY OASIS IN THE HIGH DESERTS

MUCH OF THE WEST IS ARID. BEYOND THE towering ranges of the Cascades and the Sierra Nevadas lie the dry grasslands and deserts of the continent, lands where towns are few and rock and sagebrush dominate the landscape, where water is a vital commodity to man and bird alike. Desert animals and plants have made their adaptations to this challenging country. They are at home here. Not so the migrants that pass this way, and so the few wetlands that dot this region are meccas for both land and water birds.

Nevada's Lahontan Valley is one such place. Threatened by drought and development, it's still a major destination for waterbirds on their fall migration, while nearby Pyramid

Lake is home to thousands of nesting pelicans, cormorants, and gulls. If you tire of this array, you can look for Sage Sparrows and Sage Thrashers among the sagebrush, or drive west up into the conifers of the front ranges near Reno for woodland and mountain species. And if you want a change from birding altogether, you can even head into Reno and try your luck in one of the casinos or at the ubiquitous slot machines. In fact, there's even a casino in the Best Western at Fallon, where we stay!

From Reno head east on Interstate 80 to Fernley, and continue east on Route 50 to Fallon. From here the management area is northeast of town via Stillwater Road (Route 116), which continues east when Route 50 curves south just outside town.

Be sure to check in at headquarters before leaving town for a map, checklist, and information on conditions in the area and on the roads that are open. Headquarters is in the small plaza on Auction Road just west of its intersection with Route 50—Stillwater Wildlife Management Area, U.S. Fish and Wildlife Service, P.O. Box 1236, Fallon, Nevada 89406. (702) 423-5128. There are no facilities in the area itself. Also be sure to obtain a copy of the tourist map of Fallon and Churchill County, which is invaluable for finding your way around.

The bottom lands of the Lahontan Valley were once the site of some of the richest wetlands in North America, places teeming with birds, sought by generations of Indians for the abundant life and the richness of the hunting. Sitting in the middle of this now vanishing abundance is the town of Fallon, the self-styled "oasis" of Nevada.

In the desert everything depends on water. The water in the Lahontan Valley is being channeled to a multitude of uses: the agricultural needs of the farms around Fallon, the water supplies for Reno and Carson City, needs for power; even an endangered fish species enters the equation, as Pyramid Lake is the only home of the cui-ui. These are threatened wetlands. Stillwater Wildlife Management Area,

There is a variety of accommodation in Fallon. The following is one of the better places:

Best Western Bonanza Inn and Casino—855 West Williams Ave. (3 blocks west on Route 50 from the junction of Route 95), Fallon, Nevada 89406. (702) 423-6031. Open all year. Rooms: 76 units. Amenities: Dining room, cocktail lounge, outdoor pool. Terms: Single $33–43, double $38–48. AMEX, CB, DINERS, MC, VISA.

There are a couple of campgrounds west of town, with the following well placed:

Fallon R. V. Park—5787 Reno Highway (Route 50) between Lucas Rd. and McLean west of downtown Fallon, Nevada 89406. (702) 867-2332. Campsites: 45 sites, full hookups. Some shaded sites. Amenities: Recreation room, rest rooms and showers, putting green, horseshoe pits, playground, laundry room, store, propane and dump station. Terms: Full hookup $14.

lying in the Carson Sink northeast of town, seeks to preserve some of them.

We leave Reno heading for U.S. Route 50, billed as the loneliest highway in America. It's lonely because it is a desert road, crossing desert mountains and vast expanses of desert flats, lying still and lifeless in the noonday heat. It's an improbable place to look for a wetland. Then comes the valley. Quite unexpectedly we begin to pass through tree-lined fields with cattle grazing and water standing in the open furrows.

We head out the next morning to visit Stillwater itself. At first our route runs through the lush green fields bordered by Fremont cottonwoods showing their first vivid golds of fall, and more cottonwoods marking the course of the Carson River to the north. Vast flocks of blackbirds carpet the ground around the cattle and fly up into the trees with noisy clamor. Here and there Loggerhead Shrikes wire-hop on the telephone lines ahead of us.

Then all at once we are on the refuge, most of the fields behind us. Now the landscape is one of grays, whites, and soft reds, a landscape where salt coats the ground like hoar frost and the plants stand gray and seemingly lifeless, their colors muted as though freeze-dried. In the background the mountains loom with stark red slopes and jumbles of boulders and scattered low gray shrubs.

The only water in this dry country is in the irrigation canal beside us, and landbird migrants flit ahead through the salt cedars, vanishing into feathery foliage tipped here and there with little spikes of powdery pink blossom. Out on the salt flats a bird dives abruptly into a shrub and then runs out tail cocked—a Sage Sparrow, one of the few species at home in this desert.

We need water to find more birds, and soon we spot a couple of flooded fields off to one side of the road. A Golden Eagle is sitting on one of the fence posts, looking enormous at this close range, and seeming completely disinterested in the life around it. A multitude of birds is feeding in the wet grassy areas below; a flock of ubiquitous Ring-billed Gulls, more blackbirds, and an assortment of shorebirds playing hide-and-seek in the grass. It's a foretaste of the riches to come.

Soon water begins to appear on both sides. Some of it is shallow, merging imperceptibly with the pale gray mud of the salt flats themselves; but farther on the road passes deeper pools, surrounded by dense reed beds. Western Grebes and Ruddy Ducks occupy the open water here and Song Sparrows and Marsh Wrens dive unexpectedly in and out of the cover.

Harmon Reservoir is east on Stuart Road as Stillwater Road turns north, and the S Line Reservoir is along Reservoir Road, the first north of Route 50 east of Cemetery Road. The Greenhead Club is southeast of town on Pasture Road just after this turns west south of the military base. Ask permission from the caretaker to drive the dikes.

★

One pool in particular is memorable. Out beyond the thin screen of vegetation along the edge of the road; out beyond the silver water itself on a mud flat encrusted with salt is a huge flock of avocets. Heads tucked over their backs, as pale as the salt around them, they stand motionless on slender blue legs. So still are they and so well do they harmonize with their surroundings that they seem almost negligible, like an extra-knobby patch of mud.

Then a harrier makes one of its passes too close for comfort, and the entire mass swirls up, a startling burst of black and white, and the birds circle once or twice before returning to the flat. Now, disturbed, some of them move out into the water to feed, with graceful, side-to-side sweeps of their slender upturned bills. Others move out even farther until it's hard to be sure whether they're walking or swimming, occasionally taking splashy headers under the water, like particularly inept diving ducks.

Every pool has its complement of birds, and each differs from the last. Every mud flat has its own assortment of shorebirds; phalanxes of dowitchers probing vigorously, and delicate Wilson's Phalaropes skittering about, perpetually on the brink of nervous breakdowns.

As the road curves back there are two large, dark birds on the road ahead, being dive-bombed by something smaller. This is a land where distances and sizes are deceptive, and heat haze plays tricks with shapes and colors. The threesome remain an enigma when the flying bird abruptly veers toward us, a streamlined tan shape. Suddenly we're watching a Prairie Falcon rocketing low over the flats until it finally merges into the beige background. The others? They too fly off, a pair of magnificent Golden Eagles soaring steadily upward, at first low over our heads, finally high above, then gliding away toward the distant mountains.

Stillwater has a quality all its own, but it's not the only place around Fallon where there is good birding. The backroads southwest of the refuge are worth looking at, and we drive along watching for wet fields, likely patches of scrub, and birds along the roadsides. In one place there is a small group of shorebirds and a few ducks busy feeding among

the short grasses, and in another White-faced Ibis are probing vigorously. These birds nest on the marshes of the
Greenhead Club, which itself can be full of birds. In the
brush along the field edges we catch glimpses of California
Quail and Ring-necked Pheasants skulking along, and a
Bewick's Wren bobs up briefly, its long tail wobbling around
up in the air as though trying to disassociate itself from its
owner.

Some of the small reservoirs around town are unexpectedly productive. There's particularly easy viewing at the
S-line Reservoir, where the road runs alongside the water.
Here Double-crested Cormorants sit among the dead trees,
black necks upstretched, black wings outspread like a
coven of witches celebrating some black rite. Ruddy Ducks
and coots dot the surface of the water and Great and Snowy
egrets stalk around the edges of the little islands.

Fall is probably the best time to visit Stillwater, although
there's good birding here year-round. Early spring brings
thousands of ducks to the marshes. Redheads are the commonest species present, but Mallards, pintail, Green-winged
Teal, and Northern Shoveler are abundant as well. Many of

the Gadwall, Cinnamon Teal, pintail, and Redheads that arrive remain through summer, and over 70,000 ducks have nested here.

The common breeding birds on the refuge include not only the ducks, but Eared Grebes, Snowy Egrets, and Black-crowned Night-Herons, as well as such shorebirds as Black-necked Stilt, American Avocet, and Wilson's Phalarope. American White Pelicans and Double-crested Cormorants visit from their colonies on Anaho Island to the northwest.

The largest concentrations occur in fall. In August and September huge numbers of shorebirds appear. Long-billed Dowitchers, Western and Least sandpipers—together with the avocets and Wilson's Phalaropes—are the most abundant, but some twenty species occur regularly. Up to half a million shorebirds stage in the Lahontan Valley on migration. Peak species counts of 150,000 dowitchers, 25,000 avocets, and 60,000 Wilson's Phalaropes have occurred.

Later fall brings the geese and ducks. All the spring migrant species appear again, and American Wigeon and Canvasback are also abundant. While waterfowl just do not have the rarity appeal of the shorebirds, their flights can be even more spectacular. Winter has its attractions too. Some waterfowl stay on, including large numbers of Tundra Swans joined by such diving duck as Bufflehead and Common Merganser. Flocks of White-crowned Sparrows forage along the fencerows and dikes, and blackbirds feed on the open

Lahontan Reservoir State Park is on Route 50 (not Alternate 50) some 15 miles west of Fallon. Pyramid Lake is to the northwest, via Routes 447 and 446. There are picnic areas at Lahontan Reservoir, some of the few in this area.

Because water levels in the Lahontan Valley are so critical, it might be worthwhile checking on current conditions prior to departing on your trip to avoid disappointment. The Wildlife Management Area is probably the best source of information.

★

fields. Raptors are attracted to the abundance, and Rough-legged Hawks can be common at this time, while Northern Harriers are even more common than they are during most of the year.

Pyramid Lake is noteworthy principally in the breeding season, when Anaho Island National Wildlife Refuge has huge colonies of colonial species. As many as 18,000 American White Pelicans have nested here, although in 1988 and 1989 nestings of this species here failed, apparently due to lack of food. There are up to 500 pairs of Double-crested Cormorants and 1,400 pairs of California Gulls nesting. It is not possible to land on the island, but it can be approached by boat. This is a good area for the desert landbirds as well. Black-throated and Lark sparrows can be found, as well as Sage Sparrows and Sage Thrashers. Come early and you may see a Burrowing Owl or two perched on a fence post.

Pyramid Lake and the Lahontan Reservoir can yield waterbirds in migration and winter, and Washoe and Little Washoe lakes, both south of Reno, are also noteworthy for both nesting and migratory species when water levels are suitable. Another even more productive location is Walker Lake, 40 miles to the south of Fallon on Route 95, which can have outstanding bird concentrations. This is a neglected area, as indeed are all the Nevada sites; a more lively appreciation of their value among birders could well go some way to arresting their decline. The highway runs along the west shoreline of Walker Lake, at some 30 miles in length rivaling Salton Sea in scale.

The road to Lake Tahoe is Route 431, which heads west from Route 395 some 10 miles south of Reno. Galena Creek Park is on the right just as the road starts the long grade up to Mount Rose summit.

Washoe and Little Washoe lakes are also reached via Route 395, by continuing some 8 miles past the 431 intersection, and then turning east on the road that follows the eastern shoreline of the lakes.

★

Stillwater's birdlist includes 185 species, and a visit
to the mountains adds a potential 30 or 40 more species that do not occur farther east. You can cover the
areas around Fallon in a couple of days, with perhaps
an additional day for each of Walker and Pyramid Lakes
and the Lake Tahoe area, but Stillwater and the mountains could each easily occupy another day.

Dominating Reno's southern skyline is Mount Rose, over
10,000 feet and the highest peak in the Carson Range. Its
forested slopes, and the basin of Lake Tahoe beyond, offer
a beguiling contrast to the birding in the desert wetlands.
They're a chance to see different birds in a very different
environment.

Indeed, as we head into the shady pine forests of Galena
Creek Park the sounds are the murmuring of the mountain
stream and the calls of chickadees. Kinglets forage among
the needles of the pines above, and little groups of Pygmy
Nuthatches pipe busily to one another as they fly from tree
to tree. On our way up, there were Scrub Jays on the lower
slopes, but here in the pines dark Steller's Jays peer at us
around the tree trunks as we eat lunch. The birds here have
a distinctly northern flavor to them: Hairy Woodpeckers,
Red and White-breasted nuthatches, and a Brown Creeper
join the flocks of Mountain Chickadees from time to time.
Migrants are moving here too, with occasional groups of
warblers foraging through the yellowing aspens.

From the park the road climbs sharply upward in a series
of steep curves to the pass at Mount Rose summit at 8,900
feet, with a spectacular view of the countryside around. As
with all mountains, the birds change as we head upward. At
one point we glimpse a Clark's Nutcracker high overhead,
and Cassin's Finches are foraging under the pine needles.
There is also a trail that heads up above the timberline on
Mount Rose, with Rosy Finches and American Pipits to be
found.

On the Lake Tahoe side of the mountain the forest composition changes again, and here such species as Williamson's Sapsucker and Black-backed and White-headed woodpeckers are possible. In fact, on occasion Red-breasted and Red-naped sapsuckers occur as well, making for a woodpecker bonanza!

BESIDES BIRDS AND CASINOS, THERE ARE OTHER THINGS OF INTEREST HERE

The Lahontan marshes were the site of Indian settlements for centuries. The area abounds in traces of past Indian use, and nearby Pyramid lake is both the Paiute reservation and the tribe's original homeland. The Churchill County Museum and Archive—1050 S. Maine St. 10 A.M.–4 P.M., free. (702) 423-3677—has Indian and other artifacts from the area.

Reno is noted more for other things than birding, as anyone arriving by air and negotiating the batteries of slot machines in the airport concourse cannot fail to realize. There are other things to the city than twenty-four-hour shows and gaming, however, and rockhounds will be interested in the Mineral Museum—N. Center St. 8 A.M.–5 P.M. weekdays, free. (702) 784-6987. The Fleischmann Planetarium—N. Virginia St. Hours and fees vary. (702) 784-4811—presents programs on the night sky and other astronomical events.

Lake Tahoe lies over the state line in California. It is exceptionally scenic and often very busy, with lake cruises and a host of outdoor recreational activities in the area. Hiking, fishing, and cross-country skiing are all available in the surrounding national forests. Nearer to Fallon, there are good boating and fishing at both Lahontan Reservoir and Pyramid Lake.

★   ★   ★   ★   ★

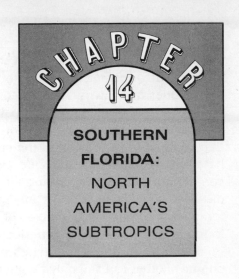

CHAPTER 14

SOUTHERN FLORIDA:
NORTH AMERICA'S SUBTROPICS

F YOU'VE EVER FOUGHT YOUR WAY AROUND MI-
ami or Tampa you probably wondered whether there was
anything natural left in Florida at all. Even outside the
cities there are miles of citrus orchards, plantations, and
vegetable fields, with only Boat-tailed Grackles and the occasional Cattle Egrets as reminders of wilder things. Yet the
natural Florida is still there—sometimes sadly fragmented,
at times hard to find at all, and always under pressure—and
the wildlife that generated such glowing accounts from
early naturalists can still be seen.

It's a fascinating place to visit. That subtropical South has
a wonderful array of habitats: swamps of mangrove and cy-

press, forests of pine and palmetto, dense tropical hammocks, and sweeping expanses of sawgrass.

There's also another, quite different habitat in the suburbs
of the cities and towns. Here in colorful array are tropical
plants from all over the world—palms of many kinds, tall
silk cottons, and vivid cascades of bougainvillea. It's here
that you can most easily find the strange set of aliens that
have arrived, sometimes accidentally and sometimes by
conscious intent, through man's agency. Spot-breasted Orioles decorate telephone wires and Canary-winged Parakeets
forage among the same species of trees they would have
found in their native South American forests. These new animals and plants, whose ultimate impact on the natives and
on one another can still only be guessed at, are now part of
the Florida environment, a sort of faunistic melting pot.

In the winter, when much of the rest of the continent is
wrestling with cold and snow, the naturalist can be excused
if his or her fancy lightly turns to thoughts of palm trees and
white sand beaches and the birds that go with them. You'll
miss a few of the Florida specialties in winter—Gray Kingbirds and Antillean Nighthawks are far to the south, and
Mangrove Cuckoos few—but most of the natives are still to
be found, and to them you can add all those water and
shorebirds that also decided to go to Florida for the winter.

We like to start at Jonathan Dickinson State Park, north of
Jupiter, a beautiful expanse of open pine woodlands. Driving
into Jonathan Dickinson after the hurly-burly of the beach
strip is like driving into another world, and perhaps it really
is akin to driving back in time. This must be how much of
coastal Florida appeared before it was overtaken by or-
anges, condominiums, and swimsuits. Tall, evenly-spaced
pine trees rise above an expanse of palmettos, the low
shrublike palms that never grow much higher than a man's
head. Their big palm-shaped leaves and stalks are armed
with formidable sawteeth—you don't take shortcuts through
saw palmettos! Interspersed through them are open, grassy
clearings dotted even in late winter with wildflowers: the

yellows of bachelor buttons and yellow-eyed grass, the mauves of roserush and pennyroyal. Chuckles of robins and the dry reels of Pine Warblers replace the steady drone of traffic.

The park road ends at the river, where the pines give way to cypresses draped in Spanish moss and a dense, still swamp of cane and cabbage palms. We camp in this enchanting spot, under the shade of the pines and surrounded by rustling thickets of palmetto. Rufous-sided Towhees scrabble noisily among the dead fronds, and the screams of the local Red-shouldered Hawks wake us in the morning if we oversleep.

In wintertime little flocks of warblers wander through the pines, and robins feast greedily in the berry thickets. For some of the locals it's almost spring: Red-bellied Woodpeckers argue noisily about prospective nest holes, and Carolina Wrens jump up to sing rollicking songs from the tops of the thickets, little chestnut bundles of energy. Near the old stables Northern Bobwhites and Common Ground-Doves are foraging in the grassy patches and an Eastern Phoebe flits from post to post.

Pine forests of this kind are home to some of Florida's most special birds. So the park checklist, for example, shows Red-cockaded Woodpeckers as uncommon residents. Just don't lay any bets on seeing one—these birds are endangered even in the heart of their range farther north. One year we found a small group here—see one of these

---

Jonathan Dickinson State Park—Day use 8 A.M.–sunset. $1.50/car. (See below for other details, also for John Prince Park)—is some 7 miles north of Jupiter on Route 1, and its entrance is well marked on the west of the road. John Prince Park is farther south, at Lake Worth. The best birding is around the campground entrance and the lagoons to the north. Both parks have picnic areas and washrooms.

★

sociable birds and you'll usually see more—but since then they have eluded us.

The Florida race of the Scrub Jay, a paler blue version of the vivid California bird, presents no such difficulties—they find us! As soon as we turn off the busy highway a flock flies low across the road. When we stop, tantalized by the fleeting glimpses of soft blues, they pour back to flit around busily, popping in and out of the scrub, chuckling and gurgling to one another. Finally one of the birds flies down onto my outstretched fingers. Finding nothing there, it looks at me with a faint air of disgust, gives my fingers a resounding peck to teach me a lesson, and the whole flock disappears into the palmettos.

It is not necessary to visit the more secluded state parks, however, to find good birding. As we continue south we camp in John Prince Park in Lake Worth, a heavily used area full of automobiles, Frisbees, picnickers, and hi-fi's, with power boats zooming up and down Lake Osborne in its center. No birdlife here, you might think, but in the swampy areas near the campground Purple Gallinules and Limpkins are wandering around casually, and in the early morning they come out to patrol the roads to see if anything worth eating has been left on the lawns. The reedy edges of the pools have a fine array of wading birds large and small, and we have lunch while a Least Bittern squats quietly in the cattails, watching for its dinner in the water next to our picnic table.

There is, of course, far more accommodation for the non-camper. From Jupiter to Delray Beach there are sumptuous oceanfront hotels aplenty, with views of pelicans and palm trees, waves and Willets. The Holiday Inn, Highland Beach, is a particularly good location. Away from the beach are more modest accommodations with more modest price tags, but great for birders who spend most of their days someplace else. Even if you locate in one of these spots you'll still find the birdlife of urban Florida, with roosting flights of Boat-tailed Grackles at dawn and dusk, and mockingbirds welcoming the sunrise.

Loxahatchee National Wildlife Refuge is just inland from this continuous strip of seafront urbanization. It covers over 221 square miles, most of it accessible only by boat. It's surrounded by 57 miles of canal, and you can boat around It If you wish, there are access ramps at both the north and south ends, as well as from the headquarters situated along the eastern boundary. But you don't need to boat for the best birding, because most of it is right there at headquarters.

We stop first at the Center for the usual checklists and brochure, and then head out onto the boardwalk that loops

---

A good beachfront location in the Delray Beach area is south of Route 806, which has exits both off I-95 and the turnpike:

Holiday Inn Highland Beach—2809 S. Ocean Blvd., Highland Beach, Florida 33487. (407) 278-6241. Open all year. Rooms: 114 units; 2 double beds, king and sofa, balconies. Amenities: Dining room, lounge, heated pool, beachfront bike and walking path, cabana service. Terms: Single $66—89, double $69—99. AMEX, CB, DINERS, MC, VISA.

John Prince Park—Exit the turnpike at Lake Worth east to Congress Ave., then ½ mile south to entrance; or I-95 exit 47 and 1¼ miles west on 6th Ave., then south ¼ mile on Congress Ave. (305) 582-7992. Open all year. Campsites: 266 electric, separate tenting area. Amenities: Flush toilets, hot showers, disposal station, nature and hiking trails, boating ramp, dock, boat rentals, fishing, playground, tennis. Restrictions: 14-day limit. Terms: $14/2 persons.

Jonathan Dickinson State Park—16450 S.E. Federal Highway, Florida 33455. (Route 1, 13 miles south of Stuart or 6 miles north of Tequesto). (407) 546-2771. Open all year. Campsites: 135, 107 electric and water. Amenities: Flush toilets, hot showers, disposal station, nature trails, boating, ramp, boat and bicycle rentals, swimming, fishing, playground, riding, grocery store— summer. Restrictions: 14-day limit. Terms: $10.

★

through the cypress swamp behind the building. Now, early in the morning, the boardwalk is deserted. Once again we are taken back into a Florida before the highways and traffic and the burgeoning population, to a quiet place where the gray-green cypress trunks reach in silent supplication from the dark waters, and huge leather ferns tower overhead. Here and there lichens paint the trunks a vivid red, like some out-of-control survey marker. This is a place for land-birds, for a Solitary Vireo or two, for warblers, and a gnat-catcher foraging among the trees.

The main entrance to **Loxahatchee National Wildlife Refuge** — Open 1½ hours before sunrise to 1 hour after sunset (don't get locked in). Free. (407) 734-8303 — is west off Route 441 between Routes 804 and 806. From John Prince go south on Congress to Lantana Road or 804, then west to 441 and turn left (south). From Highland Beach go north to 806 and then west, turning north on 441. There are washrooms at the center.

It's also a place for the unexpected. As we round a bend a sleek, sinuous form emerges onto the boardwalk ahead. We have never been this close to a wild otter before, and we freeze, expecting it to vanish as suddenly as it appeared. It looks at us, decides that we're harmless, and proceeds to roll sensually on its back, its dark fur glistening in the sunlight. Finally someone appears from the opposite direction and it vanishes quickly into the marsh, with hardly a ripple to mark its going.

Enticing though the boardwalk is, the major birding is out beyond the woodlands to the west of the road, among a series of diked impoundments. The water levels in these vary, as does the amount of vegetation. In some the high cattails allow only fleeting glimpses of open water beyond. In others water extends to the foot of the dikes, with muddy patches and a tangled growth of low weeds. Some sections are covered in carpets of water lettuce, and others appear grassy, their true depth only revealed when the head of a heron or egret pops up among the grass stalks.

Trails follow the tops of the levees, and we head out down one side, trying to choose a direction that will keep the sun behind us as much as possible—an effort only partially successful given the layout of the dikes. It is certainly worth any effort, because the place is alive with birds. Every section of the marsh has its own complement of herons and egrets, as well as little flocks of White and Glossy ibis that surge up from time to time, a contrasting medley of white and black wings, only to vanish again in the heavy vegetation.

Birds are constantly flying back and forth: the dark shapes of Little Blue Herons, immaculate white egrets, the Great Blues in their measured flight. Moorhens scuttle along the pavements of water lettuce like busy commuters at rush hour, and here and there are the irregular forms of alligators lying motionless among the weeds. At one point a Purple Gallinule wanders too close to one of those inert forms, and with a sudden splash and jerk and a couple of quick gulps it vanishes forever. But the tranquillity of the scene is barely ruffled, and the birds continue to treat the 'gators with about as much respect as the average pedestrian treats traffic.

In one of the grassier parts of the marsh are the tall gray forms of a pair of Sandhill Cranes, their red crowns bright in the sunlight. Farther out on a mud flat a huge flock of Fulvous Whistling-Ducks rests, the rich beauty of their plumage—cinnamons, browns, and white—a delightful surprise after the nondescript-looking birds of the guidebooks. Here and there Northern Harriers glide low over the reed beds, putting up swirling flocks of blackbirds and little sprigs of teal and other waterfowl.

Our walk continues, with additional species being added one by one. Here a Short-billed Dowitcher is feeding on one of the mud flats; there a flock of Smooth-billed Anis flies along the edge of one of the dikes. Small flocks of swallows hunt over the open water and a sudden flash of orange-brown reveals a gulf fritillary feeding on the flowers along the levee. Every visit to Loxahatchee is different: the only constants are the rich variety of birds and their exceptional accessibility.

A lot of first-time birders head straight down to the Everglades, leaving the urbanization of Miami somewhere off to the east of the Florida Turnpike. It is an understandable decision—who needs all that traffic!—but it bypasses the ex-

---

We recommend using the Florida Turnpike south to Homestead. The tolls are worth it for the pleasanter, more hassle-free drive. The Everglades' main entrance is via Route 27 (formerly Route 9336) southwest from Homestead to the park gate. It is 36 miles from there to Flamingo. The only accommodations in the Everglades are the two campgrounds and the lodge at Flamingo. The campsites are on a first-come, first-served basis, and reservations are usually essential at the lodge. The visitor center is open 8 A.M.–5 P.M. Be sure to pick up a park map, which has all the noteworthy points marked. Park entry fee: $5/car.

Flamingo Lodge—Marina & Outpost Resort—P.O. Box 428, Flamingo, Florida 33030. Everglades National Park. (813) 695-3101, (305) 253-2241. Open all year. Rooms: 102 units; 2 double beds, cottages with kitchenettes and suites. Amenities: Dining room, lounge, swimming pool, camp store, gift shop, canoes, cruises, tram tours. Terms: Motel $43–69, cottage $60–80, suites $105.

Everglades National Park—P.O. Box 279, Homestead, Florida 33030. (305) 247-6211. Campgrounds open all year. Restrictions: 14-day limit:

Flamingo Campground (At the south end of the park road.)—Campsites: 295, no hookups. Amenities: Flush toilets, cold showers, disposal station. Terms: $4–7.

Long Pine Key Campground (4 miles south of the park entrance, left 1½ miles.)—Campsites: 108, no hookups. Amenities: Flush toilets, no showers, disposal station, recreational program. Terms: $7.

otic riches of the Miami suburbs. Here introduced birds and natives coexist in a man-made landscape, and you are never quite sure what is going to turn up where. Homestead is a good compromise location, and if you wish to stay in the neighbourhood the hotels and motels are adequate, and far less expensive than in Miami.

For some time there had been comments on the spread of introduced Ringed Turtle-Doves in this area, until some sharp-eyed observer realized that the birds were really Eurasian Collared-Doves that had probably found their way over from the Bahamas. The difference? They're larger and darker, with gray under the tail where the Ringed Turtle-Dove is usually white. The Eurasian birds have staged a dramatic expansion over Europe, and perhaps they are now poised to do the same thing here. The rooftops around Homestead can usually be relied on to produce one or two, and while we watch them there a Loggerhead Shrike—a sorely pressed native of North America that is in serious decline—sits on the fencing nearby watching for grasshoppers.

The patchwork of gardens, fields, hedgerows, and orchards south of Miami abounds in such contradictions. The common shrub is the introduced Brazilian pepper, and in winter it seems to provide food for half the robins on the continent. At Castello Hammock wintering Painted Buntings, glorious mixtures of vivid blue, red and green, share a feeder outside the Nature Center with introduced White-winged Doves. Nearby, at Redland Fruit and Spice Park, wintering hummingbirds visit the flowers of a cultivated orchid tree.

There are few greater contrasts than between the hubbub and traffic, people and development of Miami and the sweeping expanses of the Everglades only 40 miles away, where the only sound is the wind and the only moving thing may be the shape of a harrier low in the distance. This is a subtropical wilderness where mankind seems no more than a passing interruption.

Our first stop is at the Interpretive Center, parking under

the shade of graceful mahoganies. The film on the park here puts the things we are to see into context, and they have the usual checklists and brochures, together with an unusual assortment of books and memorabilia. This is a special place, and the National Parks Service goes to some pains to help you appreciate it.

Soon we are driving through a wide, prairielike expanse of tall grassland broken here and there by stands of pine and dotted with islands of dense broad-leaved woodland, the hammocks. In places there are low clumps of straggly cypress trees looking gray and lifeless in the winter sunshine. It's a still landscape, the only life the soaring vultures and an occasional heron flying out over the grass. From time to time we pass small pools with the occasional egrets, and in one place a pale, sandy Red-shouldered Hawk is sitting on the top of a spindly cypress. Closer examination of the grasses reveals that, far from being a dry prairie, we are in reality driving through a vast marsh, and the tall, razor-edged sawgrasses in fact have their feet in water.

Soon we come to the entrance to the Royal Palm Visitor Center and the famous Anhinga Trail. It's a busy place, usually thronged later in the day. A hard-topped nature trail may not be your idea of how to see birds, but a glance at the crowds makes its practicality clear. It is easy to see why the place is so popular: we've seen wilder birds in zoos! A Green-backed Heron squats almost at our feet, and around the entrance pool other herons and egrets stand along the edges of the reeds, in orderly array as if to assure the best viewing. The birds' casual attitude toward the milling crowds continues as we head up the trail: Great Egrets pose obligingly for photographers, Little Blue Herons squat within head-scratching distance, and moorhens wander along the grassy sides of the trail like so many chickens.

When we arrive at the boardwalk loop it also is easy to see how the trail gets its name. Anhingas are everywhere: festooned around in the trees, poking their heads snakelike out of the water, and soaring stiffly overhead. There are anhingas with wings stretched akimbo in the sunlight, anhingas sitting on nests, and anhingas doing things that wouldn't make the pages of family magazines. Some of the males wave their heads around jerkily, their crown feathers raised in fuzzy little crests and their bright turquoise eye-rings giving them a wild, maniacal appearance. You expect them to shout "Wheee!" at any moment!

But there's still more to be seen. Along one more isolated pool a group of Black and Yellow-crowned night-herons sit sleepily, hunched among the reeds; and here and there Purple Gallinules flaunt their vivid blue head shields and chrome-yellow legs. Common Yellowthroats bob in and out of the vegetation, seemingly strangely out of place among all these glamour birds. Red and green bromeliads decorate the shrubs along the path like resplendent pineapple tops, and there's always a chance of a Sora or a Least Bittern.

The Anhinga Trail is a photographer's paradise, but it is well worth a visit even if you are not taking pictures. The trick is to arrive early before the crowds surge in. Then you can hope for a wider variety of birds, and also have the opportunity to watch the vultures and other raptors soaring above the canopy of Royal Palm Hammock before heading out over the sawgrass in their daily quest for food.

One of the two park campgrounds is at Long Pine Key, close to Royal Palm and so a good place to stay for an early start on the Anhinga Trail. It's handy too for Taylor Slough, along the road just north of the Royal Palm turnoff, where Cape Sable Seaside Sparrows sing gurgly little redwing-like songs at dawn and dusk. The delightful Long Pine picnic area is set among the pines around a lake and is a nice spot at any time. Pine Warblers forage methodically in the pines overhead, and little flocks of wintering warblers and sparrows are scattered here and there under the trees.

As we continue down the road we leave the pine stands behind and the prairielike quality of the vista becomes even more pronounced. The isolated hammocks seem secret, hidden places, full of potential for who knows what rarities; and in fact the flora of these dense little patches of forest is truly subtropical, with huge strangler figs and rare epiphytic orchids. Many of these plants are West Indian, and in North America occur only here and on the Florida Keys.

To visit one we turn in to the Mahogany Hammock, where a raised boardwalk winds through the middle of the woodland. At the entrance a pair of Western Kingbirds are hawking from a dead tree, but inside we find ourselves in another world. Gone are the brilliant sun and the sweeping vistas and the distant horizon; now we're enclosed by dense forest with the sun no more than a few bright specks filtered through the leaves above, and a riot of vegetation on all sides. Resurrection fern carpets the tree trunks and heavy vines dangle from the canopy. It's a silent place, and the low hooting of a Barred Owl from somewhere in the depths has an ominous quality, the answering chatter of a robin at once jarring and inappropriate. One half expects the screeches of parrots or the low hooting of a motmot.

Once again the character of the road changes and now the sawgrass is interrupted by little dark-green clumps of mangrove, the first promises of the sea ahead. Gradually the mangroves grow taller; when we stop at Paurotis Pond they're threatening to take over completely. The pond is full of coots, with Double-crested Cormorants draped around in the trees, drying their wings.

At Nine Mile Pond a pigeon sits on a dead stub across the water, its shape somehow promising more than a misplaced Rock Dove. Through the 'scope the black silhouette remains unrelievedly black and we can see the top of its head glistening in the sun, our first glimpse of a White-crowned Pigeon. A couple of days later a large flock of these birds flies across through the mangroves a little farther down the road.

West Lake is the next stop. Here a boardwalk leads through the tangled mangroves out to a large expanse of water usually—and today—covered in coots. The mangrove walk is a chance to see this fascinating community at close hand. The slender tree trunks arch up in graceful loops from the glistening mud below, and the roots are raised, stiltlike, as though the last tide had washed the soil away. On the tangle of boughs above, the smooth green-gray bark is pale in the filtered sunlight, and little groups of warblers forage through the glossy green leaves. Most are the ever-present yellow-rumpeds, feeding through the low branches of the trees; but among them is the local Prairie Warbler, a splash of gold among the dappled greens.

Flamingo is the end of the road, and, apart from the long drive out along the Keys, as far south as you can travel by road in Florida. The road emerges from the mangroves into broad lawns with shade trees and palm clumps dotted around. Along the edge of the water lies the resort complex with its marina, restaurant, and cottages, and farther along the campgrounds are clustered among the trees. You can even rent a houseboat here to penetrate into more remote areas of the park.

No matter which accommodation you choose, this can be one of North America's most enchanting destinations. The motel windows look out on the low line of shrubs bordering Florida Bay, and as we sit in the restaurant in the early evening we look out over an expanse of shimmering water painted in a multitude of light pinks, salmons, and mauves by the setting sun, with herons and shorebirds etched in silhouette on the glistening mud flats, and flocks of egrets and ibis flying past to roost in the mangroves of the scattered Keys. At dawn the picture is completely different but equally fascinating. The flats are dotted with the pinks of Roseate Spoonbills and the whites and blues of herons and egrets, and little squadrons of American White Pelicans feed busily in the shallows near the shore.

On the way to breakfast we follow little warbler flocks foraging through the trees at the side of the bay. A White-eyed Vireo peers out of one bush, and a dapper Yellow-throated Warbler explores the boughs of one of the taller mangroves. Then, deciding that the side of the restaurant might be more productive, we leave it rooting around among the cobwebs under the eaves.

One noteworthy animal at Flamingo is the mosquito. They're always around, but in some years their numbers can rival the man-eating hordes at Churchill, particularly a little later in the season. At their worst they settle on your eyelids as you try to focus your glasses, and view fly-dope as a tasty appetizer—nevertheless, you're lost without it. If you can stand them, the walk through the mangroves out along the Snake Bight Trail is one of the most productive birding trips in the park—maybe it's all that food! It is the best bet for a Mangrove Cuckoo, and at the end you just could glimpse one of the flamingos that sometimes straggle up here from the Caribbean.

The picnic area backs the marina, shaded by mahoganies and bordered by shrubs where Red-shouldered Hawks like to perch. Each post in the marina is decorated by a Brown Pelican and more stand in lines on the shore, like rows of dyspeptic elderly gentlemen who have had too much to eat. Laughing Gulls quarrel over scraps in the parking lot, and blocking the boat ramp is a solid black line of skimmers, with their improbable, mis-shapen-looking red-and-black bills.

You never know what is likely to turn up at Flamingo. Once we even located at Black Rail here, scrabbling around in the heavy vegetation at Echo Pond. We search the black-bird flocks on the lawns, eager for Caribbean stragglers, and follow the well-worn path around Echo Pond alert for Short-tailed Hawks or rarer wanderers. There are no rails on view today, but Smooth-billed Anis flop through the bushes, and a couple of Scissor-tailed Flycatchers hawk for insects from the tops of the taller shrubs, their long tails bobbling behind like strips of loose ribbon. On one day we have one of the brief, violent downpours so typical of the subtropics, and for a while the flooded lawns play host to flocks of Willets and dowitchers, with little groups of White Ibis wading in the deeper water.

Flamingo is a wonderful base for birding the productive southern part of the everglades. You can rent boats and ca-noes, but can also do very well without leaving the beaten track at all. The ponds along the lower part of the road are sometimes alive with birds, and they are all worth more than one visit. At other times there can be hardly a bird visible; it all seems to depend on the distribution of food through the marshes as a whole.

It pays to be alert, however, to more than just the birds around the water. At one pond we look up to see a huge pinwheel of Wood Storks circling at enormous height overhead, and at another a group of soaring vultures includes a smaller hawk with a yellow cere shining in the sun—the black phase of the rare Short-tailed Hawk. Short-taileds like to soar with such vulture flocks in hope that passing birds will take these ever-present watchers for granted, and not notice the predator in their midst.

From Flamingo the way west is along another legendary Florida birding route, the Tamiami Trail. Soon we are driving along with tall groves of feathery casuarinas on one side, and flat expanses of sawgrass reaching away to the horizon to the north. The road itself is bordered by broad canals,

---

Route 27 (997 on some maps; Krome, or SW 177th Ave.) north is the most direct route to the Tamiami Trail (Route 41 west). The two Homestead locations mentioned earlier are both easy to locate from Krome Ave. **Redland Fruit and Spice Park** is 2 blocks west on S.W. 248th St. (Coconut Palm Dr.) and **Castello Hammock Park** is 3 blocks east on S.W. 232nd St. (Silver Palm Dr.) and then a short distance north on S.W. 162nd Ave. (Farmlife Rd.). Redland is open 10 A.M.—4:30 P.M., free—(305) 247-5727—and Castello is open to pedestrian access at all times. Both have small picnic areas and washrooms.

---

with access points to the levees on the other side. There are even a few informal campgrounds scattered along the canals, with fishermen sitting patiently outside their campers. The levees are good vantage points for viewing the marshes and the channels. Egrets and herons come and go, and flocks of Boat-tailed Grackles are everywhere, flying along with their tails dangling behind like black paper airplanes.

Finally our perseverance pays off as a heavy-looking black hawk rises and falls above the sawgrass in the distance. It flops its way toward us, at times lifting its wings high to drop into the marsh, its white rump glistening. This, then, is the much-sought Snail Kite, a bird that can sometimes elude visitors completely. At other times we have seen bird after bird over these marshes, searching for the apple snails that constitute their major food.

As the Tamiami Trail continues westward we leave the open stretches of sawgrass, and cypresses close in along the roadside with dark pools covered in mats of water lettuce. This is the Big Cypress Swamp, the home of the endangered Florida Panther. Egrets and herons seem to be even more common here, and kingfishers decorate the wires. At the roadside rest area where we stop to have lunch there is a small boardwalk through part of the marsh, a great place for landbirds with Carolina Wrens poking in and out of the tree stubs and waterthrushes teetering around the edges of the pools.

After a couple of glimpses at cypress swamps we're ready for a real walk through one. There is no better place for such a fascinating experience than Corkscrew Swamp Sanctuary, the 11,000-acre reserve of the National Audubon Society. It lies inland from the busy Gulf Coast communities, and a visit there takes us through the full range of plant communities associated with the Florida wetlands.

The trail leads first through open pine woodlands, and then out across a wet prairie where the first spring wildflowers are beginning to bloom, purple butterworts and yellow-eyed grasses. Soon we are heading along a long strand of low cypresses with bromeliads and ferns. The real jewel of the preserve comes when we pass through the outer ring of trees into a place of giant bald cypresses, their branches misted with the delicate, feathery leaves of early spring. In this sun-spangled place a rich understory of shrubs and small trees rises from the still, dark pools, and small flocks of warblers, titmice, and gnatcatchers work their way through the branches.

In the distance there is a low, droning clamor, a noise like a multitude of small frogs celebrating spring. Finally, in one of the taller sections of the woodland, we discover that our frogs were in fact the distant voices of nesting Wood Storks. High above, a constant parade of birds is flying in and out, feeding the tall, gangly young that are standing in the nests. Even adult Wood Storks are not particularly handsome birds, with massive bills and dark warty heads, and the youngsters are downright ugly. But in flight the birds are magnificent. With their huge wings outstretched the wonderful shell-pink underwing is revealed, and the soaring

At the west end of the Tamiami Trail, Route 41 turns north to pass through the busy communities along the coast. Shortly past the point where 41 becomes a divided highway, the bypass Route 951 turns north, and it is much faster to follow this and then Interstate 75 north. The I-75 exit for Fort Myers Beach is Bonita Springs, then west on Bonita Beach Rd. to Route 865 (Estero Blvd.). The Koreshan State Historic Site is farther north at exit 19, and then west to Route 41.

Corkscrew Swamp Sanctuary is east off Interstate 75 on Route 846, which finally bears north; the entrance to the Sanctuary is where the road turns east once again. There is an excellent gift shop and a picnic area and washrooms. 9 A.M.–5 P.M. $4. (813) 657-3771.

To reach Sanibel from Fort Myers Beach, continue north on Route 865 (it becomes San Carlos Blvd.) to Route 869 west which leads directly to the Sanibel Causeway (toll). From Koreshan go north on 41 to Route 865 and then west. On Sanibel itself **J. N. "Ding" Darling National Wildlife Refuge** is right on Periwinkle Way from the causeway, and then continue on the Sanibel-Captiva road. Center 9 A.M.–5 P.M., Refuge 6 A.M.–6:30 P.M. $3/car. (813) 472-1100. There are the usual brochures and checklists.

★

bird is transformed into a creature of infinite grace and buoyancy.

This is one of the storks' last strongholds in Florida, but we are still lucky to find the birds nesting here. In recent years the water regimen in the Everglades has been such that Wood Storks have failed to nest, and when they have nested the attempts have failed. Indeed, later we are to find that this particular nesting failed as well.

It is difficult to know the real highlight of our walk through Corkscrew. Farther along the boardwalk we catch a rare golden glimpse of a Prothonotary Warbler, a rarity here in winter. Then there is the picture of the lettuce lake, with tall cypresses arched overhead and graceful festoons of Spanish moss, and a still line of White Ibis, with long, curved red bills and blue eyes, standing motionless along the branches. The Barred Owl sits quietly beside the path, its brown eyes gazing benevolently at the passersby.

It's a shock to find ourselves back in all the hurly-burly of urban Florida. Fort Myers is a busy place, and birding in this area means heavy traffic and congestion. One compensation is our hotel. The Holiday Inn Fort Myers Beach nestles comfortably on the waterfront, and a walk out the door leads straight onto the white sands of the Gulf of Mexico. To the south is a long spit, largely submerged at high tide.

At midday the beach is thronged with people, but when we get out at dawn there's only the occasional jogger in sight, and then the beach is thronged with birds. Flocks of Laughing Gulls loiter on the pale sand with groups of Royal Terns. Everywhere there are shorebirds: scattered Willets stalking purposefully along, little groups of dowitchers probing away madly, Sanderlings scuttling back and forth at the edge of the water, and nondescript gray groups of Western Sandpipers. Semipalmated Plovers are scattered around, picking daintily from side to side, and here and there is the larger, heavy-billed shape of a Wilson's Plover. Look a little closer and the shadowy forms of Piping and Snowy plovers appear, gliding ghostlike over the sand, mirroring the actions of their darker brethren.

The premier birding destination on the Gulf Coast is "Ding" Darling National Wildlife Refuge on Sanibel Island. You can stay on Sanibel if you wish, but it will cost you twice as much and you probably won't get to the refuge much faster anyway. From the mainland we drive across the long causeway, where Royal Terns, rakish-looking with their bright orange bills, dot the balustrades. The islands along the causeway are good places for a picnic lunch, and good

---

Holiday Inn Fort Myers Beach—6890 Estero Blvd. (Route 865), Fort Myers Beach, Florida 33931. (813) 463-5711. Open all year. Rooms: 103 units; 2 double beds, king and sofa, some kitchenettes. Amenities: Dining room, lounge, heated pool, coin laundry, beach. Terms: Single $62–86, double $70–94. AMEX, CB, DINERS, MC, VISA.

Camping in the Fort Myers area can be difficult. There is a host of campgrounds, but finding space in one of them in wintertime can be another matter, and many only accept campers for longer-term stays. Much the best campground is in the delightful Koreshan State Historic Park, but camping there is on a first-come, first-served basis:

Koreshan State Historical Park—P.O. Box 7, Estero, Florida 33928. (813) 992-0311. Open all year. Campsites: 60 water and electric. Amenities: Flush toilets, hot showers, disposal station, boating, ramp, fishing, nature trail. Restrictions: No pets, 14-day limit. Terms: $10. Park entry fee $1.

---

birding to boot! One day our picnic is interrupted by a Magnificent Frigatebird soaring idly overhead, its vast black wings crooked and its long, slender tail streaming behind.

The five-mile auto tour at "Ding" Darling runs along a series of pools dotted among extensive mangroves. It can be one of life's longest five miles with birds interrupting progress constantly, and it is a good idea to cover the area early if you can. The state of the tide is also important, as birds are more numerous when the flats are exposed. Whenever you visit, however, you will probably find superb birding at "Ding" Darling.

At the start of our route we are greeted by a welcoming committee of Roseate Spoonbills standing in a pool against the mangroves. Their position seems to have been carefully chosen to display their shell-pink silhouettes to the best advantage—maybe they're on the refuge payroll! But they do turn out to be accurate harbingers for the rest of the drive. Full-plumaged Yellow-crowned Night-Herons amble along the pools at the side of the road, Sandwich Terns display their yellow and black bills from the edge of one of the water-control structures, and in among the masses of waterfowl glows the orange head of a Eurasian Wigeon. Common Ground-Doves scuttle and run along the edges of the road, and at one place we look out to an Osprey nest with the sitting bird's head shining in the sun. And then there are a multitude of birds that somewhere else, at another time, would each make a visit exceptional. All the herons and egrets are here somewhere along the route. Reddish Egrets tear around frantically, little parties of Brown Pelicans plunge-dive along the canals, and ducks and shorebirds throng the flats and the pools in crowds, legions, and armies. "Ding" Darling is a fitting climax to any trip.

The route described can be covered in a week to ten days, or take two weeks or more if you wish. An average trip list could be between 130 and 150 species, with the high spots being the exceptional access to the large wading birds. 1988–89 saw exceptional droughts in Florida, but one hopes this condition will not persist.

There are two good guides to the area: James A. Lane's *Birder's Guide to Florida* (rev. Harold R. Holt; 1989, L&P Press) and *Birds of Southern Florida* by Connie Toops and Willard E. Dilley (1986, Voyageur Press).

★

IF YOU'RE DETERMINED TO DO OTHER THINGS THAN BIRD, THEN . . .

The general naturalist in Florida will have as much fun as the birder and be considerably more confused, as general references are fewer. For the botanist the Preston B. Bird and Mary Heinlein Redland Fruit and Spice Park (see above), and Fairchild Tropical Gardens in Coral Gables—10901 Old

Cutler Rd., 9.30 A.M.–4.30 P.M. $4. (305) 667-1651—are of great interest, and the marine enthusiast will find both the Biscayne National Park—S.W. 328 St. east of Homestead, 8 A.M.–sunset. (305) 247-2400—and John Pennekamp Coral Reef State Park on Route 1 at Key Largo—8 A.M.–sunset, $1.50/vehicle and driver, $1 each passenger. 1-800-432-2871—well worth detours. There are regular tours at both places with glass-bottomed boats, and for snorkeling and canoeing. Sanibel is, of course, famed for its seashells, but with so many searchers you must get on the beach at first light if you hope to find many.

Florida abounds in other attractions calculated to lure the less dedicated birder away for a few hours or days. They range from sitting on the beaches in the sun, through fishing, boating, and water sports generally, through the more structured attractions of Miami and, much farther north, EPCOT and the Kennedy Space Center. Miami has Monkey Jungle, Parrot Jungle, Metrozoo, and several museums and places of historic interest. But any attempt at a more comprehensive listing of Florida's attractions would need a chapter in itself, and the state is only too ready to supply information in abundance.

★   ★   ★   ★   ★

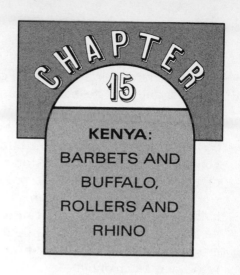

CHAPTER 15

KENYA: BARBETS AND BUFFALO, ROLLERS AND RHINO

A PRIDE OF LIONS LOUNGES INDOLENTLY IN the shade of a group of acacias, cubs scrambling and rolling over their mothers and one another indiscriminately. Out on the plain, little groups of Thomson's gazelles—Tommies—graze, their black-and-white tails in constant motion back and forth, like tiny windshield wipers. Down in the scrub along a creek stands a small herd of buffalo, with massive heads and huge horns, black and menacing, glaring ominously before stampeding in a cloud of red dust. Our van rounds a bend to find a huge elephant standing motionless in the road ahead: finally the old tusker, his thoughts reorganized, moves off and we can proceed.

Kenya is one of the very few places where the traveling birder's most treasured memories may well be of things other than birds! Birding in Africa does indeed have its distractions, and even the hardest-core lister is likely to find his or her attention diverted by mammals large and small. This said, Africa also offers some of the most thrilling birding to be found anywhere. Unlike the birds of the dense forests of South America, birds on the African savannahs are both numerous and easy to see. The problem primarily is one of storing enough data in your mental computer to be able to identify the passing array, because here—unlike more temperate zones—every bird in a flock may be a different species, and a journey of seventy-five miles can take you into a whole new batch of birds.

The style of African birding also tends to be very different. Safari travel is typically in groups of six or fewer, in small vans with open or raised roofs, and (at least in the parks) most of one's viewing must be done from the van. Walking is often only permitted in limited areas, and then in the company of a guard. At times this can be thoroughly frustrating, when some interesting-looking creature vanishes into a bush, but usually there is more than enough to keep you occupied.

Nairobi is our jumping-off point to view this splendid array of birds. We start even as the plane is landing and an African Pied Wagtail flits along the runway. More strangers appear outside the Serena Hotel as the suitcases are being unloaded. We wrestle with the identification of Streaky Seed-eaters through a haze of jet lag, watch Black Kites soaring overhead, and the yellow-and-black Reichenow's Weaver that disappears into a nearby palm is at least brightly colored.

Nairobi National Park is our first real introduction to Kenyan birding. It's only four miles from the center of the city, and by the standards of Kenyan parks is quite small. We head out onto a wide expanse of grassland, tall, gold, tawny in the morning sunlight, and dotted with low gray-green clumps of acacia. Superficially at least, it's not unlike the sagebrush country of North America, but here there are animals everywhere.

At the side of the road is the first of our mammal distractions—a warthog, on its knees rooting in the ground with its tusks. Warthogs are incredibly ugly beasts, but as we become more familiar with them they develop an almost endearing quality. They trot along, their ridiculous little tails held aloft perkily, a ready meal for almost every carnivore on the plains.

But back to the birds—and what birds! At once a Tawny Eagle flies up; nearby is a Crowned Crane, a golden starburst of feathers on its head. Here a family of Ostriches moves off in stately array, and there a tall Secretary Bird paces steadily on stiltlike legs, looking for a lizard for its next meal.

These are not just birds—indeed, it's even a little difficult to think of an Ostrich as a bird. These are the exotic denizens of the Child's First Book of Animals. They're not sup-

Nairobi has many excellent hotels, but many are located in town with little potential for birding. Both the following have well-vegetated sites, with the former having much the best facilities—and higher prices. National park entry fees are 30/- for adults and 25/- for vehicles.

Nairobi Serena Hotel—Nyerere Rd. and Kenyatta Ave., P.O. Box 46302, Nairobi, Kenya; phone 725111. Rooms: 200 units, twins, suites. Amenities: Dining room, lounge, minibus service to downtown. Terms: Following, and all below, Kenya shillings (/-). Single from 1850/-, double from 2350/-, suites 2900—3500/-, tax included.

Fairview Hotel—Bishop's Rd. off 3rd Ngong Ave., P.O. Box 40842, Nairobi, Kenya; phone 723211-10. Rooms: 110 units, most with showers or bath, family units. Amenities: Dining room, lounge. No pool. Terms: Single 360—500/-, double 580—750/-, suites 750—1200/-, tax included, bed and breakfast.

posed to appear in real life, wandering around on a patch of ordinary-looking grassland and looking for the next meal, just like the rest of the bird world. This is more than the achievement of some life birds, it's the realization of a childhood fantasy.

We hardly get started when we are stopping again, with one new experience following another. Finally we stop for lunch under the shade of a group of acacias, and are immediately besieged by a troop of black-faced vervet monkeys. They're delightful little creatures, but their potential for mayhem becomes apparent a second later. One of our group, momentarily distracted while holding his sandwich, suddenly finds it in the hand of a monkey instead. The culprit, now perched innocently on the roof of the van, is already looking for more. But there are no more sandwiches—for anyone!

A short walk along the river is both frustrating and exciting. There's an unidentifiable medley of songs and calls from invisible birds on the far side, but we also find the first of our mixed flocks—and what a colorful array it is! A Gray-headed Bush Shrike, with soft gray head and vivid green back, followed by a smaller look-alike, a Sulphur-breasted Bush Shrike, both sharing bright yellow and orange underparts. A beautiful cinnamon finch with black tail, cobalt rump, and red bill proves to be a Purple Grenadier. While we're admiring these gaudy creatures the other birds in the flock vanish, all too quickly.

Next comes our first lion kill. A kettle of vultures is soaring over a zebra carcass covered in a seething mass of screaming and fighting birds. Most are Ruppell's Griffon and African White-backed vultures, but one or two smaller Hooded Vultures scuttle around furtively at the edge of the horde. A few Marabou Storks tower over the other species, tall birds with obscene pink throat pouches and a morose air. Soon a pair of jackals arrives, putting some of the vultures to flight and embarking on a running battle with the rest, all the while snatching scraps of meat. Finally they appear to decide that the whole thing is too much trouble and wander off, leaving the field once again to the milling vultures.

A little searching reveals the provider of the feast lounging nearby, oblivious to the whole affair. No animal seems
to be able to achieve such an air of regal detachment as a
lion. The pesky little vans with their little troops of excited
occupants, all jumping about with more than a passing re-
semblance to the monkeys at lunch, are treated as though
they didn't exist. Humanity is not used to such supreme disregard. An irritated observer once suggested running over
one of the animals' tails, just to elicit some response!

My list for the day in the park is a hundred species, with
eighty-three life birds! It's no more than an average total for
a country with some thirteen hundred species of birds. Really accomplished Kenyan birders in pursuit of big days
have logged over 250 species in a day in this area. In two
weeks my own list will stand at over 400, most of the birds
wholly new.

Outside the national parks travel is through a mixture of
agricultural land and open range. The big game is absent,
but birds are not. Long-crested Hawk Eagles perch on the
telephone posts along the road, distinctive dark birds with
long, slender topknots. With them are other, less identifi-
able, raptors—a constant challenge as the van zips past. Finally we conclude, reluctantly, that most of the birds are no
more than the seemingly innumerable variations of the Augur Buzzard, that Kenyan counterpart of the Red-tailed
Hawk. Bee-eaters, shrikes, and kingfishers also decorate the
wires, and at one stop Speckled Mousebirds run lizardlike
among the branches of the bushes at the roadside.

The slopes of Mount Kenya are a very different environment from that of the relatively flat, open savannahs. Here
the road climbs up into tangles of dense bush and bamboo,
until we finally arrive at our lodge, mounted on stilts and
overlooking a water hole and salt lick.

As we arrive in the luminous sunlight of the late afternoon
a pair of Hunter's Cisticolas are singing. Many tropical birds
duet, with the male singing one part of the song and the
female the rest. The Hunter's Cisticolas are two such: nondescript little brown warblers that sit facing each other
along a bamboo stalk, bill to bill. The top bird unwinds a

whirry little song, followed immediately by the second, its reel pitched a few notes lower. Immediate is the key word: the synchronization between the ending of the first half and the start of the second is machinelike in its precision. The net effect of this remarkable performance is rather like a phonograph record with the needle stuck!

There are more showy things to be seen here as well. Hartlaub's Turacos hop through the trees, their iridescent violet-blue and green plumage glistening in the sun, suddenly flashing crimson as the birds fly from one tree to the next. Sociable flocks of Red-headed Parrots pass overhead, chattering musically.

As the evening closes in, small groups of bushbuck and elephants come in to the water hole. Bloodcurdling roars as darkness descends would do justice to a whole army of big cats, but the authors of the racket prove to be only the cuddly-looking tree hyraxes sitting all around, like teddy bears with bass voices. In the morning our stay is over, and we head back down the mountain.

Over the years Lake Nakuru has become synonymous with flamingos, and concentrations of two million birds or more have been recorded. Water levels on the lake, however, vary from time to time and on occasion it has dried up completely, leaving the nearby town blanketed in choking clouds of soda dust whenever the wind blew. In the early eighties the water levels were too high, and the flocks moved to nearby Lake Baringa and to the other soda lakes of the rift valley. It's only recently that they have returned,

---

The route to Mountain Lodge is via the Thika and Nanyuki road to Naro Moru, and the road to the lodge is between Kiganjo and Naro Moru. You should arrange to arrive at the lodge between 4 and 6.30 P.M.

Mountain Lodge—P.O. Box 123, Kiganjo, or P.O. Box 30471, Nairobi, Kenya; phone 336858. Altitude 7,200 feet. <u>Amenities</u>: Dining room. <u>Terms</u>: Single 2100—2500/-, double 2500—3000/-, full board, tax included.

★

but it's a good idea to ascertain the current status of the lake before visiting.

On our trip there's no lack of birdlife! What does two million look like? Here are densely packed lines of pink birds stretching as far as the eye can see in both directions. Farther out on the turquoise water are vast pink patches where more are feeding in deeper water. Long, straggling flocks fly

---

Lake Nakuru National Park is south of the town of Nakuru. From Mountain Lodge head south to Nyeri, then north and west to Thomson's Falls, and then south to Nakuru itself. The camp is on the east side of the lake.

Sarova Lion Hill Camp—Lake Nakuru National Park, P.O. Box 30680, Nairobi, Kenya; phone 333233. Views over lake. <u>Rooms</u>: Permanent safari tents. <u>Amenities</u>: Dining room, electricity, hot and cold running water, showers and flush toilets. <u>Terms</u>: Single from 1800/-, double from 2150/-, full board, tax included.

---

constantly back and forth, their dark flight feathers a contrast against the delicate shell-pink of their bodies. We leave the counting to the wildlife biologists, but this is the most spectacular concentration of birds we have ever seen.

When we recover from the first overwhelming impact, we're suddenly aware that the lake teems with other species as well as Greater and Lesser flamingos. Everywhere there are birds. On the flats are spruce black-and-white Blacksmith Plovers, with tiny, pale Kittlitz's Sand Plovers as dainty companions. A little farther out graceful Black-winged Stilts pace in the shallows, and dabbling behind them are Cape Wigeon, pale, bleached-looking birds with pink bills. Curlew Sandpipers, goofing off from the responsibilities of nest-tending in Siberia, are probing the silvery mud energetically. Gray-headed Gulls stand around in small groups, with clusters of Sacred Ibis and scattered, hunched Gray Herons. Constantly overhead are Whiskered and White-winged Black terns, hawking insects. Beyond the milling masses of flamingos are flocks of White Pelicans, grebes, African Pochards, and the stiff-tailed Maccoa Ducks.

Lake Naivasha, our next destination, is a striking contrast with Lake Nakuru and its turquoise water and whitish-gray mud flats. It's a freshwater lake, at once reminiscent of and very different from the large marshes of North America. There are dense beds of papyrus, and the surface is dotted with water lilies. Here and there are a few clumps of trees, and in places there are dark mud flats. There's much boating and fishing here, and the birdlife is less dramatic than that of Nakuru—it's hard to top two million flamingos—but, in its own way, equally rich.

One of East Africa's most evocative sounds is the call of the African Fish Eagle. These wonderful birds, with their shining white heads and breasts and rich chestnut underparts, sit high on the snags over the lake. Periodically one tosses its head back and utters its clear three-part cry, a wild sound that ever afterward comes to mean Africa.

Lake Naivasha is south of Lake Nakuru, on the main Nairobi road. The lodge is on the south side of the lake. To see the vultures entering or leaving their roosts in Hell's Gate, it is necessary to be there before 7.30 A.M. or after 6.30 P.M.

Lake Naivasha Hotel—South Lake Rd., P.O. Box 15, Naivasha, Kenya; phone Naivasha 13. <u>Rooms</u>: 34 units with bath or shower. <u>Amenities</u>: Dining room, lounge, swimming pool, rental boats. <u>Terms</u>: Single 1765—1845/-, double 2290—2450/-, half to full board, tax included.

★

There are other wetland birds here too—massive Goliath Herons, and slender Little Egrets prancing in the shallows. The other waterfowl seem to have just returned from a masquerade ball: there are Knob-billed Geese with their grotesque bill ornaments; Purple Swamp Hens with pink legs and massive red bills; Red-knobbed Coots, each with a pair of neat red knobs perched on its forehead, feeding among the lily pads; and splay-footed African Jacanas picking their way delicately from leaf to leaf. Occasionally a snakelike head pops out of the water as an African Darter gulps a fresh supply of air, and out along the mud at the edge of the papyrus there's a Black Crake, with bright apple-green bill and pink legs.

Not far from Lake Naivasha is Hell's Gate, recently named a national park. It is a huge gorge with precipitous rocky walls. The cliffs of this wild place are a major vulture roost, and Lammergeyer can be found.

The real wild heart of East Africa is on the open plains, with their vast herds of game animals: Nairobi National Park was no more than a foretaste. In Masai Mara Game Reserve, on the border with Tanzania, we can fully savor the enormous open sweep of the savannah, those vast golden stretches of gently rolling grassland with their dense patches of thorn scrub, scattered rocky outcrops, and flat-topped acacia trees with smooth yellow trunks marking the watercourses. This is an arid landscape, the red dust all-pervasive, and sunsets like burnished copper.

Most of our time is spent on game drives, looking for birds and large game. Herds of buffalo, zebra, and wilde-beest quickly become commonplace, together with the Yellow-billed Storks standing hunched around the water holes. Something is always happening. At one spot an old male baboon decides that the hood of the van is a comfortable resting place; at another a pair of huge black Ground Horn-bills waddle across in front of us, pausing nonchalantly to beat a lizard into pulp. Short-tailed Larks and longclaws fly up from the short grass, the Yellow-throated Longclaw a meadowlark look-alike, the Rosy-breasted with the yellow replaced by a rich salmon-red.

Some birds stand out from the constant succession of new species. Most memorable of all is the Lilac-breasted Roller, its plumage an exquisite blending of delicate blues, turquoise, mauves, and greens. It is a graceful bird, with slender, pointed tail feathers, and it sits up obligingly on the tops of the low shrubs to allow everyone a good view.

Masai Mara lies on the border to Tanzania southwest of Lake Naivasha. Continue down the Nairobi highway to the road to Narok, and then west to Ngorengore, when you turn left on the highway to the reserve.

Keekorok Lodge—Masai Mara National Park, P.O. Box 47557, Nairobi, Kenya; phone 335807. <u>Rooms</u>: Cottages; separate tenting area. <u>Amenities</u>: Dining room, lounge, swimming pool. <u>Terms</u>: Rooms—single from 2185/-, double from 2885/-, tents—single from 2135/-, double 2785/-; full board, tax included.

They're reasonably common, but I never hear anyone say, "Oh, just another Lilac-breasted Roller."

The skies over the plains are rarely empty. Vultures soar constantly, joined by Tawny Eagles and Augur Buzzards. Bateleurs hunt alone, their striking black body, white underwing, and short tail distinctive even at long distances, when they look rather like a pair of wings flying around unattached! From time to time other large raptors appear: over the escarpment at Hell's Gate, the black shape of a Verreaux's Eagle; at Thomson's Falls, the immense dark bulk of a Crowned Hawk Eagle, like a huge accipiter; and in many places the magnificent Martial Eagle, largest of the African eagles. At the other extreme a tiny Pygmy Falcon, little bigger than a starling, suddenly darts from a high perch, creating panic among a flock of even tinier finches.

There's first-class birding back at the lodge as well. A pair of Brown Parrots feeds quietly along the wooded watercourse, and an assortment of colorful barbets forage among the trees. Woodpeckers are harder to spot, but we do glimpse the small ladder-backed Cardinal Woodpecker and the larger Bearded Woodpecker, with a Pileated-like head attached to a body more reminiscent of a flicker.

Probably the most endearing bird of all is a small kingfisher. Striped Kingfishers are not much to look at, being mostly grayish-brown and white, and they are dry-country birds, feeding principally on insects. Once we see one in action we realize that this bird is the author of one of the more characteristic sounds of the African plains. Ridiculously tame, it sits in full view on the lower branches of an acacia. Periodically it celebrates life by shouting "whee-whee-whee"; at every "whee" it abruptly throws it wings wide open, as though rejoicing in the abundance of grasshoppers. The calls of this delightful little bird are to accompany us throughout the trip.

Tsavo National Park is even drier than Masai Mara, but animal life is still abundant—and different. Here we find the antelopes of arid areas, such as the fringe-eared oryx and long-necked gerenuk, looking like a gazelle crossed with a giraffe.

Wherever there is water there is birdlife, and it teems around the lodge at Kilaguni. Meals are shared with Yellow and Red-billed hornbills, crow-sized black-and-white birds with huge curved bills and the instincts of circus clowns. They share the stage with a host of smaller species such as

---

Tsavo is Kenya's largest national park, and is divided into east and west halves by the main Nairobi-Mombasa highway. Kilaguni is in the west half.

Kilaguni Lodge—Tsavo West National Park, P.O. Box 2, Mitito Andei or P.O. Box 30471, Nairobi, Kenya; phone 336858. <u>Amenities</u>: Dining room, lounge, swimming pool. <u>Terms</u>: Single from 1700/-, double from 2200/-, full board, tax included.

D'Arnaud's Barbet, with pepper-and-salt-spotted plumage, and finchlike White-billed and White-headed buffalo weavers. Out toward the water hole Marabou Storks stand around gloomily, like dyspeptic undertakers. Little flocks of guinea fowl scuttle among the scrub, and among the low branches of a creamy frangipani a Drongo sits, elegantly arrayed in black with a gracefully curved lyre-shaped tail. When night arrives, a Verreaux's Eagle Owl lands in the glow of the spotlights and sits briefly, glaring fiercely, before vanishing again into the darkness.

Most conspicuous of all are the starlings. Anyone whose contact with this family is limited to *Sturnus vulgaris* is totally unprepared for the gaudy array of brilliant birds that represent this family in the tropics. We have already met the vividly iridescent Glossy Starlings, two species decked out in varying shades of blue, green, and violet. Now we are introduced to the even more colorful Hildebrandt's and Superb starlings, which add chestnut bellies for contrast, and, in the case of the Superb, a neat highlighting of white on the breast and undertail. Even these leave us unprepared for the flock of glorious, jay-sized long-tailed birds that sweep in at lunchtime. Golden-breasted Starlings are a brilliant rich blue above, but the highlight of their plumage is the wonderful golden-yellow of the breast, a shade of an intensity unequaled in any bird I have ever seen. If I were forced—heaven forbid—to select one species as the world's most beautiful bird, I suspect this would be it.

Nearby Mzima Springs are an incredible outpouring of water for such an arid landscape. We drive to the parking lot and are welcomed by a large sign warning us of the potential dangers of wandering down the path ahead. While not exactly suggesting that we should abandon all hope, the sign does give food for thought but fails, as far as I can see, to deter anyone. And indeed, the entire path looks quite innocuous. It is difficult to remember that the herd of elephants on the far shore are wild and potentially dangerous, and that the BEWARE OF CROCODILES sign at the water's edge probably means what it says.

Rounding a corner two of us glimpse a merganserlike creature out in the water that promptly vanishes behind a clump of vegetation. Peters' Finfoot is a rare visitor to the springs, and a much-wanted bird for virtually everyone in the neighborhood. The crocodile warning is immediately put to the test as a herd of eager birders almost trip over it in their haste to get to the water's edge and see this rarity: sadly, it proves elusive and never reappears. Neither, however, do any crocodiles.

From Tsavo we head north through Mombasa up the coast to the Driftwood Beach Club south of Malindi, and a very different environment from anything we have visited so far: we're at the seaside! Before us stretches the Indian Ocean, glowing red in the sunrise with the palms rustling in the constant trade winds. The Malindi area has two draws for birders: one a shallow estuarine bay, Mida Creek, which is one of the major wintering grounds for Eurasian shorebirds on the African coast; the second the lowland Sokoke forest and the areas around the ruins at Gedi.

Mida Creek is at its best in winter when thousands of migrants crowd the flats, but it can be rewarding at any time. Near the mouth there are vast stands of mangroves; but farther up, the pale gray mud is covered with shorebirds. In summer these are principally first-year birds that have chosen to remain rather than undertake the migration back to the breeding grounds. Here and there are tall gangly Crab Plovers, relative locals that nest along the Indian Ocean; the Mongolian Plovers, running and pecking daintly along the flats, are birds of the high stony plains of the Himalayas. There are Curlew and Whimbrel and Greenshanks, all more familiar in western Europe than here; and the Terek Sandpipers with their jauntily tip-tilted bills, scuttling about actively, are visitors from the still, dark boreal forests of central Russia. In truth, however, all these birds will probably spend more of their lives right here at Mida Creek.

Malindi is on the coastal highway north from Mombasa through Kilifi, with the club south of town. The Gedi Ruins and Mida Creek are south of here again.

The Driftwood Beach Club—P.O. Box 63, Malindi, Kenya; phone 20155. Rooms: 26 cottages, most with bath and shower; twin beds. Amenities: Dining room, lounge, ocean beach. Terms: Single 560-1010/-, double 830-1330/-, family cottages 1920—4000/-, full board, tax included.

★

The most conspicuous bird here is not a waterbird at all,
but a large black-and-white creature dangling upside-down
in the nearby palms, hanging onto one of the clusters of fruit
as if its life depended on it, flapping wildly. Thus we are
introduced to the Palm-nut Vulture, or Vulturine Fish Eagle
as some books call it, with some understandable confusion
about its origins. This strange raptor eats palm nuts instead
of animal prey, although it will settle for a meal of shellfish
on occasion.

The next day we head inland to visit the ruins of Gedi, a
fifteenth-century Arab town now covered in dense tropical
forest. The trails here loop around the stone remains, and
they are a good way of getting close to some forest birds.
Birding here, like tropical forest birding generally, is difficult
and takes time. We have good looks at a Paradise Flycatcher,
its incredible tail seemingly twice the length of its body, and
a vivid Red-capped Robin Chat skulking in the undergrowth.
High above the canopy there are brief glimpses of hornbills
flying over on big floppy wings.

Kenya offers the opportunity of either organizing your
own trip, using a rental vehicle, or taking a conducted sa-

fari. There are certainly a multitude of the latter to choose from, both from North America and originating from Nairobi on your arrival in Africa. An organized tour eliminates most of the hassles that you can encounter when traveling unescorted. At best those can turn the trip into a test of endurance, and at worst into a nightmare. It is, I think, likely to be the preferred option for most travelers.

The disadvantages are that safaris are more expensive, you have no control of their schedule, and they often are not primarily oriented toward birds. It is important that you select a tour that is being organized for birding. This will assure that birds are the first priority, and you'll usually have lots of opportunity to see the big game as well.

It is also important to consider whether a safari's style is in keeping with your objectives. If you are determined to see every possible bird on your route, and have chosen a tour because its leaders are experienced and will show you more, then you are going to be frustrated by a relaxed operation that stops to photograph antelopes and buffalos. On the other hand if you would like to see more than just the birds and find a frenetic pace distasteful, you are going to be disappointed with a regimented tour that presses relentlessly from one bird to the next. Everyone's choice lies somewhere between those two extremes. Don't be too influenced by the impeccable credentials of the main leader. Remember that travel is in minibuses, and there may not be enough bird leaders to allocate one to each bus. Even though you're in a group, you shouldn't depend on someone else being available to identify all the birds for you.

Accommodation in a group is normally predetermined, but the game parks typically offer rooms in small cottages or cabins, sometimes with a tented camp option, and some safaris organize their own tenting. Tenting is usually comfortable and, while a little more spartan than the permanent accommodation, often has much better birding. It can be a good compromise between camping on your own and staying at the more structured facilities listed above.

If you're more adventuresome, then by all means organize your own trip. You should appreciate that travel in Africa is very different from travel in North America. Minor breakdowns and health problems can become major difficulties very quickly in remote parts of the country where help is not readily available. Even such simple matters as finding your way around can be a problem, because although English is an official language in Kenya you will discover that most people speak only Swahili.

A four-wheel-drive vehicle is desirable for some of the game parks, and you should carry first-aid equipment and supplies of spares with you in case of difficulties. The hazards you are likely to encounter can include problems with big game, but are more likely to be such things as theft, destructiveness by baboons, and a host of health problems from which the organized tour partially insulates you. The advantage of organizing your own trip is that you can stop as and where you wish, and visit locations that are not normally visited by safaris.

Whatever way you decide to travel, the health aspects of a Kenyan trip sound formidable. In fact, however, they represent no more than a few sensible precautions. Check with your doctor well in advance to find what shots are currently recommended for Kenya. They could include cholera, typhoid and yellow fever, and it is usually recommended to update your tetanus-polio shot as well. If you are traveling on your own and planning to go outside the main tourist routes, gamma globulin for hepatitis may be proposed as well. You will certainly have to undertake a malaria-prevention regimen, which starts before your departure and continues for a period after your return.

Once in Kenya itself you should be even more vigilant about avoiding heat exhaustion and undesirable insects than you would be in the warmer areas of the United States. Mosquitoes and biting flies here carry a variety of diseases, and it's important to be careful about using mosquito nets or, where your room is fully screened, making sure that the insects do not get in. Be meticulous about the use of insect repellent, and alert for such things as ticks and scorpions. Poisonous snakes are mainly nocturnal and are one of the good reasons for not wandering about at night. Also avoid

wandering around in bare feet and swimming in fresh water, as both can result in unpleasant infections.

With regard to food matters, avoid milk products, salads
and fruit that you have not peeled yourself, and try to stick
to cooked foods. Water is supposed to be safe to drink in
Nairobi and Mombasa, and the lodges often put a flask of
boiled water for use in the rooms, but when in doubt it is
better to stick to mineral water. In spite of all these precautions you will probably run into some difficulties, and it is
advisable to take medication with you for the treatment of
diarrhea.

The primary guide to Kenyan birds is still John Williams's
A Field Guide to the Birds of East Africa (with N. Arlott, 1980,
Collins), but C. A. W. Guggisberg's *Birds of East Africa* is now
available in the United States. This has superior illustrations
and more complete coverage, but should be used in conjunction with Lewis and Pomeroy's *A Bird Atlas of Kenya*.
Williams's *A Field Guide to the National Parks of East Africa*
(1967, Collins) is also essential equipment as it not only has
useful information on the parks themselves but also has
sections on identification of the mammals and some additional birds. If you are planning your own trip you should
obtain a copy of Ray D. Moore's *Where to Watch Birds in
Kenya* (1982, Transafrica Press), which is useful for the
many good birding areas outside the game parks.

FOR THOSE TIMES YOU'RE NOT BIRDING

Kenya's foremost attraction for the tourist is its large game,
and most of the safari trips are geared toward this. The drivers are usually good at identifying large mammals and pro-
ficient at finding them. They are not particularly good at
birding, and from time to time they had to be reminded that
we were more interested in looking over the flowering trees
on one side of the van than dashing after another possible
lion on the other; however, generally we found that it was
possible to do both. Unless you have been to East Africa
before, it is difficult to imagine any naturalist wishing to

tour the country without looking at the mammals as well as the birds.

Botanically the plains are most interesting in the rainy season (October to November and April through June), but at this time the game is more dispersed and travel is more difficult. Kenya has a fine array of plant life at any time, however, and the real shortage is of easily available material to identify the plants you find.

Most of the safari lodges have good food, comfortable accommodations, and safe swimming pools, and many people seem to prefer to spend their vacation sitting around the pool in the sun to going on dusty game drives. Scenically the Rift Valley is both beautiful and interesting, and there is much variety in the countryside, ranging from the high, forested Thomson's Falls to semidesert.

For those favoring such activity (or inactivity), there is the Indian Ocean for swimming or the beach at the Driftwood Beach Club for lounging. Scuba diving can be arranged and there are trips in glass-bottomed boats out to the Watamu National Marine Park to view the fascinating and colorful undersea fauna.

Urban attractions are fewer, but there is good shopping in Nairobi and Mombasa, both large, cosmopolitan cities. The Nairobi National Museum—Museum Rd., 15/-, 9:30 A.M.—6 P.M., phone 742131—has a good ethnological section and an interesting bird exhibit. Mombasa is a particularly attractive city, with historic old buildings and a busy port, and the country's fascinating cultural mix is particularly evident here.

★   ★   ★   ★   ★

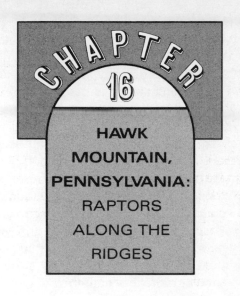

CHAPTER 16

HAWK MOUNTAIN, PENNSYLVANIA: RAPTORS ALONG THE RIDGES

MOST BIRDERS KNOW OF HAWK MOUNTAIN. IT is simply the premier spot for observing fall hawk migration in the eastern United States. Other places may record higher numbers of hawks or a greater variety of species, but in few places do the birds come so close to the observer or provide such satisfying experiences. Only at Hawk Mountain are the needs of the would-be watcher so well provided for, and the spectacle of hawk migration so well interpreted for the observer.

This begs the question, of course, of why hawk migration warrants such special attention. But hawks have always had the ability to inspire—for Hemingway even life itself was "a hawk in the sky." Few birds have the same ability to capture the imagination or generate such excitement. Those who have become ensnared by the allure of hawk watching schedule vacations and trips around their migrations, and spend hours and days at hawk lookouts.

Lookouts are those places where the migrants are channeled by accidents of topography into narrow flight paths, often following coastlines or, as at Hawk Mountain, mountain ridges. Instead of the half-dozen or so hawks that a birder might aspire to on a good day somewhere else, here the birds can pour past the observer in hundreds or even thousands. Each of these lookouts has its own distinctive character, intimately and affectionately known to its regulars. In some places the birds drift over at immense heights; at others they move almost at eye level. In some, five hundred birds makes a good day; at others you need ten thousand or more to satiate the aficionados.

Hawk Mountain Sanctuary is the most famous of these places. It was the first, and has consistently led the way both in stimulating an appreciation for hawks and developing an understanding of their movements. It is at once both remote and accessible. Much of eastern Pennsylvania is a land of small communities tucked into deep mountain valleys, with relatively little in the way of tourist accommodation, but well served by good highways. These assure easy access from the megalopolis to the northeast, yet the final approach to the mountain is as bucolic as anyone could wish. We drive past neat farms nestling among the wooded hills, crossing the Little Schuylkill River bubbling and sparkling over boulders, and head up through the tiny village of Drehersville, into the wooded hills. The road climbs steadily, narrowing until the trees close in on both sides, up through steep, forested slopes to the Sanctuary itself.

These are deciduous forests, but there are evergreens here nevertheless. In fall the dark, shiny greens of rhododendron and mountain laurel contrast with the yellows, reds, and bronzes of the falling leaves around them. A native of the Northeast is inclined to take the glorious tapestries of the autumn woodlands for granted: after all, they're there every year, and so are a source of familiar pleasure rather than of wonder and astonishment. It takes the eyes of a newcomer to really appreciate them, to marvel at the broad expanses of color, the subtle blending of hues, and the bold contrasts of vivid reds and golds. They're one of the world's splendid spectacles.

The scenery is an incidental but important part of the experiences at Hawk Mountain. A regular visitor during the autumn movements will come first during the oppressive days of August with Ospreys and American Kestrels passing, watch the first colors change in September as kettles of

Hawk Mountain is most easily reached from Route 61, which runs between Interstates 81 and 78. South of Pottsville take Route 895 east to Drehersville, turn right over the bridge, and then bear left up the hill.

Accommodation in the immediate area is limited, but there are several motels along Route 61, including the following, some 5 miles away:

Best Western Dusselfink Motor Inn—From Interstate 81, Exit 36S, south 13 miles; Exit 9A Interstate 78, north 13 miles). R.D. 3, Box 3728, Pottsville, Pennsylvania 17901. (717) 385-2407. Open all year. Rooms: 100 units; double, queen- and king-size beds. Amenities: Dining room, cocktail lounge. Terms: Single $34—52, double $42—60. AMEX, CB, DINERS, MC, VISA.

There is primitive camping in Appalachian Trail huts on the Sanctuary. The nearest serviced campground is: **Christmas Pines Campground**—From junction of Routes 61 and 895, go west 2 miles on 895, then north ½ mile on paved road, then ¾ mile east on gravel road. P.O. Box 375, Auburn, Pennsylvania 17922. (717) 366-8866. Open April 15—October 15. Campsites: 92 sites, 89 water and electricity, 3 no hookups. Shaded sites. Separate tenting area. Amenities: Rest rooms and showers, sewage disposal, laundry room, store, propane, ice, recreation room, basketball, volleyball, shuffleboard, horseshoe pit, playground. Terms: $8—11/4 persons.

★

Broad-winged Hawks spiral over, look out over the multi-hued hills of October as Red-taileds and accipiters fly by, and brave the cold winds and starker vistas of November when Golden Eagles and Rough-legged Hawks can be the rewards. The changing panorama, the huge vistas from the top of the mountain, the interplay of light and shadow below—all these are as intrinsic to Hawk Mountain as the hawks themselves, and much more predictable.

When we arrive, the Sanctuary is cloaked in low cloud. Even so, this is a wonderfully scenic place, with the gnarled oaks and dark laurels looming mysteriously out of the mist around the Center; but the weather is not good for seeing anything, let alone hawks. Fortunately the Center itself is full of interesting things to see and do—and buy!—and as

---

The Sanctuary is open 8 A.M.–5 P.M., and entry costs $3. There are toilets at both the Center and on the way to the lookout, and picnic lunches can be eaten at the lookouts themselves. There are no other meal facilities, and it's recommended that you carry something to eat even if you don't plan to stay all day. Also take a cushion to sit on; the rocks get hard after a while. You should wear hiking boots or good walking shoes, and take warm clothing, as the lookouts are exposed and can be cold.

There is much valuable material on hawks for sale at the store. An invaluable introduction is *The Mountain and the Migration* by James J. Brett, which discusses the location, the mechanics of migration, and the birds themselves, and includes lists and maps (1986, Hawk Mountain Sanctuary Association, Route 2, Kempton, Pennsylvania 19529. $9.43). The Center can sometimes assist in advising the prospects for watching on a given day; phone (215) 756-6961.

Two books that are good background reading are Maurice Broun's own *Hawks Aloft: the Story of Hawk Mountain* (1984 Dodd, Mead) and Michael Harwood's *The View from Hawk Mountain* (1973 Scribner's).

★

we wait for the weather to clear, chickadees and nuthatches dash in and out of the feeder by the window.

Weather is, indeed, a key element in hawk movement. We've seen hawks moving along the ridges in rain but they dislike such conditions, not to mention the problems of visibility the observers themselves face in a downpour. Even on seemingly ideal days, however, birds may be few. Hawk migration, like so much else in migration watching, is spotty; mind-boggling on some days and dead the next. Anecdotes of hawk migration in action are often composites, built of a memorable experience here, a huge flight there; to experience them fully you must be prepared to wait at the pleasure of hawks and weather!

When conditions finally clear we hike up the rocky three-quarter-mile trail to the mountain's main viewpoint, the North Lookout. Appropriately enough, it faces northeastward, a jumble of rocks over 1,500 feet high looking down nearly 1,000 feet to the thin line of the Little Schuylkill River far below. From here there's a sweeping panorama of Pennsylvania countryside, and the long, wooded line of the Kittatinny Ridge stretches ahead, its higher points along the skyline each thoroughly familiar to the regular watchers. Each is assigned its own number, one through five, to assist in locating approaching hawks, when the cry may be "Hawk over number one!" or, perhaps more precisely, "Osprey over number two!" To the right of the lookout lies an outlier of the ridge and the South Lookout, lower and with less spectacular views but often yielding a different mix of migrants.

Even the start of a day's movement has an excitement to it. In the fields and woods below, fall migrants are scattered through tangles of aster and goldenrod, and among trees just beginning to hint at their fall colors. All at once a hawk appears, soaring low over the treetops: a Broad-winged, it soars idly and vanishes. A moment later there is another from another part of the woodland, surely not the same bird. But then there is another, and another and yet another. Gradually the entire patch of woodland has broadwings soaring low over the canopy and swinging out over the open areas in search of rising air currents that will provide lift. Soon hawk after hawk is passing overhead, and then they are gone. Suddenly the morning seems empty—until another group appears.

Why is Hawk Mountain such a good place for watching these movements? The high points along the Appalachian ridges are natural viewing platforms for watching birds flying along them. Hawk Mountain is one of the very best: that exposed eminence of jumbled rocks faces out over the main line of the birds' movement.

Birders like to joke that hawks are lazy birds and prefer soaring to flying. In fact, soaring demands a lot less energy than direct flight, an important matter when the next meal is always uncertain. Soaring is the preferred mode of travel particularly for the Broad-winged Hawks and other buteos. They like to migrate by gliding southward from one rising current of warm air—the thermal—to the next, and using these thermals themselves to soar up and gain the altitude necessary for the next glide.

As the birds head south they encounter the long ridges of the Appalachians running southwest, and ideal conditions for a free ride along their journey. The northerly winds hit the slopes of the mountains and are pushed upward, creating a line of rising air that follows the line of the ridge. The hawks can start at one end and soar all the way along the crest of the ridge with a minimum of effort. In places the topography is broken and the birds continue south to the next ridgeline, and as Kittatinny forms the easternmost of the ridges, the birds will concentrate along it.

Even those hawks that are less well adapted for soaring than the buteos are only too ready to make use of the long lines of rising air. The accipiters, those elusive woodland hawks, migrate in steady flight with a few quick wing beats alternating with short glides, but they readily follow the ridgeline. Even the falcons, supreme fliers that often head out over open water on migration, also join the flights.

Hawks have an almost uncanny ability to locate rising air currents. My most dramatic recollection of this has nothing to do with Hawk Mountain, but everything to do with hawks. I think back to one late October morning, camped on a point on Lake Ontario. An icy northwest wind gusts leaden clouds over our heads, driving the remaining yellowing leaves from the trees. The fields are sere and brown, and here and there a few melancholy asters hang as reminders of the glories just a week or two earlier. Flocks of sparrows forage along the hedgerows, and a few late Tree Swallows rush past, regretting having postponed departure so late. In the sheltered lee of our vehicle we start to prepare breakfast on our camp stove. All at once we become aware that low, just over

our heads, soaring in the only rising column of warm air for miles, are a Red-tailed Hawk and a handful of Turkey Vultures. Where they came from and how they found our minuscule source of warmth is one of those mysteries of migration. But it is a weak thermal indeed; soon they drift off in search of something more sustaining, and we are left with another memory.

Once a good updraft is located, the birds' ability to exploit it can be dramatic. On another day we watch a Broad-winged Hawk appear at treetop height, flying with the characteristic short flaps that broadwings use when they have to fly at all. All at once it begins to soar, immediately joined by other birds moving down behind it, maybe twenty or thirty in all. They plane upward effortlessly, idly turning and banking to exploit every eddy in the rising air, and still continuing drift southwestward. But the slow-motion ballet is an illusion; in a mere quarter of a mile or so they are almost out of sight, tiny dots in the sky far above.

Such experiences are part of the mystique of hawk watching. Then there are the numbers. Broad-winged Hawks in particular can move in huge flocks. One fine morning finds us sitting quietly, watching the clouds in that mixture of hope and anticipation that always precedes a good day. Finally someone spots a kettle of broadwings far to the northeast, spiraling like a pinwheel of gnats against the fluffy white clouds. As we watch we become aware of more birds much closer, here moving at treetop height, then spiraling rapidly upwards to peel off high above with their wings set, gliding rapidly southwestward. Meanwhile more birds join the column of rising air, until we are looking at a gigantic column of spiraling broadwings. Then there are more to the south, to the west, to the east and, finally, all around. Within half an hour it is all over, but it seems as though all the broadwings of the world have just flown by and had staged the event especially for us.

In all, fifteen species of hawks appear annually at Hawk Cliff. Mid-September is perhaps the best time to see both numbers and a good variety of species, as the Broad-winged Hawk flight peaks then. American Kestrels and Ospreys are also at their most numerous, and most of the other species can be seen then as well. October brings the peak of the Sharp-shinned and Cooper's hawk flights, and the larger buteos—Red-taileds and Red-shouldereds—are more common than they are in September. By November the movement tails off, although Red-tailed numbers may peak at this time and it is the best period for seeing such rarer species as Northern Goshawk, Rough-legged Hawk, and Golden Eagle. Some movement even continues into December. Some species, like Northern Harriers, can occur throughout, and the same seems to hold for some of the more uncommon birds at the Mountain, such as Bald Eagles, Peregrine Falcons, and Merlins.

The weather conditions that stimulate hawk flights are the same as those that encourage southbound migration generally. The southward movement of a body of cold air is usually associated with the passage of a "low," with poor weather, heavy cloud, and rain. The winds then swing into the north and west, skies clear, and temperatures begin to fall. Now the ideal conditions for autumn migration are all present: good weather, favorable following winds, and cold, a potent warning of things to come. The birds don't reason it all out, but they do fly—millions of them. Hawk Mountain records confirm that the best flights occur when a low-pressure system with bad weather has passed to the north, with a cold front moving down from the Great Lakes and two or three days of northerly winds.

It's possible, of course, for most or all of the season to pass without these conditions developing. Some autumns have day after day of beautiful sunny bluebird weather, and others seem to be one long sequence of cloud and rain. The birds still move, and some of them are seen from the lookouts, but those are the years when the enthusiasts shake their heads sadly and start looking forward to next year! Yet there are other birds to be seen here as well as the hawks. Waterfowl and loons fly over, and flocks of robins or Blue Jays may pour past. Warblers may flit through the treetops below, a tempting snack for a passing sharp-shin.

The knowledge of what can be seen when, and how hawk migration is influenced by the weather doesn't come easily. Indeed, even so simple a matter as whether hawk numbers are increasing or declining cannot be achieved without systematic counts taken over long periods of time. In recent years such counts have become commonplace at many lookouts, but Hawk Mountain led the way. Systematic daily counts have been taken here each fall—except for a brief break during the war years of the 1940s—since 1934. Over 20,000 hawks are seen in the average fall migration.

While autumn has a particular enchantment on these Pennsylvania ridges, the other seasons have their delights as well. In spring brightly colored warblers move through the trees along the slopes. Hawks can be seen in the spring as well, but the ridges do not concentrate the birds in the way that they do in fall, and the movements are small. Wood Thrushes and Ovenbirds sing from the shady forests of summertime, and Red-bellied Woodpeckers dispute noisily. In places rarer southern warblers can be found—Hooded, Worm-eating, and Kentucky, and Louisiana Waterthrushes. Screech and Great Horned owls call at night, answered at times by Barred Owls from the swampy woodlands below.

Today Hawk Mountain is a center for those who wish to watch, admire, and learn about hawks. It was not always so. In the past we have been strangely ambivalent about these magnificent birds. Raptors have been at once admired and persecuted as "vermin." The mountain has more than its share of memories of those days. As the migrants moved along the line of the ridge, passing the lookouts at eye level, at one time those standing there didn't just watch the passing birds; they shot them.

In fact, the story of Hawk Mountain is the story of the change in attitudes toward birds of prey. It was the killing at the mountain that first drew attention to the place. The early tales of the carnage that used to occur at the mountain are appalling to us today—lines of hunters firing freely at every bird that passed, with the killing continuing through much of the hawk migration. Those who visited in those days found the ground below the lookout carpeted with dead and maimed hawks.

It was then that Richard Pough first visited the place and photographed long lines of dead birds that he had picked up below the lookout. The history of his efforts and those of

Rosalie Edge to stop the carnage and found the Sanctuary in 1934 is an inspiring story of conservation in action. But it took the dedicated efforts of Maurice Broun, the first curator, to make protection a reality and develop a true sanctuary on the mountain.

Broun and his wife retired in 1966, but their foundation was a good one and the sanctuary has continued to prosper. In fact it is almost too successful. There are over 50,000 visitors a year here now, and there is a limit to the capacity of the lookouts, the trails, and even the facilities around the center itself. Facilities have been expanded with new parking areas, but the problem of overcrowding remains. It is best to visit Hawk Mountain on a weekday and even then you are likely to find it crowded.

The mountain continues to be the preeminent venue for hawk watching, and nowhere else has quite its character, or its facilities. Nevertheless, there are other locations along the ridges where people now watch the migration. Well to

---

Bake Oven Knob is north from Allentown on Route 309 to the intersection of Route 143. Continue on 309 for 2 miles to County Road 39056 and turn right, then 2.1 miles and left on an unmarked road, bearing left up a steep hill to the parking area. The two lookouts are about ½ mile along the Appalachian trail to the right. From Hawk Mountain both Bake Oven Knob and the Route 183 location can be reached by driving east or west respectively on Route 895, but this road intersects with Route 309 north of turnoff on 39056, so you must then turn south on 309 and left on 39056.

Leaser Lake is west on Route 143 from the intersection with 309 described above, to the village of Jacksonville. The road to the lake is on the right just past the village, and there is a network of small roads around the lake that can yield the landbirds mentioned. Lake Ontelaunee is about 7 miles northeast of Reading on Route 222 to Maiden Creek and then left on Route 73.

★

the southwest is the Pulpit east of Chambersburg, and Waggoners Gap north of Carlisle. The two alternative locations nearest Hawk Mountain are on Route 183 as it crosses the ridge south of Pottsville, and Bake Oven Knob, which lies to the northeast. The birds at all these places are much the same as you can hope to see at Hawk Mountain itself.

Farther afield in the east there's excellent hawk watching at Cape May, and along the lower Great Lakes, Holiday Beach and Hawk Cliff on Lake Erie, west and east respectively of Point Pelee, are fine venues in fall (but not spring); while in spring flights occur at Grimsby in Ontario and Derby Hill in upstate New York.

While you are in the area of Hawk Mountain waiting for the weather to clear, there are some other places you can visit in the general area. The two closest wetlands are Leaser Lake, which is east of Hawk Mountain near Wanamakers, and Lake Ontelaunee near Reading. The latter is noteworthy for migrant waterfowl, and the area around Leaser Lake has had nesting Acadian Flycatchers, Golden-winged and Blue-winged warblers together with Grasshopper Sparrows, although these species would not be expected at the time of the main hawk migration.

THINGS TO DO WHILE IT'S RAINING

The beautiful countryside around Hawk Mountain abounds in outdoor recreational activities, with the Appalachian Trail running right through the Sanctuary. Locations of more passive interest are relatively few. This is Pennsylvania Dutch country, and at Lenhartsville, east on Interstate 78, is the Pennsylvania Dutch Folk Culture Center with special exhibits and shows—¼ mile south on Route 143 from Interstate 78; 10 A.M.–5 P.M., $3.00, (215) 562-4803.

There is much of historic interest farther south, with Valley Forge National Historic Park outside Philadelphia, and Philadelphia itself with its historic buildings and many interesting museums and galleries.

★   ★   ★   ★   ★

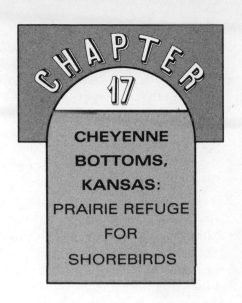

CHAPTER 17

CHEYENNE BOTTOMS, KANSAS:
PRAIRIE REFUGE FOR SHOREBIRDS

ANSAS IS A PLACE OF MEETINGS. IT IS A PLACE where the eastern forests meet the prairie, where southern birds meet northern birds, and—farther west—where the long-grass prairie meets the sagebrush and dry prairie of the far west. It's also a place that birders often zip through on their way to somewhere else, but in doing so they miss exciting birding, for here they can sample many kinds of habitats and the birds of each.

In the middle of all this, almost in the geographic center of the state, lies Cheyenne Bottoms, a wetland where some 30 percent of the continent's shorebirds stage on their way north. Not that shorebirds for a few weeks in spring is all the Bottoms has to offer. It's a major staging ground for other waterbirds as well, both spring and fall, and home for an abundance of nesting waterbirds, including a strangely isolated population of Mottled Ducks. Some twenty-five miles to the south is Quivira National Wildlife Refuge, another superb area of quite a different character, and with rather different birds. Together they form a premier birding destination, particularly in spring.

Great Bend is a convenient center for visiting both places. Otherwise it's unexceptional, and Cheyenne Bottoms itself is not a place that forces its presence upon you. Even as we drive down the highway to town it's not very noticeable, simply a wide expanse of low-lying land stretching off to the west. But it is wonderfully accessible, and once we turn on to the access road we find ourselves driving with wetland on either side, and ahead of us a road that loops up through the heart of the marsh with abundant opportunities for stopping, looking, and listening.

The marshes themselves are varied, a large central pool with extensive stands of cattail and some wide stretches of open water, and outer "pools" occupied by grass and sedge marsh, patches of open water, and reed beds. In the fall there's extensive hunting here, and these outer sections are evenly dotted with low mounds for the use of hunting blinds, but outside the hunting season these form convenient resting places for gulls and cormorants, and enough ducks to drive a hunter green with envy.

Shorebirds are dotted about over the flats, yellowlegs tripping about daintily pecking from side to side, Black-bellied Plovers trendily decked out in immaculate whites, grays, and blacks, and busy crews of dowitchers probing madly in the mud. Flocks of peep are scattered around, challenging identification even in bright spring plumages, and roly-poly little Semipalmated Plovers scuttle about with their stubby little orange-and-black bills, looking formally attired for their invertebrate lunches.

The fall numbers are spectacular, but not as spectacular as some of the spring peaks that can be seen here. Visualize 25,000 Long-billed Dowitchers, thousands of Hudsonian

Godwits and Baird's Sandpipers, and a single flock of 10,000 White-rumped Sandpipers! Fully 90 percent of the eastern populations of many of these species stage at Cheyenne Bottoms between late April and the end of May. Some of the 3,000 or so Wilson's Phalaropes stay to breed, and the same is true for the American Avocets that stop here.

There are other species as well. Out in one of the grassy areas are the dark backs of a flock of White-faced Ibis, and the rich cinnamon of drake Cinnamon Teal glows through the remains of last year's reeds. From time to time the birds raise their heads to scan the marsh warily with ruby eyes,

---

To reach Cheyenne Bottoms take routes 156 or 281 south from Interstate 70. The Bottoms are just northeast of Great Bend, lying between these two highways. The main entrance is east off 281 north 6 miles from the junction in town with Route 56.

Accommodation in Great Bend is concentrated in a strip just west of town. The following is one of the better locations:

Great Bend Holiday Inn—3017 West 10th (Route 56, 1 mile west of downtown), P.O. Drawer D, Great Bend, Kansas 67530. (316) 792-2431. Rooms: 175 units, suites, standard and king-size rooms. Amenities: Dining room, lounge, supper club, coffee shop, exercise room, indoor pool, whirlpool, sauna and steam, mini golf. Terms: Single $38–50, double $43–55. AMEX, CB, DINERS, MC, VISA.

There is little camping in the area. A primitive campground (free; no facilities except a picnic table) is along the west access road to Cheyenne Bottoms, in a pleasant wooded area. Otherwise the following has rather limited camping available:

Colossal Wash Systems—Overnight Park—On Route 56 east of downtown Great Bend. For information write to Colossal Wash Systems, 5292 Timber Creek, Great Bend, Kansas 67530. (316) 792-1483. Campsites: Electricity and water. Terms: $7.

★

and a Northern Harrier, one of the reasons for their alert-
ness, quarters low over the cattails beyond. Meanwhile
Great Blue Herons come and go, and from somewhere in
the distance come the rhythmic pumping sounds of a bittern.

And indeed sound is one of the most memorable facets in
the experience of these prairie wetlands. There is the constant hubbub of the Franklin's Gulls, the creaky songs of
Yellow-headed and Red-winged blackbirds, and the wails
and squawks of coots and Pied-billed Grebes. From time to
time from the fields surrounding the marsh we can hear the
distant songs of Western Meadowlarks, joyous liquid
phrases that somehow seem to epitomize all that is delightful about the prairie spring.

Quivira is a very different but equally enjoyable experience. The road to the refuge is bordered on either side by
flat fields of sorghum, and its entrance is a sandy graveled
road to the modest headquarters building. The refuge is a
long strip of prairie with pools and salt marshes following
the course of Rattlesnake Creek, and as soon as we leave
the headquarters we find ourselves skirting the first of
these, a large expanse of open water surrounded by reeds,
called the Little Salt Marsh. It has many of the same water-

The access road to the Bottoms from Route 281
passes the camping area on the right and then arrives
at the headquarters building. The only privies are here,
and maps and checklists are available. The road then
continues east, and finally divides to become a loop
that forms a rough circle with large pool in the center
and more wetlands on the outside. There are three side
roads running off the loop, dividing the areas on the
outside into a series of four pools. Two of these roads
head north to join a dirt crossroad, and the third runs
out to Route 156. There is a highway picnic area on 156
just north of here. All these roads can be worthwhile,
but some can be impassable in wet weather.

★

Quivira is south of Great Bend, via Route 281. Drive to County Road 973: the refuge guide identifies this as Road 636, but in any event it is a hard-surfaced road running east, some 22 miles south of the Route 50 intersection in town. Drive east about 14 miles to the Zenith road, which runs south, and the refuge entrance is on the north. Go into the headquarters for a map and checklist, and to check on road conditions. The roads on the refuge are usually satisfactory, but the east-west road at the north end, which leads back to 281, is both very sandy and clayey in places and can be difficult, particularly when wet. There are no public facilities on the refuge.

★

birds as Cheyenne Bottoms, and our interest is captured more by the prairie landbirds in the sandy grasslands through which we are driving.

North of the marsh itself the wires along the side roads have a rich array of birds; Eastern and Western kingbirds, Loggerhead Shrikes, and Scissor-tailed Flycatchers with their long, slender tails streaming loosely behind them, revealing wonderful patches of crimson as they fly up in pursuit of passing insects. Bell's Vireos sing jumbled little songs, Brown Thrashers root around in the areas of bush, and Lark Sparrows spook from the sandy patches along the road. In the distance a Mississippi Kite soars low over one of the shelter belt plantings. At one point a short detour leads through a prairie dog colony, where the tubby little animals sit in the mouths of their burrows flicking their black-tipped tails, people-watching.

The wetland highlight at Quivira is at the north end of the drive, where there is a one-way loop through the Big Salt Marsh, and once again we find ourselves surrounded by all the excited bustle of a prairie marsh. As we have lunch by the biggest pool, male Ruddy Ducks are displaying, snapping tails back and forth, blowing little bubbles and jerking their cobalt bills up and down with tooty noises, while the girls respond with excited, squeaky little quacks. Egrets stalk in the shallows, and on a mud flat in the distance a group of American White Pelicans sits sedately, like a group of portly gentlemen after a heavy dinner.

As the road turns north a series of shallow salt-encrusted pools opens up on our right, and above them, hovering daintily, are Least Terns. This is one of the few places in Kansas where this endangered species can be found. These

---

An excellent reference to the state as a whole is *A Guide to Bird Finding in Kansas and Western Missouri* by John L. Zimmerman and Sebastian T. Patti—1988, University Press of Kansas, Lawrence, Kans. 66045. The Kansas hotline is (316) 343-7061.

There were shorebirds to be seen at the Bottoms in spring 1989, but given the uncertain water supplies it might be worthwhile to check on current conditions when planning a visit. The relevant phone numbers are: Cheyenne Bottoms Wildlife Area (316) 793-7730 and Quivira National Wildlife Refuge (316) 486-2393.

Quivira and the Bottoms combined list over 330 species, although sheer numbers of shorebirds are the main features of a spring visit here. The heavier movements occur between mid-April and mid-May, a time when many prairie birds are also at their most visible. You can cover each area comfortably in a day, but you'll likely want more than one visit, and a trip can easily be extended into a week or more with visits to the prairie areas elsewhere in the state.

---

white crystalline flats are also home to Snowy Plovers, those pale phantoms of the salt flats. Quivira has other delights as well, including Black-necked Stilts and several species of rail. King, Sora, and Virginia can all be found along the route we have just driven, and Black Rails are reputed to occur in the wet fields on the north side of the township road west of the loop drive.

Both areas have much to offer in fall as well, although the vast concentrations of shorebirds do not occur at this time, and the birds are more difficult to locate due to the heavier vegetation. Cheyenne Bottoms in particular attracts enormous numbers of waterfowl—in places the water becomes black with them—and huge flocks of roosting blackbirds that are a spectacle in themselves. But for us the most exciting features of a fall visit are the flights of Sandhill Cranes. They're common here in the spring as well, but by May they have already moved on.

It's late afternoon when the Sandhills start to return to the Bottoms. We can watch this scene for an hour or more and never tire of the big birds and their wild calling; we set out to tour the marshes, and end up sitting watching cranes. At first small flocks appear, then larger groups, massing in the grassy wetlands around the refuge like herds of small gray cattle. As evening approaches the flocks become more and more numerous, until straggling lines and clusters of flying birds are approaching slowly from every direction, the more distant no more than wisps, smokelike against the luminous sky. As the birds come closer some drop directly into the marsh, but many of the larger groups instead soar upward in a final celebration of the power of flight, their throaty calls echoing in a kind of evensong. They soar and bank slowly, almost idly, the flocks breaking into smaller groups that spiral independently, crisscrossing in an intricate, slow-motion ballet. Gradually the birds begin to descend, wings set and legs outstretched, like interceptors returning to the flight deck of some supercarrier, until they finally land with heavy wing beats among the rest.

Once—just once—there was a larger bird in one of the little groups, and we glimpsed white plumage and black wing tips as the flock dropped into the distant reedbeds. Whooping Cranes are rare but regular visitors with the Sandhill flocks at both locations.

Cheyenne Bottoms and Quivira are similar in size— 19,857 and 21,820 acres respectively—but they are under different jurisdictions. Quivira is a National Wildlife Refuge, but the Bottoms are a State Wildlife Area established in the 1950s, and the present system of five pools (one in the middle and the others around the outside) and dikes was constructed at that time. There is a system of canals to divert water from the Arkansas River, and neighboring creeks supplement the water supply. The aim is to maintain water depths at around 24 inches with the pools drained in rotation, but water supply is always uncertain, with too much water in some years and not enough in others. As the result of the exceptional drought of 1988 the Bottoms dried up completely in the following spring, and Quivira was not much better.

Some of the other noteworthy Kansas species are easily accessible from Great Bend. To the northeast along Interstate 70 in the vicinity of Manhattan, there are areas of long-grass prairie where such typical species as Greater Prairie-

Chicken, Upland Sandpiper, Dickcissel and Grasshopper sparrow can be found. Farther east again, near the border with Missouri, oak-hickory forest begins to replace prairie, together with a variety of distinctively eastern forest species. For a taste of the drier west, the high plains in the southwest corner of Kansas can yield Lesser Prairie-Chicken, together with Scaled Quail, Cassin's Sparrow, and Lark Bunting. The Cimarron National Grasslands near Elkhart are the best places to find these species.

Just as Kansas offers a fascinating mix of north and south, east and west in its birdlife, so does the flora change from oak-hickory forest to the east, through long-grass prairie, to short-grass prairie in the west. Hence the state offers much to the botanist as well.

OTHER POINTS OF INTEREST
NEAR GRAND BEND

Pawnee Rock State Monument, 13 miles southwest of Great Bend on Route 56, preserves a huge red sandstone outcrop that was a landmark on the Santa Fe Trail. It was the scene of many engagements between wagon trains and Indians, and among the Indians themselves. The Santa Fe Trail itself is commemorated in the Santa Fe Trail Center Museum and Cultural Center some 12 miles farther southwest at Larned—2.5 miles west on Route 156; 9 A.M.–5 P.M., $2 (316) 285-2054. East of Great Bend at Lyons, the Quivira Relics County Museum—105 W. Lyon St. 8.30 A.M.–5 P.M. Free (316) 257-3941—includes historic artifacts from this period and from the earlier Indian cultures.

Both Great Bend and Hutchinson (east of Quivira) are oil towns; the latter is also a major salt-mining center, and its grain elevator is one of the largest in the United States. The Kansas Cosmosphere and Space Center here—1100 N. Plum St. (316) 662-2305—features regular shows ($4) that simulate space travel.

★   ★   ★   ★   ★

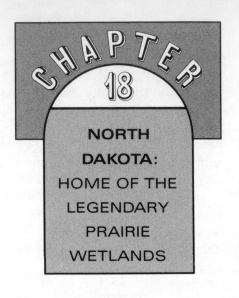

CHAPTER 18

NORTH DAKOTA: HOME OF THE LEGENDARY PRAIRIE WETLANDS

F OR MANY, A TRIP ACROSS THE PRAIRIES IS AN exercise in boredom. For a birder it's an adventure, an expedition into places teeming with life and rich with species that can be found nowhere else on the continent. Some of North America's most wanted birds live on the prairies.

In many ways North Dakota is the quintessential prairie state. Here are the sweeping vistas, the wide grain fields and endless sky. It is a land of extremes, bitter cold in the winter and often hot in summer. And the landscape may be parched for weeks, and then deluged in violent storms that batter the very crops they promise to save.

Yet the land is neither as flat nor as arid as it might first appear. Tucked into the gently rolling landscape are innumerable hollows, each with its own small pothole of water, with its own complement of water plants and birds, while on a much larger scale broad rivers etch their way into the landscape, meandering through steep-sided valleys, their courses garnished with woodland. Both habitats are alive with birds, and together they make the state one of the premier birding venues on the continent.

It is early when we set out from Minot. Dawn in North Dakota has a clear brilliance; a huge expanse of sky tinted in soft reds and blues, with little fluffy pink clouds. The features of the flat landscape seem inconsequential on such a vast canvas. I had an aunt who once saw a picture of such a prairie sky, and asked what the little things at the bottom were. They were grain elevators.

Our destination today is the Des Lacs National Wildlife Refuge to the northwest. North Dakota has more National Wildlife Refuges than any other state, and Minot is a handy center for visiting several of them. To the south lies Audubon N.W.R., a part of the Garrison Dam wetlands, while to the north lie a group of refuges formed by the damming of the Souris River as it loops down from Canada and back up again on the way to its appointment with the Assiniboine. On the eastern side of the loop is the J. Clarke Salyer Refuge, while farther west the Upper Souris lies a few miles north of Minot. Des Lacs is farther northwest again at Kenmare, on a tributary of the Souris River. Lostwood National Wildlife Refuge is an associated area a few miles west of the river. It preserves native prairie plant and animal associations. Each of the refuges has a distinctive character all its own.

Des Lacs was the site of the first American Birding Association convention, in 1973. The residents of Kenmare know about birders! Few communities are so intimately associated with a wildlife refuge: it sits on the east bank of one of the refuge's main lakes, and one of the best birding routes runs south from town. For the birder wishing to stay close to the refuge itself there is limited accommodation right in town, although we prefer to stay in Minot, which has far more facilities. On our arrival at Kenmare we head straight for the refuge headquarters to pick up a map and check-list—the latter covering all the Souris Bend refuges.

Des Lacs consists of almost 19,000 acres along the Des Lacs River, here impounded to form a series of narrow lakes. The reserve is a strip along some thirty-five miles of river, but from a birding point of view only the bottom twelve miles or so, north and south from Kenmare, are accessible. The road roughly bisects this into two sections: the Upper Lake, which includes the entire area north of Kenmare, and the Middle and Lower lakes, running south from

---

Access for those flying to Bismarck, the state capital, is by driving the 110 miles north to Minot, an interesting drive that passes a host of pothole marshes and Audubon National Wildlife Refuge; alternatively you can fly direct to Minot, which, however, has much more limited service.

There's a wide range of accommodation in all price ranges at Minot. We found the areas on the north edge of town to be the most convenient, and there are several restaurants and fast-food outlets there:

Best Western International Inn—1505 North Broadway (on Frontage Rd. off Route 83, north edge of Minot), P.O. Box 777, Minot, N.D. 58701. (701) 852-3161. Open all year. Rooms: 270 units. Amenities: Dining room, cocktail lounge, indoor pool. Terms: Single $37–47, double $47–57. AMEX, CB, DINERS, MC, VISA.

There are several campgrounds southeast of town. None seems especially birdy, but likely the best—because it backs on a slough—is:

Minot KOA Campground—R.R. 4, Box 180, (6 miles southeast of Route 83 on 52 East) Minot, N.D. 58701. (701) 839-7400. Fully open April 15–October 15. Campsites: 65 sites, 15 full hookups, 9 water and electricity, 26 electricity only. Shaded or sunny sites. Tents welcome. Amenities: Game room, volley ball, playground, laundry room, store and sewage disposal. Terms: Base rate $10/2 adults; water $1, electric $2, sewer $1.

★

To reach Kenmare from Minot, take Route 52 north-west some 50 miles. For the Refuge turn left in town on County Road 2, crossing the lake and bearing left. The entrance to the Headquarters is a short way up the hill off County Road 1A, which continues on to Tasker's Coulee. The lake road along the east shore of the Middle and Lower Lakes runs southeast from Kenmare to join Route 52, and the road that follows the west bank of the Upper Lake is right off County Road 2 (bear right at the bottom of the hill after leaving town). It is inadvisable to attempt any of these roads if they may be wet without first checking on their condition at headquarters, as they can be impassable.

there. On the lower lakes we find the most abundant waterbird nesting areas.

We head south from town on the dirt road along the east bank of the lakes, passing open expanses of water interspersed with reedbeds. Scattered through here, some resting out in the middle and others busy with nesting duties, are Western Grebes. They're striking birds and, together with their close relatives the Clark's Grebe, the most elegant of the family. Their immaculate white breasts and forenecks contrast sharply with their black upper parts, and a dagger-like yellow bill and bright ruby-red eye complete the effect.

The resting birds are no more than black and white mounds out on the water, but from time to time we are treated to glimpses of courtship displays from the other birds. Periodically pairs rear up, their necks in graceful curves, and race across the water side by side like runaway figureheads from the prow of some Paleolithic ship, their breasts gleaming and eyes glistening in the sun. In another display the birds face each other and pull clumps of vegetation from the water, offering these soggy masses to each other, apparently a guaranteed turn-on in the grebe world.

Eared Grebes, nesting in shallower parts of the wetland, present a totally different but equally fascinating picture.

The colonies rest on little mounds of vegetation dotted over the water like tiny islands. Each mound is topped by a grebe, its dark plumage relieved by a golden sunburst of feathers on the side of its head, its tiny bill tip-tilted upward at a jaunty angle. Placid they're not—the entire colony is a hive of activity as pairs greet one another, reach out to squabble with neighbors, or steal hunks of vegetation from adjacent mounds.

Waterbirds are far from the only features of interest on this road. To the east are grassy hillsides with scattered thickets of shrubs. From each come the distinctive Bronx cheers of Clay-colored Sparrows, the pale sandy little singer usually perched on one of the outer branches of the bush. Along the brow of the hill a Swainson's Hawk is hanging, wings uptilted, watching for movement in the grassland below.

We have lunch in the picnic area in Tasker's Coulee, a beautiful wooded bowl that is alive with birds. An Eastern Phoebe hangs around the washrooms here, and Black-billed Magpies flap laboriously across the clearing, their long tails dangling behind. Over lunch we quickly locate most of the commoner birds of wooded areas on the prairies.

The third good access point to birding at Des Lacs is a dirt road following the west shore of the Upper Lake. It runs through wooded areas below the bluff for a few miles to a delightful picnic area on the shoreline, before heading back up the hill to return to the county roads. It's particularly good in migration periods when there are good views of Snow Geese out on the water, and migrant passerines working their way through the wooded areas. In the nesting season we find more grebes, together with all the other typical birds of the prairie marshes: Forster's Terns hovering airily out over the pools, and Yellow-headed Blackbirds gurgling from the tops of the cattails. A Sora whinnies from somewhere in the reeds, and high overhead a flock of American White Pelicans soars in slow motion, the sun flashing on their white plumage as they bank in unison, their wing tips blacker than black itself.

At the far end of this road is an observation blind at a Sharp-tailed Grouse dancing ground. You must be very early in the morning to see the birds in action, and obtain permission from the refuge first. It's worth the effort. The males gather at dawn to posture and dance, heads lowered, wings drooping, and purple throat sacs distended, their feet stamping rapidly and their pointed tails erect. The whole affair is sharply reminiscent of some of the dances of the Plains Indians, and these displays were obviously the source of the Indian inspiration.

Lostwood National Wildlife Refuge is west of Des Lacs, and consists mainly of mixed grass prairie with scattered potholes and small lakes. Several of these are alkaline, and

---

To reach Lostwood National Wildlife Refuge drive west on County Road 2 to Route 8 and turn south, or alternatively use Route 50 west. The entrance to Lostwood is 6.3 miles north of the junction of Route 50 and 8. Note that the tour road may be closed in wet weather, and from September 14 to May 1. There are no facilities here.

---

they are nesting habitat for Piping Plover and American Avocet, while the prairie areas can yield such species as Sprague's Pipit, Lark Bunting, Baird's Sparrow, and Chestnut-collared Longspur. There is a 7.5-mile tour road that covers some of the better habitat, and several hiking trails.

Upper Souris National Wildlife Refuge is on the Souris itself north of its confluence with the Des Lacs River. Like Des Lacs, it consists of a series of wetlands nestling under the high bluffs that bound the flood plain of the river. Once again we visit the refuge headquarters for a map and for the leaflet giving directions to the area's "unique" bird species. There's less area to cover at Upper Souris than at the other two refuges, but in many ways it is our favorite.

The auto tour road runs up over the prairie and then down past a series of large pools, and a series of hiking trails loop out over the prairie and around the pools themselves. Walks out on these yield both Sharp-tailed and Le Conte's sparrows singing their buzzy little songs. The access road continues north for a short distance along the side of Lake Darling, the area above the dam, to a picnic area and views of the waterbirds at the bottom end of the lake.

A little farther on the right is the field where Sprague's Pipit and Baird's Sparrow can be found, although heard is a more accurate description, at least initially. The pipit soars high overhead, no more than a dot in the sky, pouring out descending cascades of light, silvery notes; while the sparrow has an even more silvery trill, a beautiful little song originating from some ill-defined spot out over the grassland.

Just southwest of the refuge headquarters a road leads down to another picnic area and hiking trail along the river. This is a particularly delightful birding spot. While we are wandering through here a Great Horned Owl calls from the woodlands opposite and a Prairie Falcon appears unexpectedly, following the course of the water and spooking a pair of Hooded Merganser that are swimming nearby. The woodlands have the typical prairie mix of orioles and Yellow Warblers, Least Flycatchers and House Wrens—all very visible and, to eastern eyes, surprisingly abundant.

Northeast of Minot is the largest and most remote of the three Souris Loop refuges, the J. Clark Salyer National Wildlife Refuge. It encompasses some forty miles of the east loop of the river, running up to the Canadian border, and covers 58,700 acres in all, but unlike the other refuges the terrain is relatively flat, at least in the main areas to the

---

Upper Souris is about twelve miles north of Minot between Routes 52 and 83, and is accessible from either one. County Road 6 runs west from 83 to cross the refuge and then connect with 52 near Carpio. The refuge headquarters is on this road east of the dam. It also has folders on mammals and native grasses.

★

south. The auto tour road here is 22 miles long, with a separate 5-mile "trail" farther north, devoted specifically to prairie grasslands.

A fall visit to J. Clark Salyer gives an idea of how rich these refuges are outside the breeding season. It's October, and apart from a few cars on the township roads we have the place to ourselves. Soon the morning overcast clears to a sparkling blue autumn day, and the tour road loops south to cross the main marshes. Here are walls of cattails, but in the openings there are vistas of wide mud flats and pools dotted with ducks.

We're surprised at the number and variety of shorebirds. Most are snipe, dozens of them, all probing away as though their very lives depended on it—which, I suppose, is literally

---

J. Clark Salyer National Wildlife Refuge is east off Route 14 with its main entrance 3 miles north of Upham. From Minot the best route is probably north on Route 83 and then east on surfaced and good gravel roads to Upham. The last 14 miles of the auto tour road and the grassland trail farther north are dry-weather roads only. There are privies and picnic areas at the refuge headquarters and, about halfway along the tour, at the Thompson Place, an old homestead site.

★

---

quite true! But there are some peep here too, and dowitcher, with Killdeer and Pectoral Sandpiper. Here and there are yellowlegs, picking their way delicately across the flats as though afraid of getting their feet dirty.

In October the Snow Geese arrive from their nesting grounds on the tundra, carpeting the marsh white. During lunch, flock after flock flies over in irregular lines and V's, glistening white against the blue of the sky, the groups spotted here and there with the darker shapes of the blue geese. One by one the birds drop down to join those already in the marsh, their clamor rising and falling as newcomers land. Finally the large dark bulk of a Bald Eagle passes over, and the entire mass erupts into flight, like enormous feathers

Audubon National Wildlife Refuge is about 50 miles south of Minot on Route 83, immediately east from the south side of the causeway across Lake Sakakawea. The dam itself can be reached via Route 48, which runs south from Coleharbor, just south of the refuge, to Route 200 and then westward. It is the areas on the south side of the road that are of interest. There are picnic areas at Garrison Dam and on the north side of the Route 83 causeway, but no facilities at Audubon itself.

bursting from a gigantic mattress. But the disturbance is only temporary and the birds soon settle back, the din of voices subsiding to a low hubbub in the distance.

The open country around the marsh has its own birdlife. American Pipits are calling overhead, and in a couple of places small flocks of brown birds whirl up from the roadside, flashing white as they bound away, Lapland Longspurs going south. Hawks—Red-taileds and harriers—appear from time to time moving steadily southward, and a smaller bird sitting unsteadily in the topmost boughs of a distant cottonwood turns out to be a Northern Shrike.

Finally the road turns west to parallel the river, and we enter riverside woodlands with chickadees and Downy Woodpeckers. Sparrow flocks forage along the field edges. They're mainly White-crowneds, but in almost every flock there are Harris' Sparrows, striking larger birds with black faces and bold pinkish bills. Along one of the wooded creeks ducks materialize under the spreading boughs, dark birds until they emerge into the sunlight, when they are transformed into exquisite studies in rich reds and maroon: drake Wood Ducks.

In summertime this refuge has all the marsh species that you will find in the other two but is particularly reliable for Le Conte's Sparrows; in fact, there is one stop on the tour route specifically designated for this species. Sedge Wrens are particularly common in this sector, Short-eared Owls oc-

The only bird-finding guide to this area is rather dated, but still useful. It is *A Birder's Guide to North Dakota* by Kevin J. Zimmer (1979, L. & P. Press, Box 21604, Denver, Colo. 80221). It's one of the late James Lane's series of finding guides, and follows the same general approach and format.

North Dakota is a destination more for the special prairie species you can find here than for big lists. Nevertheless, the Souris Loop checklist alone has 293 species, including 23 accidentals. Some 150 species nest. Des Lacs and J. Clark Salyer will occupy a minimum of a day each, and although the other two areas need less time you will probably need four days to a week to have enough time to cover everything well.

★

cur, and Yellow Rails have also been reported from these areas of the marsh. The riverside woodlands and sandhill areas give access to upland habitats that are not present to the same degree on the other reserves. Sharp-tailed Grouse and Gray Partridge are among the species that can be found in these wooded areas, and both Say's Phoebe and Moun-

tain Bluebird are local nesting birds. Sandhill Cranes have nested at J. Clark Salyer in the past, but you are more likely to see these birds passing over in migration.

The other good areas are located south of Minot. Audubon National Wildlife Refuge is a 14,735-acre area at the east end of the Garrison Dam impoundment. There is a 7.5-mile auto tour road here covering prairie and wetland habitats along the south shore of Lake Audubon, and most of the prairie species that can be found at the Souris Loop reserves are here as well. Canada Geese breed, and Greater White-fronted Geese occur more frequently on migration than in the other refuges.

Garrison Dam itself is of interest more in winter, when the waters below the dam are one of the few areas of open water in a frozen landscape and hence waterfowl, gulls, eagles and other hawks concentrate in numbers. It can be good in migration times as well, particularly as there are a few areas of sheltered cottonwoods that can attract landbird migrants.

SOME OTHER FEATURES OF
INTEREST AROUND MINOT

Whatever your views of Garrison Dam, it is an imposing structure, one of the world's largest earth-filled dams. There are free guided tours of the power house in the summertime, and ample boating and fishing opportunities both below the dam itself and on Lake Sakakawea.

Minot had an early reputation for lawlessness, but today is more noted for its winterfest in February and Norsk Hostfest in mid-October when the local Scandinavian culture is celebrated. There's a Pioneer Village and Museum — 1¼ miles east on Route 2B, Tuesday–Sunday 1–8 P.M., May 31–October 31, $1. (701) 839-0785 — with artifacts from the area's past.

To the south the pleasant town of Bismarck is the state capital, and has a number of places of general interest, including the capitol building itself.

★   ★   ★   ★   ★

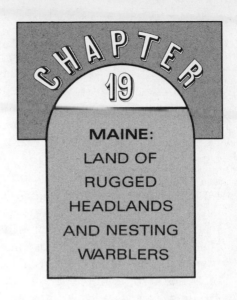

CHAPTER 19

MAINE: LAND OF RUGGED HEADLANDS AND NESTING WARBLERS

ONE THING THAT HELPS MANY EASTERN BIRD-ers through the long winters is anticipation of the war-bler migration. For a week or two in spring the wood-lands are filled with a kaleidoscope of bright colors as the birds pass on their way north. It's a fleeting delight; dingy fall plumages dominate the return movement, and we have to wait until another spring rolls around to see the vivid mites again. At one time or other we all covet a closer glimpse of these enchanting creatures on their breeding grounds, a remote vastness vaguely identified as "the north woods."

Maine is a part of that mysterious region, and it offers not only an array of breeding warblers, but magnificent scenery, unparalleled atmosphere, and the seacoast to add the tang of coastal waterbirds to the mixture. The best birding on the entire coast is on Mount Desert Island, connected to the mainland by a short bridge, and a place of rugged headlands, deep, sheltered fjords, winding roads, and little fishing villages. Large parts of the island are occupied by Acadia National Park, and it is there that some of the finest birding can be found.

The island forms a transition zone between southern birds and more northern species—ironically the northerners occur in the southwest, and the more southern species are in the woodlands to the east—and in all, twenty warbler species nest. It's also a great place in migration time, and many rare wanderers have ended up here. In fact, over 320 of Maine's some 400 species have been recorded from Mount Desert Island. Add in the *Bluenose* ferry, which crosses the Gulf of Maine from Bar Harbor to Yarmouth, Nova Scotia, and is probably the easiest way of seeing pelagic birds in season, and you have an exciting mixture available nowhere else in the United States.

The island got its name from Samuel de Champlain in 1604. He called it L'isle de Monts Deserts, probably from the ancient granite mountains that dominate the place. Cadillac

Mount Desert Island is reached via Route 3 from Ellsworth, itself southeast of Bangor via Route 1A. The island is almost cut in half by the deep fjord of Somes Sound. Route 3 leads to Bar Harbor and then loops down to parallel the coastline of the eastern section before heading up to join Route 198, which continues up to rejoin 3 just south of the bridge back to the mainland. For the best birding, however, enter the national park at Hulls Cove (north of Bar Harbor off Route 3) and follow the one-way loop road, which runs close to the sea. The western section of the island is accessible via Routes 102 and 102A, the latter with the bog and other good areas along it. Be sure to obtain a map at the park entrance, which shows the full road network in detail.

★

Mountain is the highest, at 1,530 feet the highest point on the Atlantic coast north of Rio de Janeiro. The rounded tops of these exposed heights are the home of alpine flowers, and are great places for watching hawk movements in the fall.

Cadillac Mountain looms ahead of us as we head down from Ellsworth, but you cannot sense the real quality of the island until you enter the national park itself. Soon we're driving through forests of spruce and fir, along a road that offers tantalizing glimpses of the sea. A rugged rocky shoreline looks even more fascinating in the frequent mists than it does in bright sunshine, when it is merely enchanting. These northern forests have a beauty all their own. The dark gray trunks of the conifers rise from a thick carpet of lush green mosses, their trunks encrusted in lichens and the branches festooned in yellow-green usnea lichens.

We head over to the southwest, to the woods near Bass Harbor Head. Here the spruce grow tall and dense, and from the matted tangles of boughs above come the songs of warblers, the sleepy lisp of Black-throated Green and thin notes of a Bay-breasted. We could be anywhere in the boreal forest, until the malevolent laughter of a passing Great Black-backed Gull puts things back into context. Somewhere, just beyond those dense, tangled branches, is the sea.

Some of the park's best birding areas are clustered in this southwest section, close to the Seawall campground. The small salt marsh at Bass Harbor can yield Sharp-tailed Sparrows, and two nearby trails lead out onto small headlands. The first is the Ship Harbor Trail, and the second is called Wonderland. Don't let the Hollywood terminology put you off—both trails really are wonderful: tranquil walks through aromatic spruce forests and across flower-spangled grassy clearings and lichen-encrusted ledges close to the shore. These are places for northerners such as Boreal Chickadee and Gray Jay, and both Olive-sided and Yellow-bellied flycatchers have bred. One day we glimpse that dark phantom of the spruce forests, a Black-backed Woodpecker, vanishing silently through the tall trees like a ghost. Eighteen species of warbler nest here in these woodlands, and they're one of the places we come back to again and again.

Yellows are the dominant motif with the breeding warblers. Yellow with bold black stripes for a Magnolia, bright yellow with red stripes for a Yellow, lemony yellow and dark

---

The best camping is in the park, where there are also the usual day-use facilities (park entry fee $5/vehicle). Only Blackwoods campground will accept reservations, no earlier than 56 days prior to the date required. Both campgrounds are usually full in season (this is the most heavily visited national park in the United States), but there are a dozen private campgrounds on the island:

Acadia National Park— P.O. Box 177, Bar Harbor, Maine 04609. (207) 288-3338. Amenities: Rest rooms with cold running water, dump station, nature program. Hot showers and supply store within ½ mile of both campgrounds. Restrictions: 14-day limit.

Blackwoods Campground—off Route 3, five miles south of Bar Harbor. Open all year, full facilities mid-May—mid-October. Campsites: 310, no hookups. Terms: $10.

Seawall Campground—on Route 102A, four miles south of Southwest Harbor. Open late May to late September. Campsites: 211, no hookups. Terms: $8 drive-in site; $5 walk-in site.

There is ample accommodation in Bar Harbor, but vacancies can be difficult to find in the summer. The following is close to the ferry terminal, and not far from the park entrance:

Holiday Inn Bar Harbor Regency—123 Eden St., Bar Harbor, Maine 04609 (on Route 3 adjacent to Bluenose Ferry Terminal). (207) 288-9723. Open May through October. Rooms: 224 units; 2 double beds, king-sized beds, and sofa. Amenities: Oceanfront dining room, lounge, exercise room, heated pool, sauna, whirlpool, golf, tennis, beachfront jogging, nature path, fishing. Terms: Standard $69–159, king $79–159. AMEX, CB, DINERS, MC, VISA.

★

green for a Wilson's, yellow with a delicate necklace for a Canada. Then there are the ones with yellow touches to the decor: rump, crown, cheeks, undertail. They're all here, and unlike those transitory spring migrants, they stick around! To find them you must seek out their habitats. Magnolias in spruces, Yellows in shrubbery, and Canadas in swampy woodlands. Alder thickets are places for Wilson's Warblers—thickets like those around the Big Heath.

The Big Heath is just over the road from the trails. It's one of the best-ordered sphagnum bogs I know, as though someone had carefully read a textbook on sphagnum bogs before putting it together. It's a large, orderly, bowl-shaped area with its trees neatly graduated around the sides, finally giving way to tangles of sheep's laurel and leatherleaf, which in turn yield to open mats of yellow-green sphagnum dotted with red pitcher plants and sundews. Here and there little pools of dark water are covered with the yellow flowers of bladderwort, their stems rising leafless from the water like masses of minute flagpoles bearing tiny yellow banners.

Fascinating though bogs may be, they're not particularly productive places for birds. White-throated Sparrows whistle their clear songs from the heavy woodland along the edges, and in the wetter areas Common Yellowthroats and Swamp Sparrows skulk among the shrubbery. But there are some specialties to be found here as well: among the tamaracks Palm Warblers wag their tails unceasingly, and a lively three-part song reveals a Lincoln's Sparrow somewhere deep in a tangle of roots.

The Bass Harbor area has some of the rather limited shorebird habitat on the island. There's more back in the town of Bar Harbor, a sharp contrast to the relative quiet and seclusion of the park. This busy community, one of the most popular destinations on the east coast, teems with tourists. Off Bridge Street a low bar stretches out toward Bar Island when the tide is out. It's often thronged with people too, but nevertheless shorebirds and gulls loiter and feed here.

Not all of the park is devoted to heavy coniferous forest, and to add the deciduous forest species to our list we head for the woods around Sieur de Monts Spring. There is a nature center here as well as a wildflower garden, and the whole place becomes crowded with tourists later in the day. Even then, however, we find quiet areas along the paths and carriage drives through the woods, with such typical species as Great Crested Flycatcher, Eastern Wood-Pewee, Least Flycatcher, and Red-eyed Vireo.

Acadia National Park has two outliers, both of them worth a visit. Isle au Haut is a small island lying some twenty miles southwest of the rest of the park. It too has heavy forests of spruce, but it is perhaps most noteworthy as a migrant trap and as a good place for viewing oceanic species, particularly when there is a brisk east wind. Wintering Harlequin Ducks sometimes hang around the island until well into June.

The second outlier is Schoodic Point, which lies immediately east of Mount Desert Island on the other side of Frenchman Bay. It is a rugged area of forested headland, scenic even for this beautiful part of the world, and another good place for more northern species. Common Eiders nest offshore here, and the woodlands are as good a place as anywhere in the park for finding Gray Jay and Boreal Chickadee. Common Ravens patrol the headlands, and with luck and perseverance you might even locate a Spruce Grouse here, or a Black-backed Woodpecker.

If you want to get offshore, Bar Harbor has the answer, because the M. V. *Bluenose* ferry crosses the Gulf of Maine to Yarmouth, Nova Scotia, leaving in the morning and re-

---

Isle au Haut is accessible by ferry from Stonington via Route 15, south from Route 3 west of Ellsworth. There's very limited camping, which must be booked far in advance from the national park (request a ferry schedule when applying). Schoodic Point is south on Route 186 from West Gouldsboro, which is east of Ellsworth on Route 3. Drive south to Winter Harbor and follow the signs. There is a picnic area but no accommodation on the Point.

★

The best time for pelagics from the *Bluenose* ferry is from late summer through early fall. The crossing takes six hours, and reservations are required if you plan to take your automobile across. Call or write Marine Atlantic, P.O. Box 250, North Sydney, N.S., Canada B2A 3M3; (207) 288-3395, toll-free U.S. 1-800-341-7981, Ont./ P.Q. 1-800-565-9411, NB, NS and PEI 1-800-565-9470. $36.25/adults, $67/auto. The boat leaves Bar Harbor at 8 A.M. and returns at 4:30 P.M. Crossings can, of course, be rough, and very cold out on the water even when it is pleasantly warm on shore.

Valuable articles on pelagic birds from the *Bluenose* are "Pelagic Birds in the Gulf of Maine" Parts I and II, by Davis W. Finch, William C. Russell, and Edward V. Thompson (*American Birds*, 32 #2, March 1978, pp. 140–55; #3, May 1978, pp. 281–94).

turning in the later afternoon. The Holiday Inn is located conveniently close to the terminal. It's a six-hour voyage and a must for anyone interested in pelagic birds, those oceanic wanderers that regard land as hostile terrain to be avoided at all costs. The rich waters of the Gulf of Maine and the Bay of Fundy draw these elusive creatures closer to shore, and the *Bluenose* cuts across their feeding grounds. On the right day the crossing can be spectacular.

Pelagic birding has a quality all its own. It also has a down side. In good weather birds may be few and far between. In bad weather you may lose interest in birds rather quickly! When we set out there's a choppy swell that seems a compromise of sorts, but soon the more queasy passengers start a procession below decks. Fortified by Dramamine and wedged along the side, those who stick it out find the gymnastics of the boat tolerable.

From the start there's lots to look at. At first the action is all with gulls, and the customary mix of species keeps the boat company, always on the lookout for something edible: many Herring, a few Ring-billeds, the odd Great Black-backed. It's not until we're well away from shore that something new appears—a Greater Shearwater, dark, long-winged, moving rapidly toward the boat. No landbird flies like this: turning and banking effortlessly low over the waves, a few rapid beats of the narrow wings and then a smooth, fluid glide.

There are several useful references to the area. Most recent is Richard K. Walton's *Birdfinding in New England* (1988, David R. Godine). *A Birder's Guide to the Coast of Maine* by E. C. and J. E. Pierson (1981, Down East Books) is more specific to the area, and James Bond's *Birds of Mount Desert Island* (1958) is old and out of print but still of interest. The Maine hotline is (207) 781-2332.

The park checklist has seasonal bar charts of abundance, which show over 140 species as regular during the summer. A June visit will assure the best warblers, but will be rather early for most shorebirds and pelagics. Later summer should yield a little of everything, but the landbirds are more difficult to find. Three days should enable you to sample the island's habitats; a week would be better.

The shearwater is just the beginning. Soon several more are skimming low around the boat, until someone dumps a mass of scraps from the galley and they descend upon it, a shrieking, fighting tangle of birds. They're joined by a Sooty Shearwater, looking all black from our vantage point above. At one point a group of Red-necked Phalaropes rises from the surface of the water and flies off, white wing bars flashing in unison. Wilson's Storm-Petrels appear, small dark birds dipping and fluttering just above the waves, looking too insubstantial to survive in this wind-lashed environment. Later a Leach's Storm-Petrel flies quickly past with jerky, erratic wingbeats, ignoring the boat and the other birds around it.

Finally Yarmouth looms up ahead and a new group of gulls flies over in search of an easy meal. Someone starts throwing popcorn, and the quarrelsome crew fight and scream over the offerings, snatching them in midair. Suddenly a dark, immature jaeger dashes into the group, twisting and turning with buoyant grace and pursuing the other birds with a savage intensity, only to vanish as abruptly as it appeared. Then the mud flats of the harbor are close at hand and small groups of turnstones and Willets fly up in alarm as the boat passes. The voyage is over.

We're accustomed to the birds of summer being local nesters, or at least nonbreeding youngsters that are wandering around while their elders get on with the serious business of rearing a brood. Leach's Storm-Petrels fit the mold well. They're actually one of the commonest birds in these waters, nesting in thousands on offshore islands, but they're not given to following boats so views of them are usually limited to quick glimpses in passing. But on this trip the phalaropes are on their way south from the Arctic; and the shearwaters and Wilson's Storm-Petrels are wintering birds, migrants from the Antarctic seas, idling away the stormy southern winter here off the balmy east coast of North America.

Acadia National Park is one of those places that challenge a birder's single-mindedness. Plant life lures, whether the carnivorous plants of the bog, the salt-marsh vegetation along the shore with its daily inundation of saltwater, or the carpets of mosses under the conifers with their subtle variations of texture and growth form and their shades of green. Rhodora, the delicate rhododendron of the northeast bogs, is common here; and in the salt marshes mauve sea lavender dips its toes in the sea twice a day.

Along the rocky shores themselves low tide reveals a dramatic zonation from periwinkles above to kelp mats below. Between the two are rock pools, each different from the last and each a miniature garden of tiny sea anemones, algae, and sponges, dotted with shells and concealing a lively assortment of minute crabs, shrimps, fish, and other animals that dash unexpectedly out of the fairyland forests of sea-weed on the bottom.

And then there's the scenery: rugged headlands with gnarled conifers half hidden in fog; Thunder Hole, where the breakers explode up through the rocks like a giant fountain; and Cadillac Mountain, offering vistas over the entire park, where the vegetation is stunted by the winter storms and dainty three-toothed cinquefoils dot the thin soil around the parking lot. Then there is always the sea, flat and silvery under the fog banks or dark blue and flecked with white-caps against a blue sky, with pudgy Black Guillemots bobbing just offshore.

THINGS TO DO IF IT'S TOO FOGGY TO BIRD

Mount Desert Island is of geological interest as well, and the park has available for rental a tape tour that describes the geology, ecology, and history of the area. Another notewor-

thy feature is the Bar Harbor Garden Club's wildflower garden at Sieur de Monts Spring, which is divided into 10 habitat groupings and has a good cross-section of the 300 or so local species labeled.

Just north of Bar Harbor on Route 3 is a Natural History Museum and store in the College of the Atlantic—$2. (207) 288-5015—and at Southwest Harbor the Wendell Gilley Museum—corner Main St. and Herrick Rd. $1. (207) 244-7555—features bird carvings. There's also an Oceanarium there—1 mile east on Clark's Point Rd. $3.50. (207) 244-7330.

Route 3 from Ellsworth passes (1 mile south of Route 1) the home of Maine's pioneer ornithologist, Cordelia Stanwood. There is a small museum on the site, and a 100-acre Birdsacre Sanctuary with nature trails and picnic facilities—Museum 10 A.M.–4 P.M., June 15–October 15. $1. (207) 667-8671.

Cruises featuring sightseeing, fishing, and whale-watching are all available from Bass, Northeast, and Bar harbors. Bar Harbor itself caters heavily to tourists with an abundance of souvenir and antique shops.

★   ★   ★   ★   ★

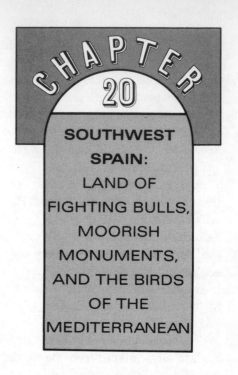

CHAPTER 20

SOUTHWEST SPAIN: LAND OF FIGHTING BULLS, MOORISH MONUMENTS, AND THE BIRDS OF THE MEDITERRANEAN

NDALUSIA IS A COUNTRY OF RED-BROWN hills and olive groves. The town plazas are lined with orange trees, and black fighting bulls, lithe and lethal, stare ominously from cactus-fenced fields. The Moors occupied this land for centuries, and their influence is tangible—in the rich blue tilework, in the exquisite filigree, and in the narrow white streets hiding shady courtyards and sparkling fountains, with verdant, tranquil little gardens. Down the street, in jarring contrast, there's the social center of every town, the bullring, with its ritualized brutality every Sunday afternoon.

It's all as different from the gentle, lush countrysides of the nations to the north as one could imagine; this sun-drenched landscape and its handsome, swarthy people seem more suited to the Middle East than to Europe. And their attitudes are different too. The Englishman cossets his birds in reserves, the Spaniard views them along the barrels of a gun if he thinks of them at all. Yet somehow the hand of man has laid less heavily on the wildlife of Spain, and here you will find the last refuges of birds long vanished elsewhere in Europe, together with Mediterranean species—rollers and orioles, bee-eaters and bustards—that were never more than exotic waifs farther north.

In the nature of things, however, our introduction to Andalusia must wait, and our welcome to Spain is from Common Swifts rocketing and screaming around the buildings of Madrid airport at dawn. Also in the way of things, they're the last birds we're to see for a little while, unless you count the inevitable Rock Doves and sparrows (not a Spanish Sparrow in the lot) of downtown Madrid.

But the setting is an enticing one, with the forested heights of the Sierra de Guadarrama looming to the north. Given an enforced stopover in the capital, the mountains can yield good birding of a kind we will not encounter farther south, so we leave the city and head north up the road to the ancient town of Segovia. The main mass of the Sierra Guadarrama lies 90 km. (60 miles) or so northwest of Madrid, and rises to heights of almost 8,000 feet. Soon we find ourselves driving through dense silent forests of pine, towering trees with striking rust-colored trunks. Finally the road reaches the pass, and inviting patches of open grass appear among the conifers.

It was hot in the capital, but it's early spring here, and the close-cropped sward is jeweled with yellow mountain buttercups and with low patches of thrift like drifts of pink candy floss. Glowing under the trees are tiny clumps of dainty, perfect daffodils no bigger than your little finger, nestled among the dead leaves like errant sunbeams. Ahead a splash of crimson in the trees reveals a Greater Spotted Woodpecker, looking as though it had inadvertently sat in a patch of red ink. The bird is shy and it quickly moves off, a

There is an enormous range of accommodations in Madrid, from modest hostels to luxury hotels. The two listed below offer two price ranges, are well located for sightseeing in the center of the city, and have contrasting styles. There are better-situated hotels than those listed, but they are classed as residential; this means that they do not offer meals apart from a continental breakfast. While this may be acceptable to some travelers, many persons could find it annoying. Hostels tend to be more spartan, but some of them are excellent, and they are a more economical choice of accommodation.

Plaza — Plaza de Espana, Madrid, Spain, phone (91) 247-1200. Open all year. Superb view! <u>Rooms</u>: 306 units, twin beds. <u>Amenities</u>: Dining room, lounge, elevator, rooftop swimming pool. Terms: Double from 14,580 pesetas.

Tryp Victoria — Plaza Del Angel 7, Madrid, Spain; phone (91) 531-4500. Open all year. Historic old hotel with stained-glass windows and decorative cupola. <u>Rooms</u>: 110 units, twin beds. <u>Amenities</u>: Dining room, lounge, elevator. <u>Terms</u>: Double from 7,150 pesetas.

To reach Segovia take the A-6 Autopista out of Madrid to Exit 1 at Villalba, and then head north on the N-601 through La Granja to Segovia.

flash of black, white, and red among the pervading rusts and dark greens.

We sit on the rocks looking out over the slopes and the highway below, with its muted drone of traffic. Above a Woodlark circles constantly, pouring out sequence after sequence of rich song, each an exquisite cascade of notes; and joined from time to time by Citril Finches, flying up from the tops of the pines to circle erratically, with their own ecstatic flight songs. To the east a Booted Eagle glides unsteadily, its pale underparts a striking contrast against the dark of the pines.

Outside Madrid the state-run paradors often offer the most interesting and attractive accommodations, particularly for naturalists who are often looking for something different from the usual city hotels. To reach Mazagón leave Seville on route N-431 to Huelva, and then take the C-442 coast road southeast. The continuation of this road runs to Torre de la Higuera (Matalascanas), where it joins route H-612 (C-445 on some maps), for access to the Doñana, as below.

Parador De Mazagón—21130 Mazagón, Huelva, Spain, phone (955) 37-60-00. Open all year. Picturesque, beach. Rooms: 43 units; twins, 1 suite. Amenities: Dining room, lounge, swimming pool, garden, tennis. Restrictions: No dogs. Terms: 7,000–10,000 pesetas.

Segovia itself is a beautiful old town, full of ancient churches, with a huge Roman viaduct straggling across the valley. Black Redstarts sing from the tops of the old walls, and the restaurants serve succulent meals that induce sleep on the return drive to Madrid rather than birding. It's an excellent day trip.

The gateway to Andalusia is through Seville, a beautiful but busy city where Lesser Kestrels hawk around the towers of the great cathedral. It's a short flight but a long drive from the capital, and from here we drive over ever narrowing roads to Mazagón, where the parador is decked in a riot of blossom overlooking the beach. There's excellent birding nearby, but just twenty kilometers south is the Doñana National Park, probably the premier birding area in southern Spain and one of Europe's birding meccas. It consists of over 50,000 hectares of wetlands and forested dunes on the north side of the estuary of the Guadalquivir.

So we find ourselves bumping along in a Land-Rover over a dusty trail through the heavy scrub that dominates much of the dune country of the Doñana. At first there's not much to be seen, just the occasional Red-legged Partridge scuttling madly across the track ahead. Stop beside one of the heavier tangles and Dartford Warblers fuss and scold and skulk, popping up to glare at the intruders—little maroon bundles of indignation with tails cocked high and topknots askew, dashing back into cover again for fear of giving someone a good view through their binoculars.

Dotted through the rolling scrubland are huge cork oaks, venerable old giants with massive trunks and wide spreading crowns like enormous mushrooms. Melodious Warblers sing their delightful songs in the tops of the trees, carefully staying on the side opposite to us. In places are little clumps of stone pine, the low weather-beaten pines of the dunes, great sites for nesting hawks.

Southern Spain is a place for raptors, and the Doñana is particularly famous in this respect. It is one of the last strongholds in Europe for the Imperial Eagle—the endangered Spanish race is distinct from the birds that occur farther east—and there is a multitude of other hawks. Over the pine woods kites maneuver elegantly, the ever present Black Kite joined here by the Red Kite, a bird whose habits are totally belied by its beauty, with pale sandy head, rich rufous body and tail, and bold white patches at the base of the primaries. The tail is long and forked, and the birds soar effortlessly, their long tails fanning and parting with every fluctuation in the breeze. In one place a pair of Bonelli's Eagles is soaring high overhead, and at another stop our driver points out a dark tangle in the top of a distant tree, the nest of an Imperial Eagle. But there are no Imperial Eagles to be seen.

Finally the scrub opens out and we look over a vast flat expanse of grassy marsh. Near the water's edge a group of Collared Pratincoles are hawking for insects, looking like enormous swallows. Pratincoles are special: one of those birds that arrest the fingers when casually flipping through the bird guide, and that develop a "must see" quality ever after. The reality is worth the wait; graceful long-winged shorebirds with rich chestnut underwings, striking white rumps, and long forked tails, they look just as elegant on the ground as they do hawking gracefully in the air. Closer, they are even more beautiful, with a warm buff throat neatly outlined in black and a striking red base to the short bill.

Farther along we arrive at a group of trees covered in heron nests, a kind of avian apartment building with a few storks and Gray Herons in the penthouses and Cattle and Little Egrets ranged in the boughs below, together with scattered Black-crowned Night-Herons. It's a typically chaotic scene, with the birds constantly flying in and out, and nest-relief ceremonies and the feeding of young going on everywhere. In the grass beneath the trees we glimpse the dark forms of European wild boar, and while we are standing there a long-tailed brown-and-white bird flies across the clearing, a Great Spotted Cuckoo.

Doñana National Park has two reception centers off route H-612 (C-445), the Almonte—Matalascanas Road. The northernmost is at the village of El Rocío, where the information center La Rocina has a nature trail. A road runs 7 kilometers west from here to the Acebron Palace, where there are exhibits and another trail. The main reception center is at El Acebuche — closed Mondays and during the El Rocío festival at the end of May; 8:30 A.M.—5 P.M., phone (955) 44-23-40 and 43-02-11 — which is 1.5 kms. from the road farther south at kilometer 29. There are exhibits here, a coffee shop and souvenir stand, and another trail. The interior can only be visited by Land-Rover, and these are available from the Acebuche center and operated by Cooperativa Marismas del Rocío (Parque Nacional Doñana, Centro de Recepción del Acebuche, Matalascanas, Huelva, Spain). Cost per person, with a minimum of 8 passengers in one vehicle is subject to revision, but plan on some 1,500 pesetas. Alternatively a vehicle and driver can be hired for about 15,000 pesetas for a full day. It is essential to book well in advance of your trip, and current charges and schedules can be obtained from the address above. Four separate day trips are available.

★

But we still haven't seen an Imperial Eagle.

Doñana has a wealth of birds, and to expect to see them all on a short visit is naïve. There are flamingos here most of the year and a wealth of waterfowl, including such rarities as Ruddy Shelduck and White-headed Duck. The herons include both Purple and Squacco, and there's a good variety of landbirds. The raptors are exceptional: Marsh Harriers quarter the marsh constantly, and the dark, streamlined shapes of Hobbies strike terror to the flocks of swallows.

Some persons even see Imperial Eagles.

But it is not necessary to enter the national park to have good birding, as there are marshes and pine woods along the highway as well, and all of these can be productive. On our last day we work through the pines just north of the visitor center, and find noisy flocks of the beautiful Azure-winged Magpies foraging through the trees, while the inevitable Dartford and Sardinian warblers scold from the thickets. Back at the vehicle, we're standing in the road discussing where to have lunch when a dark shape looms overhead. A huge raptor soars above us, its dark body relieved by a pale head and white forewings shining brilliantly in the sun. The Imperial Eagle circles idly a couple of times and then starts to climb, finally becoming just another hawk high in the heavens, and then gliding off eastward over the park, to play hide and seek with some other group of birders.

There is excellent birding all along the Atlantic coast south to Gibraltar, itself a famed crossing point for raptors moving to and from Africa on migration. The areas on the south bank of the Guadalquivir offer some attractive birding, with marshes at Cádiz particularly attractive to waterbirds.

The Laguna Medina is even easier to find and very easy to bird. When we arrive, it's covered in waterfowl, with the pink dots of a few flamingos at the far end. Great Crested and Black-necked grebes (the North American Eared) are dotted over the surface with little flocks of Pochard, and Red-crested Pochards with their striking orange heads. Ferruginous and White-headed ducks are possible here too, although we fail to find any.

Instead our attention is distracted by the chorus of busy, hurried songs coming from the reedbeds and thickets of brush along the shoreline. Many European warblers are great skulkers, and the marsh species are particularly notorious in this respect. After much effort we manage to dig out Reed Warblers and Great Reed Warblers, Cetti's and Savi's warblers. The little Fan-tailed Warblers don't need any finding. They are everywhere, flying over the reed tops with jerky little song flights—if a raspy "zeep-zeep-zeep" can be called a song.

The countryside yields its own birding delights. Little flocks of Serins bounce along the roadside. Slender Montagu's Harriers, the most graceful of their kin, glide low over the fields; and here and there on the telephone wires gold and green Bee-eaters sit, making periodic sorties after passing insects. Hoopoes flop across the road, their bodies an improbable shade of pink and their wings zebra-striped, flashing in the sun. Burly blue-green Rollers hunt from the tops of telephone posts, and now and again embark on erratic tumbling display flights.

Even the sun-drenched little white towns have their attractions. On the rooftops Spotless Starlings gurgle contentedly, shiny, dapper counterparts of their cousins farther north. Some of the taller buildings boast White Stork nests, vast piles of sticks with the owners gazing solicitously over broods only a stork could love. Elaborate ceremonies accompany the nest exchanges, when the pairs wave their bills high in the air and clatter their mandibles in a kind of ciconiid flamenco.

And then there are always the swifts. Swifts tearing along the streets just above the traffic; swifts hurtling around buildings and through alleyways in a reckless, endless game of tag; swifts screaming like a whole army of schoolgirls on a steep roller-coaster; swifts ever continuing the timeless tradition of the world's first—and best—aeronautic display. They're characterful birds.

To reach the areas east of the Guadalquivir, return to Seville and then head south on the A-4 Autopista to Exit 4 (Jerez). From here the Laguna de Medina is some 5km. on the left along the C-440 road running south to Medina-Sidonia, and is easily visible from the road. There is a picnic area here. (The Cádiz marshes are visible from the N-IV, the major route just west of the A-4.) Arcos de la Frontera is east from Jerez on route N-342. The Parador's site is spectacular:

Parador de Arcos de la Frontera — Plaza de Espana, 11630 Arcos de la Frontera, Cadiz, Spain; phone (956) 70-05-00. Open all year. Rooms: (Recently renovated) 24 units; singles, twins. Amenities: Dining room, lounge, elevator. Restrictions: No dogs. Terms: From 9,500 pesetas. AMEX, DINERS, MC, VISA.

Our base for this leg of our trip is the parador at Arcos de la Frontera, with dizzying views from the edge of the gigantic cliff overlooking the broad valley below. Here we can look down on—yes, the swifts—together with Lesser Kestrels playing effortlessly in the wind currents along the cliff edge.

It is a scene that is to be repeated at our next destination, the town of Ronda, where the gardens of our hotel again overlook a precipice. It's a wonderful place, perched high on sheer cliffs, the two parts of town separated by a chasm where Rock Sparrows forage. In the dry hills nearby we find

From Arcos the C-344 runs east to join the C-339, which continues southeast to Ronda. Route C-341 running southwest from town is also a good birding road. The Victoria is another splendidly situated hotel:

Reina Victoria — Jerez 25, Ronda, Spain; phone (952) 87-12-40. Open all year. Rooms: 89 units. Amenities: Dining room, lounge, elevator, swimming pool, garden. Terms: Singles 7,000—8,900 pesetas.

Black Wheatears, and handsome Rock Buntings tastefully attired in gray and chestnut.

We spend the evening in the hotel garden, looking down at the toy houses and the minute trees below, with the faint songs of Nightingales drifting upward in the still air. Above, in front of us, and all along the cliff face below there is a milling throng of birds: black crowlike Choughs tumbling and soaring gracefully in the wind, their slender red bills vivid in the sun; swifts again, parties of them—Common, Pallid, and Alpine—hurtling back and forth on sickle wings in their lifelong celebration of the power of flight; and swirling flocks of swallows and martins, including a newcomer, the Crag Martin. All at once sharp alarm notes sound and a Peregrine Falcon flies rapidly along the cliff face: then, with little conscious lapse of time, a flash of steel blue drops out of the sky, and the Peregrine is perched on the ledges below, calmly dissecting the swallow it has just captured.

And so to Granada, a Moorish stronghold for centuries, and a city where the flamboyance of the Spanish Renaissance contrasts with the exquisite grace and restraint of that miracle of medieval Arab architecture, the Alhambra. But there are birds here too. In the wooded slopes below the Alhambra the rich songs of Blackcaps soar over the roar of the tour buses climbing the hill, and in the hidden gardens of the Generalife Blue Tits poke in and out of the thick hedges and Nightingales sing in the trees along the moat.

The Sierra Nevadas tower south of Granada, dominated by the peaks of Mulhacén and Velata rising to over 10,000 feet to the southeast. The highway winds up through the orange groves of the lower slopes and the scrub to end at the ski lodges high above, surrounded by banks of snow even in late May, and with bare sweeps of scree and stark gray rock faces dotted with scattered clumps of alpine flowers. From these heights we look out over the heat haze in the valley below and down on the back of the occasional Griffon Vulture soaring over the valley. It's a quiet place where the road ends, with the lodges silent and inactive and birdlife scarce.

The climb up the Sierra Nevadas takes us, in effect, gradually northward. Near the base, Black-eared Wheatears sit on the rocky outcrops, little patches of pink and black against the reddish soil. Near the summit, the roadside is decorated with the grays and black of Northern Wheatears. Lower down, the little stream valleys are occupied by Blue

Probably the best route from Ronda to Granada is to follow the C-341 northeast to the C-342, and then continue east. If flamingos eluded you on the coast, watch for the N-334 some 20 km. east of the C-341 intersection. About 15 km. north on this road is Fuente de Piedra, and a short distance west of town (on the MA-454 side road) is the Laguna de Fuente de Piedra, a shallow salt lake where the birds breed intermittently.

Granada is another large city in a truly magnificent setting, but with most of the accommodation in urban areas. The woods up the hill to the Alhambra offer some respite, although the roads are very busy. Much the most desirable—and expensive—location is the Parador, located within the Alhambra itself. The Alhambra Palace is also expensive, but the best situated for the wooded areas up the hill. You can hear Scops Owls calling from here at night. There is an abundance of less expensive accommodation.

Parador San Francisco—Alhambra, 18009 Granada, Spain; phone (958) 22-14-40. Open all year. Located in an old convent within the precincts of the Alhambra. Rooms: 39 units; 35 twins, 4 single. Amenities: Dining room, lounge, garden. Restrictions: No dogs. Terms: From 14,500 pesetas. AMEX, DINERS, MC, VISA.

Alhambra Palace—2 Pẽna Partida, Granada, Spain; phone (958) 22-14-68. Open all year. Rooms: 132 units. Amenities: Dining room, lounge, elevator, garden. Terms: Double from 12,000 pesetas. AMEX, DINERS, MC, VISA.

The highway up the Sierra Nevada, the GR-420, is southeast of town; snaking some 45 km. up the Pico Veleta to the skiing lodges of Solynieve.

★

Rock Thrushes shouting loud songs; farther up, the orange-breasted Rock Thrush flashes its white rump as it vanishes behind the boulders with harsh alarm notes.

To the botanist one of the most fascinating places on the climb is the hedgehog zone, where the plants seemingly have responded to centuries of browsing by goats and ibex by developing low prickly mounds, reminiscent of the European hedgehog. Superficially they all look alike, but we poke into one mound and discover yellow pea flowers in blossom, while nearby another displays the cross-shaped blossoms of a member of the mustard family. In spite of the orderly, attractive look of the hedgehog zone it's an uncomfortable place to walk, but we do manage to startle a Tawny Pipit.

Well over 300 species can be seen in the places we have visited, but many of these are either wintering birds or are otherwise unlikely to be encountered in May. This is probably the optimum time. It can be very hot later, and it is advantageous to visit during the peak birdsong period, particularly as the warblers can be difficult to see at the best of times. Depending on your luck and energy, you can probably expect between 150 and 170 species in a couple of weeks, and if your only previous contact with Europe has been in Britain or the north, some 75 species are likely to be new to you.

People in Spain—surprise!—speak Spanish, and if you cannot speak the language yourself some advance preparation with a phrase book is recommended. Even on a conducted tour you'll be faced with menus and the like. For a do-it-yourself trip, the hotels listed are selected more with a view to their locations than their costs, and both less expensive accommodations and camping are available for those wishing to economize.

A keen birder can find Spanish eating habits frustrating in the extreme. Breakfasts are typically continental, which means coffee and a roll, and while this is satisfactory for some persons, others prefer something more substantial before embarking on an active day in the field. Sometimes it is almost impossible to obtain an early breakfast, and both lunch and dinner are served at hours that are long past the mealtimes of the average North American. It is not unusual to find lunch just getting under way at 2 P.M., and dinner does not usually start until about 9 P.M. and is frequently much later, particularly in the capital. Thus you are forced into an eating regimen which is totally opposite to the early-to-bed, early-to-rise pattern of many keen birders.

One partial solution to the meal problems, in Madrid at least, is to look for the cafeterias, where light sandwich meals can be acquired outside normal mealtimes. These cafeterias are unlike those in North America, and more resemble cafés. There are several chains in the city—California, Nebraska, Morrison, and Manila—and fast-food outlets such as McDonald's are also becoming increasingly com-

mon. These may not offer much in the way of culinary adventure, but at least they're predictable. Outside the capital there is less choice available, and you may have to settle for being hungry all morning and having indigestion all night. Bring snacks—granola bars and the like.

Spain is an easy country to get around in, with good highways, automobile rentals at the airports (an International driver's license is desirable), and good air links between Madrid and both Seville and Granada. Be warned that traffic—particularly in the cites—is extremely heavy, the streets are often very narrow, and the Spanish approach to driving has much in common with bullfighting. Some of the routes described, such as those around Ronda and up the Sierra Nevadas, also entail typical mountain driving with hairpin curves and steep drop-offs. If all this makes the whole thing seem too much trouble to cope with on a holiday, by all means look for a conducted tour. There are several nature tour operators, both in North America and the British Isles, who cover Spain regularly (some of the U.K.-based operators offer a wider range of alternatives).

A couple of references are useful, in addition to the usual guidebooks. John Gooder's *Where to Watch Birds in Britain and Europe* (revised 1988; Christopher Helm) has a good section on Spain. Andy Paterson's *Birdwatching in Southern Spain* (1987 Golf Area, S.A.) is an irritating book, but one with much useful information, although it covers neither the Coto Doñana nor Madrid. The field guides suggested for Britain are the appropriate ones here too.

There are the usual "nasties" here such as mosquitoes and biting flies, and you should be conscious of scorpions if you do any camping—shake out your shoes in the mornings. Some of the snakes are venomous, so they all should be avoided. One unfamiliar hazard is with cattle: the bulls are very dangerous and very fast, and cows are not too friendly either. Stay out of occupied fields.

OTHER THINGS TO SEE AND DO IN SPAIN

Botanically this area is even richer than it is for birds, with a host of rare and exciting species. Reptiles and amphibians are well represented, although mammals are rather scarce. Swallowtails and peacocks are among the host of showy butterflies and moths.

Madrid has all the attractions of a large European city including an abundance of shopping and many fine old buildings. Probably the most famous location is the Prado Museum—Tuesday–Saturday 9 A.M.–7 P.M., 400 pesetas; phone 468 09 50—which has an incomparable collection of Veláz-quez, El Greco, and Goya paintings.

There are some pleasant parks in Madrid. The entrance to the Botanical Gardens is adjacent to the Prado, and it has a collection of over 30,000 different species of trees and plants from all over the world, most of them labeled. The largest park is the Retiro with 130 hectares of woodland.

While we are not proposing a stay in Seville, there should be ample time for sightseeing while passing through. The magnificent Cathedral (10 A.M.–1 P.M. and 4:30–6 P.M., Mon-day–Friday, 200 pesetas) is the largest in Spain, and the third-largest in the Christian world. It dates from the fif-teenth century. Immediately adjacent is the huge tower called La Giralda, one of the most famous landmarks of Se-ville. Also of great interest is the Alcázar, the old Moorish fortress with some beautiful architecture, and there are many other fine old buildings.

The jewel of Southern Spain, and indeed one of the world's most magnificent buildings, is the Alhambra in Gra-nada (9 A.M.–8 P.M., 450 pesetas. Note that large bags and backpacks are prohibited). In its day it was a city within a city, a combination of fortress, royal residence, church, and summer garden. No words are adequate to describe the Al-hambra, and no one should miss it.

Granada is full of noteworthy buildings, especially the op-ulent renaissance cathedral, and there is a scenic gypsy quarter, the Sacro Monte (watch out for pickpockets).

In fact, all the old towns along our route have their places of interest: old churches, ancient castles, and picturesque houses. Enumerating them all is quite beyond the scope of this section. There are a multitude of other things to see and do, ranging from bullfights to lounging on the beach at Ma-zagón. Andalusia is famed for its flamenco dancing, pa-rades, and festivals, and Jerez de La Frontera is the center of the sherry industry (you can book a tour of the wineries).

★   ★   ★   ★   ★

SCIENTIFIC NAMES OF SPECIES MENTIONED IN THE TEXT

(Species names that are consistent with the current AOU Check List are excluded)

Acacia, Yellow-barked (*Acacia xanthophloea*)

Agave (*Agave desertii*)

Alder (*Alnus rugosa*)

Alligator (*Alligator mississipiensis*)

Anemone, Yellow (*Anemone richardsonii*)

Antshrike, Black-crested (*Sakesphorus canadensis*)

Archangel, Yellow (*Lamiastrum galeobdolon*)

Ash (U.K.) (*Fraxinus excelsior*)

Avocet (U.K.) (*Recurvirostra avosetta*)

Azalea, Alpine (*Loiseleuria procumbens*)

Baboon (*Papio anubis*)

Baby Blue Eyes (*Nemophila phacelioides*)

Bakeapple Berry (*Rubus chamaemorus*)

Barbet, d'Arnaud's (*Trachyphonus darnaudii*)

Bachelor-button (*Polygala nana*)

Bateleur (*Terathopius ecaudatus*)

Bear, Polar (*Ursus maritimus*)

Bearberry, Alpine (*Arctostaphylos alpina*)

Bee-eater (*Merops apiaster*)

Bellbird, Bearded (*Procnias averano*)

Bellwort (*Uvularia grandiflora*)

Beluga (*Delphinapterus leucas*)

Birch (U.K.) (*Betula pendula*)

Bistort, Alpine (*Polygonum viviparum*)

Bittern (U.K.) (*Botaurus stellaris*)

Blackbird (U.K.) (*Turdus merula*)

Blackcap (*Sylvia atricapilla*)

Blackfly (Simuliid spp.)

Bladderwort (*Utricularia cornuta*)

Bluebell (*Endymion non-scriptus*)

Boar, Wild (*Sus scrofa*)

Bobcat (*Felis rufus*)

Bougainvillea (*Bougainvillea spectabilis*)

Bromeliads (*Tillandsia fasciculata* and others)

Buffalo (*Syncerus caffer*)

Bunting, Reed (*Emberiza schoeniclus*)

Bunting, Rock (*Emberiza cia*)

Bushbuck (*Tragelaphus scriptus*)

Bushmaster (*Lachesis muta*)

Buttercup, Mountain (*Ranunculus gregarius*)

Butterwort, Purple (*Pinguicula caerulea*)

Buzzard (U.K.) (*Buteo buteo*)

Buzzard, Augur (*Buteo rufofuscus*)

Cacao, cocoa (*Theobroma cacao*)

Calypso (*Calypso bulbosa*)

Campion, Alpine (*Lychnis alpina*)

Cane (*Arundinaria gigantea*)

Caribou (*Rangifer tarandus*)

Casuarina (*Casuarina equisetifolia*)

Cat-tail (*Typha* spp.)

Cedar, Eastern Red (*Juniperus virginiana*)

Cedar, Salt (*Tamarix* spp.)

Cedar, Western Red (*Thuja plicata*)

Chaffinch (*Fringilla coelebs*)

Chat, Red-capped Robin (*Cossypha natalensis*)

Cherry, Choke (*Prunus virginiana*)

Chiffchaff (*Phylloscopus collybita*)

Cholla, Teddybear (*Opuntia bigelovii*)

Chough (*Pyrrhocorax pyrrhocorax*)

Cinquefoil, Three-toothed (*Potentilla tridentata*)

Cisticola, Hunter's (*Cisticola hunteri*)

Coffee (*Coffea arabica*)

Conebill, Bicolored (*Conirostrum bicolor*)
Coot, Red-knobbed (*Fulica cristata*)
Coquette, Tufted (*Lophornis ornata*)
Cottonwood (Eastern) (*Populus deltoides*)
Cottonwood (N.D.) (*Populus sargentii*)
Cottonwood, Fremont (*Populus fremontii*)
Crab, Ghost (*Ocypode quadrata*)
Crake, Black (*Porzana flavirostra*)
Crane, Crowned (*Balearica pavonina*)
Creosotebush (*Larrea tridentata*)
Crocodile (Af.) (*Crocodylus niloticus*)
Crow, Carrion (*Corvus corone*)
Crowberry (*Empetrum nigrum*)
Cuckoo, Great Spotted (*Clamator glandarius*)
Cui-ui (*Chastmistes cujus*)
Curlew (U.K.) (*Numenius arquata*)
Curlew, Stone (*Burhinus oedicnemus*)
Cypress, Bald (*Taxodium distichum*)
Daffodil (*Narcissus rupicola*)
Darter, African (*Anhinga rufa*)
Dipper (U.K.) (*Cinclus cinclus*)
Dolphin (*Delphinus delphis*)
Dove, Eurasian Collared (*Streptopelia decaocto*)
Drongo (*Dicrurus adsimilis*)
Duck, Ferruginous (*Aythya nyroca*)
Duck, Maccoa (*Oxyura maccoa*)
Duck, White-headed (*Oxyura leucocephala*)
Dunnock (*Prunella modularis*)
Eagle, African Fish (*Haliaeetus vocifer*)
Eagle, Bonelli's (*Hieraaetus fasciatus*)
Eagle, Booted (*Hieraaetus pennatus*)
Eagle, Crowned Hawk (*Stephanoaetus coronatus*)
Eagle, Imperial (*Aquila heliaca*)
Eagle, Long-crested Hawk (*Lophoaetus occipitalis*)
Eagle, Martial (*Polemaetus bellicosus*)
Eagle, Tawny (*Aquila rapax*)
Eagle, Verreaux's (*Aquila verreauxii*)
Ebony, Texas (*Pithecellobium flexicaule*)
Elephant (*Loxodonta africana*)
Euphonia, Violaceous (*Euphonia violacea*)
Falcon, Pygmy (*Polihierax semitorquatus*)
Fer de lance (*Bothrops asper*)
Fern, Interrupted (*Osmunda claytoniana*)
Fern, Resurrection (*Polypodium polypodioides*)
Fig (*Ficus* spp.)
Finch, Citril (*Serinus citrinella*)
Finfoot, Peters' (*Podica senegalensis*)
Fir, Douglas (*Pseudotsuga menziesii*)
Flamingo, Greater (*Phoenicopterus ruber*)
Flamingo, Lesser (*Phoenicopterus minor*)
Flycatcher, Paradise (*Terpsiphone viridis*)
Flycatcher, Pied (*Ficedula hypoleuca*)
Fox, Silver & Cross (*Vulpes vulpes*)
Frangipani (*Plumeria alba*)
Fritillary, Gulf (*Agraulis vanillae*)
Frog, Cricket (*Acris crepitans blanchardi*)
Gazelle, Thomson's (*Gazella thomsonii*)
Gerardia (*Gerardia purpurea*)
Gerenuk (*Litocranius walleri*)
Goose, Graylag (*Anser anser*)
Goose, Knob-billed (*Sarkidiornis melanotos*)
Goose, Spur-winged (*Plectropterus gambensis*)
Gorse (*Ulex europaeus*)
Grape, Wild (*Vitis* spp.)
Grass, Cord (*Spartina* spp.)
Grass, Yellow-eyed (*Xyris fimbriata*)

Grebe, Great Crested (*Podiceps cristatus*)

Greenfinch (*Carduelis chloris*)

Grenadier, Purple (*Granatina ianthinogaster*)

Guineafowl (*Numida meleagris*)

Gull, gray-headed (*Larus cirrocephalus*)

Gum, Sweet (*Liquidambar styraciflua*)

Hackberry (*Celtis occidentalis*)

Harrier, Marsh (*Circus aeruginosus*)

Harrier, Montagu's (*Circus pygargus*)

Hawthorn (U.K.) (*Crataegus monogyna*)

Hazel (U.K.) (*Corylus avellana*)

Hedysarum (*Hedysarum alpinum*)

Heron, Goliath (*Ardea goliath*)

Heron, Gray (*Ardea cinerea*)

Heron, Purple (*Ardea purpurea*)

Heron, Squacco (*Ardeola ralloides*)

Hobby (*Falco subbuteo*)

Hoopoe (*Upupa epops*)

Hornbeam (U.K.) (*Carpinus betulus*)

Hornbill, Ground (*Bucorvus leadbeateri*)

Hornbill, Red-billed (*Tockus erythrorhynchus*)

Hornbill, Yellow-billed (*Tockus flavirostris*)

Huisache (*Acacia smallii*)

Hyrax, Tree (*Dendrohyrax arboreus*)

Ibis, Sacred (*Threskiornis aethiopicus*)

Immortelle (*Erythrina micropteryx*)

Indian Blanket (*Gaillardia pulchella*)

Iris, Blue (*Iris versicolor*)

Jacana, African (*Actophilornis africana*)

Jack-in-the-Pulpit (*Arisaema triphyllum*)

Jackal (*Canis mesomelas*)

Jackdaw (*Corvus monedula*)

Javelina (*Dicotyles tajacu*)

Jay (U.K.) (*Garrulus glandarius*)

Kestrel, Lesser (*Falco naumanni*)

Kingfisher, Striped (*Halcyon chelicuti*)

Kite, Black (*Milvus migrans*)

Kite, Red (*Milvus milvus*)

Lark, Short-tailed (*Pseudalaemon fremantlii*)

Laurel, Mountain (*Kalmia latifolia*)

Laurel, Sheep's (*Kalmia angustifolia*)

Lavender, Sea (*Limonium nashii*)

Leatherleaf (*Chamaedaphne calyculata*)

Lemming (*Dicrostonyx torquatus*)

Lettuce, Water (*Pistia stratiotes*)

Lily (*Lilium philadelphicum*)

Linnet (*Carduelis cannabina*)

Lion (*Panthera leo*)

Lizard, Coachella Fringe-toed (*Uma inornata*)

Longclaw, Rosy-breasted (*Macronyx ameliae*)

Longclaw, Yellow-throated (*Macronyx croceus*)

Macaw, Red-bellied (*Ara manilata*)

Madrona (*Arbutus menziesii*)

Mahogany (*Swietenia mahogani*)

Magpie, Azure-winged (*Cyanopica cyana*)

Mandarin (*Aix galericulata*)

Mangrove (*Rhizophora mangle*)

Manzanita (*Arctostaphylos glandulosa*)

Maple, Red (*Acer rubrum*)

Martin, Crag (*Ptyonoprogne rupestris*)

Martin, House (*Delichon urbica*)

Meadow-rue, Alpine (*Thalictrum alpinum*)

Mesquite (*Prosopis glandulosa*)

Mistflower (*Eupatorium coelestinum*)

Monkey, Black-faced Vervet (*Cercopithecus aethiops*)

Moose (*Alces alces*)

Moss, Reindeer (*Cladonia rangiferina* and *C. alpestris*)

Moss, Spanish (*Tillandsia usneoides*)

Mousebird, Speckled (*Colius*

striatus)
Nightingale (*Luscinia megarhynchos*)
Nuthatch (U.K.) (*Sitta europaea*)
Nutmeg (*Myristica fragrans*)
Oak (U.K.) (*Quercus robur*)
Oak, Cork (*Quercus suber*)
Oak, Garry (*Quercus garryana*)
Ocotillo (*Fouquieria splendens*)
Oleander (*Nerium oleander*)
Olive (*Olea europaea*)
Orchid Tree (*Bauhinia variegata*)
Orchis, Early Purple (*Orchis mascula*)
Oryx, Fringe-eared (*Oryx beisa callotis*)
Ostrich (*Struthio camelus*)
Otter (*Lutra canadensis*)
Owl's Clover (*Orthocarpus purpurascens*)
Owl, Scops (*Otus scops*)
Owl, Tawny (*Strix aluco*)
Owl, Verreaux's Eagle (*Bubo lacteus*)
Palm, Coconut (*Cocos nucifera*)
Palm, Date (*Phoenix dactylifera*)
Palm, Fan (*Washingtonia filifera*)
Palmetto, Saw (*Serenoa repens*)
Paloverde (*Parkinsonia florida* and *P. microphylla*)
Papyrus (*Cyperus papyrus*)
Parrot, Brown (*Poicephalus meyeri*)
Parrot, Red-headed (*Poicephalus gulielmi*)
Partridge, Red-legged (*Alectoris rufa*)
Partridgeberry (Nfd.) (*Vaccinium vitis-idaea*)
Peacock (*Nymphalis io*)
Pelican, White (*Pelecanus onocratalus*)
Pennyroyal (*Piloblephis rigida*)
Pine (Fla.) (*Pinus elliottii*)
Pine, Caribbean (*Pinus caribaea*)
Pine, Coulter (*Pinus coulteri*)
Pine, Stone (*Pinus pinea*)
Pine, Torrey (*Pinus torreyana*)
Pine, Yellow (*Pinus ponderosa*)
Pipit, Meadow (*Anthus pratensis*)
Pipit, Tawny (*Anthus campestris*)

Plover, Blacksmith (*Vanellus armatus*)
Plover, Crab (*Dromas ardeola*)
Plover, Kittlitz's Sand (*Charadrius pecuarius*)
Pochard (*Aythya ferina*)
Pochard, African (*Netta erythrophthalma*)
Pochard, Red-crested (*Netta rufina*)
Poinciana, Dwarf (*Caesalpinia pulcherrima*)
Poppy, Mexican (*Eschscholtzia californica*)
Prairie Dog, Black-tailed (*Cynomys ludovicianus*)
Prairie-clover (*Petalostemum purpureum*)
Pratincole, Collared (*Glareola pratincola*)
Redstart (U.K.) (*Phoenicurus phoenicurus*)
Redstart, Black (*Phoenicurus ochruros*)
Reedling, Bearded (*Panurus biarmicus*)
Retama (*Parkinsonia aculeata*)
Rhododendron (*Rhododendron maximum*)
Rhododendron, Lapland (*Rhododendron lapponicum*)
Rhodora (*Rhododendron canadense*)
Robin (U.K.) (*Erithacus rubecula*)
Rockcress (*Arabis* spp.)
Roller (*Coracias garrulus*)
Roller, Lilac-breasted (*Coracias caudata*)
Rook (*Corvus frugilegus*)
Roserush (*Lygodesmia aphylla*)
Saguaro (*Carnegiea gigantea*)
Sawgrass (*Cladium jamaicensis*)
Saxifrage, Yellow Mountain (*Saxifraga aizoides*)
Scrambled Eggs (*Corydalis micrantha*)
Sea Lion, California (*Zalophus californianus*)
Sea Spurrey (*Spergularia marina*)
Seal, Gray (*Halichoerus grypus*)
Secretary Bird (*Sagittarius serpentarius*)

Seed-eater, Streaky (*Serinus striolatus*)

Serin (*Serinus serinus*)

Shag (*Phalacrocorax aristotelis*)

Shelduck (*Tadorna tadorna*)

Shelduck, Ruddy (*Tadorna ferruginea*)

Shooting Star (*Dodecatheon clevelandii*)

Shrike, Gray-headed Bush (*Malaconotus blanchoti*)

Shrike, Sulphur-breasted Bush (*Telophorus sulfureopectus*)

Shrimp Plant (*Beloperone guttata*)

Silk Cotton (*Ceiba pentandra*)

Skylark (*Alauda arvensis*)

Snail, Apple (*Pomacea* spp.)

Snake, Coral (*Micrurus* spp.)

Spanish Bayonet (*Yucca torreyi*)

Sparrow, Rock (*Petronia petronia*)

Sparrow, Spanish (*Passer hispaniolensis*)

Spicebush (*Lindera benzoin*)

Spinetail, Stripe-breasted (*Synallaxis cinnamomea*)

Spruce, Black (*Picea mariana*)

Spruce, Sitka (*Picea sitchensis*)

Squirrel, Richardson's Ground (*Spermophilus richardsonii*)

Starling, Glossy (*Lamprotornis* spp.)

Starling, Golden-breasted (*Cosmopsarus regius*)

Starling, Hildebrant's (*Spreo hildebrandti*)

Starling, Spotless (*Sturnus unicolor*)

Starling, Superb (*Spreo superbus*)

Stork, Marabou (*Leptoptilos crumeniferus*)

Stork, White (*Ciconia ciconia*)

Stork, Yellow-billed (*Mycteria ibis*)

Sumac, Stagshorn (*Rhus typhina*)

Sundew (*Drosera rotundifolia*)

Swallow, White-winged (*Tachycineta albiventer*)

Swallowtail (*Papilio* sp.)

Swamphen, Purple (*Porphyrio porphyrio*)

Swift, Alpine (*Apus melba*)

Swift, Common (*Apus apus*)

Swift, Fork-tailed Palm (*Reinarda squamata*)

Swift, Pallid (*Apus pallidus*)

Sycamore (Ariz.) (*Platanus wrightii*)

Tamarack (*Larix laricina*)

Tanager, Silver-beaked (*Ramphocelus carbo*)

Tern, White-winged Black (*Chlidonias leucopterus*)

Thistle (Ariz.) (*Cirsium neomexicanum*)

Thrift (Nfd.) (*Armeria maritima* var. *labradorica*)

Thrift (Sp.) (*Armeria juniperifolia*)

Thrush, Blue Rock (*Monticola solitarius*)

Thrush, Rock (*Monticola saxatilis*)

Thrush, Song (*Turdus philomelos*)

Tit, Blue (*Parus caeruleus*)

Tit, Great (*Parus major*)

Toucan, Channel-billed (*Ramphastos vitellinus*)

Treecreeper (*Certhia familiaris*)

Trillium (*Trillium grandiflorum* and *T. erectum*)

Turaco, Hartlaub's (*Tauraco hartlaubi*)

Usnea (*Usnea barbata*)

Verbena (*Stachytarpheta jamaicensis*)

Violets (*Viola* spp.)

Vulture, African White-backed (*Gyps africanus*)

Vulture, Griffon (*Gyps fulvus*)

Vulture, Hooded (*Necrosyrtes monachus*)

Vulture, Palm-nut (*Gypohierax angolensis*)

Vulture, Rüppell's Griffon (*Gyps rüeppellii*)

Wagtail, African Pied (*Motacilla aguimp*)

Wallflower (*Cheiranthus cheiri*)

Warbler, Cetti's (*Cettia cetti*)

Warbler, Dartford (*Sylvia undata*)

Warbler, Fan-tailed (*Cisticola juncidis*)

Warbler, Garden (*Sylvia borin*)

Warbler, Great Reed (*Acrocephalus arundinaceus*)

Warbler, Melodious (*Hippolais polyglotta*)
Warbler, Reed (*Acrocephalus scirpaceus*)
Warbler, Sardinian (*Sylvia melanocephala*)
Warbler, Savi's (*Locustella luscinioides*)
Warbler, Willow (*Phylloscopus trochilus*)
Warbler, Wood (U.K.) (*Phylloscopus sibilatrix*)
Weaver, Reichenow's (*Ploceus baglafecht*)
Weaver, White-billed Buffalo (*Bubalornis albirostris*)
Weaver, White-headed Buffalo (*Dinemellia dinemelli*)
Whale, Gray (*Eschrichtius robustus*)
Whale, Humpback (*Megaptera novaeangliae*)

Whale, Killer (*Orcinus orca*)
Wheatear, Black (*Oenanthe leucura*)
Wheatear, Black-eared (*Oenanthe hispanica*)
Wildebeest (*Connochaetes taurinus*)
Willow, Woolly (*Salix lanata*)
Wolf (*Canis lupus*)
Woodlark (*Lullula arborea*)
Woodpecker, Bearded (*Dendropicos namaquus*)
Woodpecker, Cardinal (*Dendropicos fuscescens*)
Woodpecker, Chestnut (*Celeus elegans*)
Woodpecker, Greater Spotted (*Dendrocopos major*)
Woodpecker, Red-crowned (*Melanerpes rubricapillus*)
Yaupon (*Ilex vomitoria*)
Zebra (*Equus burchelli*)

★   ★   ★   ★   ★

ABOUT THE AUTHOR

CLIVE EDMUND GOODWIN'S *first recollection of watching birds was at the age of seven, and he has been fascinated by them ever since. Born in Leeds, England, he is an experienced and active birder who has lived in Toronto for over forty years. He was Ontario regional editor of* American Birds *for seventeen years, and is author of* A Bird-Finding Guide to the Toronto Region *and* A Bird-Finding Guide to Ontario *as well as numerous magazine articles. Professionally Mr. Goodwin served as Executive Director of both the Toronto Civic Garden Centre and of the Conservation Council of Ontario; and in 1977 was elected an Honorary Member of the latter body. He is a recipient of the Federation of Ontario Naturalists' Distinguished Service Award and is a past president of the Toronto Field Naturalists, as well as a member of several other ornithological and nature organizations. For the past ten years he and his wife, Joy, popular bird tour leaders, have operated their own naturalists' business, teaching and leading tours to destinations both in North America and overseas, including some to places described in this book.*